Andrea Della Robbia and His Atelier, Volume 1

Allan Marquand

PRINCETON MONOGRAPHS IN ART AND ARCHAEOLOGY XI

ANDREA DELLA ROBBIA
AND HIS ATELIER

BY

ALLAN MARQUAND
PROFESSOR OF ART AND ARCHAEOLOGY IN
PRINCETON UNIVERSITY

VOLUME I

PRINCETON UNIVERSITY PRESS
PRINCETON
LONDON: HUMPHREY MILFORD
OXFORD UNIVERSITY PRESS
1922

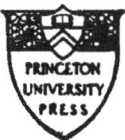
PRINCETON
UNIVERSITY
PRESS

PREFACE

After the monograph on Luca della Robbia one naturally expects a monograph on Andrea della Robbia. Andrea was Luca's nephew, received his art education from his uncle, and in the field of glazed terra-cotta was his natural successor. Had Andrea, like his uncle, remained a bachelor or had his sons engaged in diverse professional lines, my task would have been an easier one. But Andrea had twelve children and of his sons five followed their father's profession. The output of Andrea's atelier was enormous and it is no easy matter to distinguish the individual style of each of these five sons. Through the circumstance that two joined the Dominican order of S. Marco and carried the art of their father southward to the Marches, and two followed François I to France, the individuality of Giovanni, who remained in Florence, is easier to define. This I have attempted in a special monograph. Similarly the characteristics of Benedetto and of Santi Buglioni were not difficult to determine and have been set forth in a separate catalogue of their works. The comparative scarcity of documents and dated monuments led me to consider separately the heraldic devices in Robbia ware, many of which are dated. To a certain extent this helped to bring order into chaos. The little that I have been able to gather concerning the works of Fra Mattia, Fra Ambrogio, Luca, and Girolamo della Robbia I reserve for a separate monograph. This leaves a large mass of material of which I have attempted to treat in this volume. From the very outset of his career Andrea's activity was so great that he could not supply the demand without considerable assistance. It is not always possible to distinguish Andrea's personal handiwork from the work done under his supervision and in his atelier, and I do not expect my judgments to receive universal acceptance. I claim only to have made an attempt to present an orderly catalogue of the monuments which issued from the workshop of Andrea. In this work I have had the good fortune to have the coöperation of my friend Mr. Rufus G. Mather, who has revised all the known documents and added many here published for the first time.

CONTENTS

I. INTRODUCTION

1. *Biographical.*—The genealogical tables A and B were prepared by Mr. Rufus G. Mather. They follow, in the main, the tables published by Milanesi, Cavallucci and Molinier, and Miss Cruttwell, with such corrections and additions as a revision of Robbia baptismal, death, and tax records enabled us to make. Table A will be useful as displaying the family connections of Luca della Robbia, while Table B records the descendants of Andrea della Robbia. It is the latter to which readers of this volume will most frequently refer. The birthdays of Andrea and his children are gathered from the baptismal records with greater accuracy than from the more variable tax records. Document 1 preserves for us the birthday of Andrea, while Documents 2-19 give those of his children, of Giovanni's children, and of Luca, the litterateur. It would be useless for our purpose to search out and publish the baptismal records of all of Andrea's descendants. The marriage records (Docs. 20-25) are less complete. They are taken from XVII century Mss., which, however, were copied from original records. They give us the names of the married couples, and usually the amount of the dowries. The death records (Docs. 26-30), preserved sometimes in the Libro dei Morti of the Ufficio delle Grascia and sometimes in the records of the guilds, are also incomplete. But we are able to publish the records for Andrea's father and mother, for himself and his brother Simone and his son Piero. Mr. Mather has also brought to light (Docs. 31-32) interesting information regarding two daughters of Andrea, Caterina and Margherita. Both became sisters in the Dominican convent of S. Lucia, Caterina in 1496 and Margherita in 1502. Caterina, who became Suora Speranza, was the oldest of all the nuns, and was known as the Madre del Monasterio. She lived in seclusion there for 69 years, having entered at 16 years of age. Her sister Margherita lived as a nun in the same convent for 62 years and was known as Suora Agnolina. Provision was made for their support by Andrea and his sons (Docs. 33-34, 67).

Andrea's ancestors were more or less prosperous farmers—his grandfather Simone in 1427 returns for taxes some nineteen pieces of property (Doc. 55). It was Simone's removal to Florence that determined the artistic careers of his son Luca, and later of his grandson Andrea. He rented a house in the Via Sangiglio (S. Egidio) in the district of S. Piero Maggiore, and it was here that Andrea was born on October 10th,

1435. Here he lived until 1446 when his father Marco and uncle Luca took a more commodious house with a garden in the Via Guelfa (Docs. 49-50). It was in this house that much of his work, and that of his sons, was produced. Andrea received the best of training as a sculptor under his uncle Luca and was matriculated in the Arte dei Maestri di Pietra e di Legnami in 1458 (Doc. 35). His accounts with that guild for 1466-1524 show that he was several times Syndic and many times a member of the Council (Docs. 40-46).

He was an ardent follower of Savonarola and took part in the fight at S. Marco in his defense. For this he, with some three hundred others, was "admonished" and for two years deprived of the right to hold public office (Docs. 36, 36a). Several of his sons shared in his devotion to Savonarola; Francesco became Fra Ambrogio in S. Marco in 1495 and Marco became Fra Mattia in 1496. His son Luca became a lay brother in the same monastery. Luca and his brother Giovanni and Girolamo are named as eligible to the Grand Council of the city of Florence in 1525 (Docs. 38-39). Andrea appears to have worked in Florence for the greater part of his life, and from his atelier in that city his works were transported to remote quarters of Italy. In 1506 he obtained a passport to go to Rome (Doc. 37), apparently a short visit only, as the Viterbo lunettes were sent from Florence in 1507-1509.

The accounts of the Campagnia di S. Luca or l'Arte delle Pittura for 1472 show that he was a member and Camerlingo also of that guild (Docs. 47-49).

In his will, dated Feb. 19, 1471, Luca left his half interest in his house in the Via Guelfa to his nephew Simone di Marco. Simone lived and worked here with his brother Andrea for a while, but both having families, Simone on July 2, 1485, surrendered his rights to the Capitolo and henceforth the house was rented to Andrea and his male descendants (Doc. 50). Hence the debits and credits in the books of the Capitolo from 1475-1489 stand in the name of Simone or of Andrea (Doc. 51), but after Andrea's death (Aug. 4, 1525) the accounts (1531-1553) though standing in his name concern his heirs at law (Docs. 52-54).

The tax returns also furnish us with material useful for biographical purposes. These began to be recorded in 1427. Andrea's grandfather, Simone di Marco, made his return in that year and it is preserved to us (Doc. 55). He owned various pieces of property in the vicinity of Florence, and in that city itself in the district of S. Piero Maggiore he owned (or rented on long lease) a house on the Via S. Giglio (S. Egidio) with its "sale, palchi, camere, terreno, corte, cucina e volta, e pozo," where he lived with his wife Margherita and their sons Marco, Ser Giovanni and Luca. Documents 56-57 give Simone's returns for 1430 and 1433; Documents 58, 61, the returns made by Andrea's father Marco di Simone, and Document 62 a return for the children and heirs of Marco di Simone.

Andrea's personal tax returns for the year 1470 (Doc. 63) reports several pieces of property owned by him in common with his uncle Luca and his brother Simone. His age is given as 33 (he was actually 35), that of his wife 21. The ages of his children Antonia, Marco and Giovanni, given as 3, 2, and 1, seem to be correct. By 1481 his tax return (Doc. 64) shows an increase in property and his family of three children now increased to seven by the addition of Paolo, Lisabetta, Luca, and Francesco, whose ages are given as 8, 7, 6, and 4. According to the baptismal records only those of the two younger are correct. It may also be noted that 600 florins are set aside as a dowry for the eldest daughter Antonia, whereas Lisabetta is recorded as having no dowry. This return must have been made in August, 1480, since it records a child as expected at any day, and we know from the baptismal records that the next child Caterina was born Aug. 19, 1480. Andrea's next tax return (Doc. 65) known as that of 1498, was made out, according to Mr. Mather, in April 1495. He has reduced his possessions by the sale of five pieces of property, but enlarged his holdings on the Via Guelfa by the purchase of an adjoining house and grounds. The increase of his business as well as of his family may have rendered this necessary. In addition to the seven children, mentioned already, five more, Caterina, Piero, Margherita, Girolamo, and Maria were added during the years 1480-1492.

The business of Andrea della Robbia, mentioned in his uncle Luca's will as very profitable, naturally attracted the services of his sons. Giovanni, Luca, and Girolamo seemed to have worked in the house in the Via Guelfa until the latter two went to France; while Marco and Francesco, who entered the Dominican monastery of S. Marco, where they were known as Fra Mattia and Fra Ambrogio, worked with their father and brothers before establishing furnaces of their own in the Marches. Andrea's brothers seem also to have had some sort of a partnership in the business, the firm being known in 1491 as Andrea della Robbia e fratelli (see p. 112, Doc. 5). His brother Simone received payment for many of the medallions made for the Hospital of S. Paolo.

On the 4th of September, 1522, Andrea made his will (Doc. 67) in the presence of seven Brothers of S. Marco. He makes provision for the payment of the registration fee, for masses in S. Marco for his daughters, his wife and his sons Giovanni, Luca, and Girolamo. What interests us chiefly in this will is the disposition made of his furnace and mixing troughs in a room opposite the kitchen and known as the *anticucina* in the house on the Via Guelfa. Here it was that Andrea had made his many monuments. The will assigned it at first to Girolamo, but this legacy was apparently not accepted as satisfactory to the other sons, for in the Codicil (Doc. 68) other arrangements are made and the *anticucina* is allotted to Giovanni. This probably failed to satisfy Luca and Girolamo and accounts for the Revocation of the will on June 3, 1524 (Doc. 69). Andrea then died intestate. On July 2, 1529, Giovanni applied for his third of his father's estate (Doc. 70). Luca and Girolamo by this time had gone to France to work for François I, and the use of the furnace in the Via Guelfa fell into Giovanni's hands. However, he did not long enjoy its use, since death overtook him before the close of 1529 or in the early months of 1530.

2. *Monuments and Style.*—In the classification of the monuments attributed to Andrea della Robbia we are confronted with many a difficult problem. Cavallucci once told me that unless he had a document to guide him he was at sea in the attribution of Robbia monuments. Well he might be, for their number is legion and the style exceedingly variable. But the documents themselves are uncertain guides. In biographical matters names and dates are often inaccurate and a keen critical sense is required to ascertain what may be accepted as historical fact and what as ignorant fiction. Even when payments are recorded for specific monuments, the documents often lead us astray. For example, the records of the Compagnia di San Frediano show payments made in 1494 to Luca della Robbia for a frieze made for their chapel in San Frediano; and in 1495 to Andrea della Robbia for the same frieze. This probably means that the account stood in the name of the elder Luca as late as 1494, although he died in February 1482 (old style, 1481), inasmuch as Andrea in these books is recorded as Andrea di Luca della Robbia. It is possible, however, that the first payments were made to Luca di Andrea della Robbia, one of Andrea's sons who worked in his atelier. In the accounts of S. Maria delle Carceri for 1491 payments for the medallions of the Four Evangelists were made usually to Andrea di Marco della Robbia, but once to Andrea di Marco della Robbia *e fratelli*. The output of the Robbia establishment during Andrea's lifetime was so enormous that it is particularly difficult to isolate certain monuments as Andrea's personal handiwork and to partition the rest amongst his brothers and sons.

Andrea's brothers may be disregarded, as they played an insignificant part in his atelier, but his sons were more individual. Giovanni developed a marked style of his own and has been considered in a separate volume of the Princeton Monographs. Luca, Girolamo, Fra Mattia, and Fra Ambrogio are more difficult to differentiate, although some attempt will be made to distinguish them in a forthcoming volume in this series. There remain a large number of monuments in which Andrea's directing agency is manifest, but his personal share was more or less limited. I have accordingly divided this volume into two parts entitled: (1) Andrea della Robbia, and (2) Atelier of Andrea della Robbia. I have not hesitated occasionally to disregard the documents, and to assign to Andrea's atelier various monuments which show little or no trace of his personal handiwork, and on the other hand to attribute to him many important works for which we have no written documents. When the works of all of Andrea's sons are more accurately understood some of the monuments here classed in the Atelier of Andrea may be withdrawn and attributed to a specific author, but it would be a mistake to do so at the present time. Whether to assign a monument to Andrea himself or to his atelier has been in many cases more or less arbitrary, but on the whole an attempt to isolate the personal works of a master from those of his workshop, in which his personal share was more or less limited, cannot be wholly without value.

The classification of the monuments of Andrea or his atelier into decades has not been always an easy matter, nor has it been altogether arbitrary. A large public would doubtless be grateful to know to what decade the Innocenti Bambini are to be assigned. Some day we may have more definite knowledge on this question, as a Florentine savant is said to have in his keeping the document which would solve that problem. But so long as he jealously guards his information the public can only be served with unsubstantiated guesses. For the monuments as a series these guesses are not wholly unsubstantiated. A careful perusal of the volume will show that in most cases historical considerations govern the classification by decades.

The following summary of dated or documented monuments will serve in general as a justification for the chronological position assigned to those monuments for which dates and documents are lacking.

1470-1480.

1475.	Buondelmonte stemma (Fig. 134).	
1475.	Madonna of the Architects (Fig. 19).	Documented.
1478.	Della Stufa stemma (Fig. 37).	Dated.
1479.	Brizi Adoration (Fig. 41).	Chapel dated.
"	Tornabuoni stemma (Fig. 155).	Dated.

1480-1490.

1481.	Two Angels for the Duomo, Florence.	(Documented).
1484.	Altarpieces at Montepulciano (Fig. 51).	Documented.
"	Salviati stemma (Fig. 158).	Dated.
"	S. Pietro Martire.	Documented.
1487.	Arte della Lana stemma (Fig. 60).	Documented.
1488.	Painted lunette (Fig. 178).	Documented.
1489.	Madonna and Angels (Fig. 179).	Documented.
"	Prato Cathedral lunette (Fig. 86).	Dated and documented.
"	Arte dei Giudici e Notai lunette.	Documented.

1490-1500.
    1490.   Davanzati stemma (Fig. 76). Dated.
    1491.   Wooden Crucifix. Documented.
    "   Prato Evangelists (Fig. 77-80). Documented.
    1492.   Prato Frieze (Fig. 81-82). Documented.
    "   Trotti stemma (Fig. 85). Documented.
    1494.   Bivigliano altarpiece (Fig. 189). Documented.
    "   S. Frediano frieze. Documented.
    1496.   S. Zenobi lunette (Fig. 226). Documented.
    1498.   S. Paolo medallions (Fig. 98-106). Documented.
    1499.   Guasconi stemma (Fig. 109). Dated.
1500-1510.
    1502.   Foiano altarpiece (Fig. 259). Dated.
    1505.   Pistoia lunette and vault (Figs 123-124). Documented.
    1507.   Ginori stemma (Fig. 279). Dated.
    1507-8.   Viterbo, La Quercia lunettes (Figs. 125-7). Documented.
    1507.   Montalcino altarpiece (Fig. 283). Dated.
    1509.   Viterbo, Fiorentini lunette (Fig. 290). Documented.
1510-1520.
    1510.   Almadianus bust (Fig. 128). Documented.
    1513.   Certosa, Christ and S. Lorenzo. Documented.
    1513-'20.   Bibbiena altarpieces (Figs. 292-293). Dated within limits.
    1514.   Heads, for Guido Magalotti. Documented.
    "   Pieve S. Stefano altarpiece (Fig. 299). Dated.
    1515.   Pian di Mugnone Nativity (Fig. 300). Documented.
    1517-1518. S. Frediano Resurrection. Documented.
    1518.   Empoli, Madonna (Fig. 302). Dated.
    1522.   Stemma of Guido Magalotti. Documented.

This list is presented as of provisional value and open to criticism, but nevertheless will be helpful in the final establishment of a chronological series of the works of Andrea and his atelier. The character of the monuments made by Andrea and his atelier deserves a passing notice. His uncle Luca della Robbia lived at a time when the architects, and especially Brunelleschi, led the artistic activities of Florence. Sculpture was needed for the adornment of buildings. Andrea, however, lived when the sculptors and painters had secured the ascendancy. The list of his monuments includes many large altarpieces, innumerable shrines and ciboria, and a number of portrait or ideal busts. During his lifetime the civic buildings of Tuscany were literally covered with heraldic memorials made by the Robbias to commemorate those who had held various civic offices. The activity of Andrea's atelier must have been extraordinary, so great is the quantity of monuments that issued from the furnace of the house in the Via Guelfa.

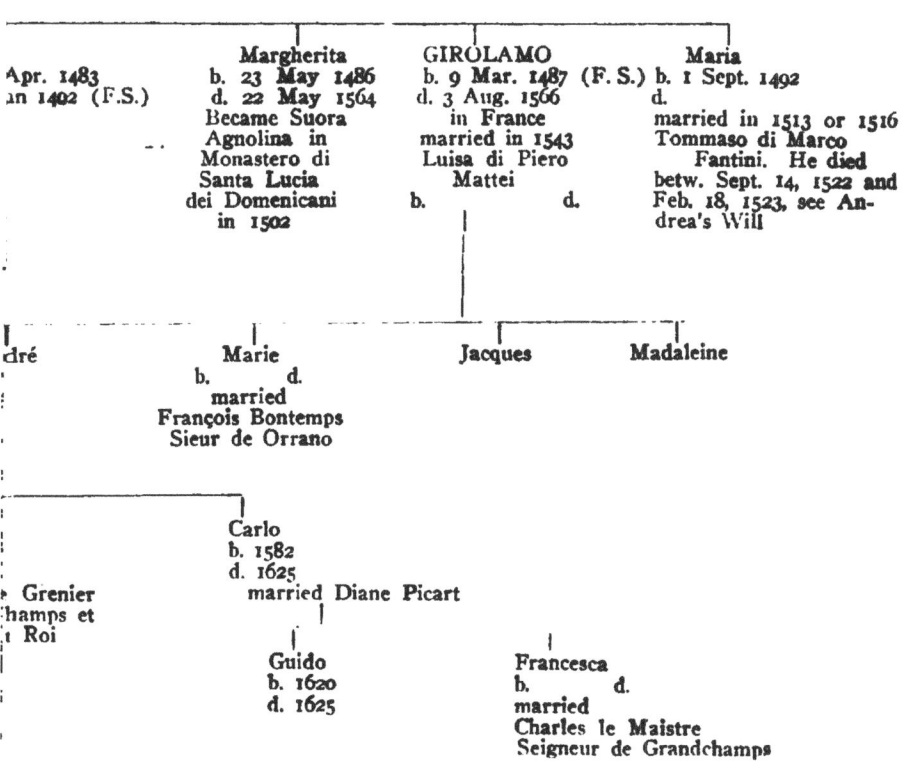

Apr. 1483
ın 1492 (F.S.)

Margherita
b. 23 May 1486
d. 22 May 1564
Became Suora
Agnolina in
Monastero di
Santa Lucia
dei Domenicani
in 1502

GIROLAMO
b. 9 Mar. 1487 (F. S.)
d. 3 Aug. 1566
in France
married in 1543
Luisa di Piero
Mattei

b.   d.

Maria
b. 1 Sept. 1492
d.
married in 1513 or 1516
Tommaso di Marco
Fantini. He died
betw. Sept. 14, 1522 and
Feb. 18, 1523, see An-
drea's Will

dré

Marie
b.   d.
married
François Bontemps
Sieur de Orrano

Jacques

Madaleine

Grenier
:hamps et
: Roi

Carlo
b. 1582
d. 1625
married Diane Picart

Guido
b. 1620
d. 1625

Francesca
b.   d.
married
Charles le Maistre
Seigneur de Grandchamps

It may no longer be assumed that the Robbias had a furnace wherever the name Fornace is found upon the map. The records of Pistoia, of Viterbo, and of Rome show payments not only for the monuments themselves but for their transportation from Florence as well. Many irregularities in the setting up of the monuments—cornices misplaced, pilasters set upside down, garlands in part reversed—indicate also that while the products of his atelier were being spread abroad, the master remained at home.

The style of Andrea was essentially decorative. He was attracted by form rather than by colour. He put ornament above expression, he gave a touch of refinement and grace to whatever he undertook, whether it were an architectural moulding or an elaborate reredos. In composition he was content with the simplest kind of balance. This usually consisted of a central figure or group with lateral figures of equal value. In the school pieces this degenerated of course into a dull uniformity. But Andrea did not hesitate to introduce a certain amount of asymmetry. In the Vieri Canigiani altarpiece (Fig. 33) a landscape on a small scale with S. Francesco receiving the stigmata is balanced by a larger and more sculpturesque group of Tobias and the Angel. But asymmetry strong as this, evidently did not please him. The limit of asymmetry which appealed to Andrea may be seen in the Coronation altarpiece at the Osservanza (Fig. 45). Here the balance between an imposing God the Father and a smaller Virgin is preserved by a skillful distribution of cherub heads, and in the foreground the group of three saints to the right close together is balanced by two to the left set further apart. In the Brizi Adoration (Fig. 41) we find a similar amount of asymmetry; but we observe here that Andrea was keener to preserve a lateral than a vertical balance. The composition as a whole is top-heavy, more so than in later compositions where adoring angels were reduced in size. In the large reredos at Aquila (Fig. 122) he has attempted to combine a Coronation and a Resurrection, binding them together by means of musical and adoring angels and avoiding top-heaviness by reducing the size of the upper, and adding weight to the lower group.

The types which he created are characterized by refined grace and charm. His Madonnas are not motherly peasants, but aristocratic ladies, with delicate features and clad in fine linen. He was no admirer of blue-eyed beauties, but dark eyes made a stronger appeal to his taste. For eyebrows and pupils he used dark blue or violet pigments, and for the irises yellow. In very many cases, however, he secured a more naturalistic effect by fusing the pupils and irises, not into round dark spots as Giovanni was accustomed to paint them, but by the use of copper colour, both dark and light, so as to produce the effect of hazel eyes. In a general way we may say that Luca della Robbia was fond of blue eyes, Andrea of hazel, and Giovanni black.

In the portrayal of religious subjects, which of course occupied his attention almost exclusively, we are sometimes at a loss to determine whether the scenes are portrayed as in heaven or on earth, as there is sometimes no clear distinction made, though often both heaven and earth are indicated. The heavens are indicated by a characteristically refined blue sky—covered with clouds. These are distributed from the top to the base of the picture and painted in dark blue and white. Golden tinged clouds, which appealed to Giovanni della Robbia and to the two Buglioni, are seldom seen in the works of Andrea. Landscape backgrounds of course occur in Nativities, in La Verna, or in Desert scenes, but the colouring is more or less arbitrary. Huts, sheep, dogs are used when needed to elucidate a theme. It was left to Giovanni and others to distribute insignificant animals throughout the landscape as if the object were to create a menagerie.

In the construction of frames Andrea exhibits the same qualities. If he uses architectural mouldings, it is not the heavy, clumsy variety found in some works of the Robbia school, but delicate moulding of graceful outline well proportioned and happily combined; if he decorates his pilasters with arabesques these are worthy of attention for their regularity and decorative charm; he makes an attractive innovation in the use of cherub heads for friezes and frames, either singly or in conjunction with floral or fruit garlands. Floral garlands were treated more or less realistically by Luca della Robbia; in the hands of Andrea they become more conventional. In the seventies they were less conventional, as for example in the Madonna of the Architects (Fig. 19) or in the Sassetti altarpiece (Fig. 20); in the eighties they became stereotyped into triplex bunches set at regular intervals, modified only by rhythmical alternation of form (Figs. 56, 158). Similarly the fruit garland, naturalistically treated by Luca, became in Andrea's hands subject to schematic arrangement. Seldom do we find a single file of fruit (Figs. 28, 134), and infrequently groups of two (Fig. 162), or of complex groups (Fig 110); the much more common type being that of triplex groups (Fig. 38) composed of fruits of the same kind set 2 and 1, separated from fruit of another kind similarly arranged, with a rhythmic alternation of colour and united into a garland by means of ribbons of rectilinear or serpentine outline. These fruit garlands, when used to decorate pilasters or upright friezes, usually spring from vases. The La Verna Crucifixion (Fig. 68) illustrates how decorative the fruit garland became in the hands of Andrea della Robbia. In the hands of his successors the same motive became a vulgar concatenation of fruit and flowers, without distinction or charm. This degeneracy is supposed by some to have begun with Andrea himself and that the chief glory of the Robbias departed with the death of Luca. Such a judgment fails, however, to give to Andrea sufficient credit for his masterpieces. Luca della Robbia, with all his insight, his originality, and his power, produced few works which in grace, refinement, and decorative charm can compare with the Osservanza Coronation (Fig. 45) or the La Verna Crucifixion (Fig. 68).

DOCUMENTS

[Copied by Mr. Rufus G. Mather.]

1. Birth of Andrea della Robbia.
   "Andrea di Marco di Simo(ne) della Robbia
   adi 20 dottobre 1435"
[Archivio di Stato. Libro Approvazione di Età dal 1432 al 1512. Cod. Carta Sec. xvi, segnato Tratte, Cod. 42, c 1.]

2-13. Births and Baptisms of Andrea della Robbia's children.
   2. "Mercoledi adi 21 di decto (Gennaio) 1466 (modern style 1467)
   Anto° et Margherita dandrea di Marco de Larobbia
   nacque di decto hore sette et batezato di decto   ba(tezata) di 21"
[Archivio dell' Opera di Sᵃ Mᵃ del Fiore. Libro dei Battezati, 1466-1473, c. 6.]

   3. "Mercoledi adi 7 di decto (Aprile) 1468
   Marco et Giovanni de Andrea di Marco p. di San
   Lorēzo nacque adi 6 ahore 17   baᵗᵒ adi   7"
   [Idem, c. 31.]

   4. "Adi 20 di decto (Maggio) 1469
   Giovāni et Anto° de Andrea di Giovāni (error—should be Marco) p. di San
   Lorēzo nacque adi 19 ahore 3   baᵗᵒ addi 20"
   [Idem, c. 53ᵗ.]

   5. "Venerdi adi 2 di decto (Novēbre) 1470
   Paolo et Santi de Andrea di Marco delarobbia
   p. di S° Loreᵗᵒ nacque adi due
   hore 12-   baᵗᵒ adj   2"
   [Idem, c. 84ᵗ.]

   6. "Sabato adi 18 di decto (Septēbre) 1473
   Lisabetta et francesca de Andrea di Marco delarobbia
   nacque adi 18 ahore 6—   baᵗᵃ adj   18"
   [Idem, c. 145.]

   7. "Sabato addj 26 Dagosto 1475
   Lucha et bartholomeo Dandrea di marcho della
   robbia p. di santo lorenzo naq addj 25 hore 23—   ba addj 26"
   [Archiv. idem, Libro dei Battezati, 1473-1481, c. 29.]

8. "Mercoledi adi 23 di decto (Luglio) 1477
Franc° et iac° dandrea di (Iac written and cancelled)
Marco p. di San Lorēzo nacque adi 23 ahore 14—   ba adi 23"
   [Idem, c. 66.]

9. "Sabato adi 19 di decto (Agosto) 1480
Caterina et lodovica dandrea di Marcho delarobia
nacque adj 19 hore 15—   ba adi 19"
   [Idem, c. 110ᵗ.]

10.   "Aprile 1483
         Lunedi adi 14 daprile 1483
Piero domeco (domenico) et ro(mo)lo dandrea di marcho
p. di san lorēzo nacq. adi 13 hōr 24   ba adi 14"
   [Arch. di S. Maria del Fiore, Lib. dei Batt., Maschi, 1481-1492, c. 22.]

11.   "Martedi adj 23 di maggio 1486
Margherita zanobia e romola dandrea di marcho della robbia
p°. di s° lorenzo nacq. adj 23 hore di
   [Arch. idem, idem, Maschi e femine, 12 Aprile-2 Ottobre 1486.]

12.   "Lunedi addi 10 di marzo 1487
girolamo domenico dandrea di marco dellarobia
p° dj scō lorēzo nacque addi 9 ore 21."
   [Arch. idem, Lib. dei Batt., 1479-1489; also Milanesi, Miscell. 43 III
P, c. 149.]
"Lunedi adi 10 di marzo 1487
girolamo et domenic° dandrea di marcho della robbia
p° di s/co lorēzo nacq. adi 9 h(o)re 12.   ba adi 10"
   [Arch. idem, Lib. dei Batt., Maschi, 1481-1492, c 98ᵗ.]

13.   "Sabbato adi primo di Septembre 1492
Maria et magdalena dandrea di marco della robbia
p° di s L°. adi p° hō 23.   ba adi 2"
   [Arch. idem, idem, Femmine, 1491-1501, c. 165ᵗ.]

14-18. Births and Baptisms of Giovanni della Robbia's children.
   14. "Martedj adj 19 d(e)c(t)o (Decembre, 1503).
Marcho et romolo di giovan(n)j dandrea dellarobbia
p. di scō lorēzo n(acque) adj 19 di detto mese hore 4½."
   [Arch. idem, idem, 1500-1507; also idem, 1501-1511, c. 34ᵗ.]

   15. "Venerdj Addj 11 (Aprile, 1505)
Filippo et Ro(mo)lo Di giovan(n)j dādrea dellarobbia
p. di s° p° mᵉ N(acque) addj 11 hore 15½".
   [Arch. idem, idem; also 1501-1511, c. 57.]

16. "Martedi addi XIIIj di d(e)c(t)o (Aprile, 1506)
Lucant° et romolo di giovanni dandrea della robbia
p. di s° piero maggiore N(acque) addi 13 h. 16½"
[Arch. idem, idem; also 1501-1511, c. 72ᵗ.]

17. "Sabbato addi 21 di decto (Ottobre, 1508)
Lexa(n)dra et orsola di giovan(n)i dādrea della robbia
po. di S. Lorēzo n. addi decto h. 6."
[Arch. idem, Femmine, 1507-1516; also idem, 1501-1511, c. 112ᵗ.]

18. "Domenicha adi 27 di detto (Aprile, 1511)
Simone et ro(mo)lo di giovan(n)i dādrea della robbia
po. S. Lorēzo N(acque) del di deto h. 4."
[Arch. idem, idem, Maschi, 1507-1516; also, idem, 1501-1511, c. 163.]

19. Birth and Baptism of Luca della Robbia, Latinistà.
"Mercoledi adi 19 di decto (Maggio) 1484
Luca et zanobi di simone di marcho, p. di san
lorēzo nacq(ue) adi 19 hor(e) 16   ba adi 19"
[Arch. idem, idem, Maschi, 1481-1492, c. 38ᵗ.]

20. Marriage of Andrea della Robbia.

della Robbia
            "Andrea q(uondam) Marci Simonis della Robbia
            Intagliator p(o)p(o)li S. Laurentij recepit
            in dotem

Pagoli
            D(o)n(n)ae Ioa(nn)ae eius ux(or)is et filiae
            Ser Laurentij Paoli F(lorenos) 266   223"
[Spogli dello Strozzi. Cod. Carta Sec. XVII, Segnato Magliab. Cl.
XXXVII Cod. 299, c. 223, Libro D 116 Qᵗᵗ S. Gio', 1465; M. *L. d. R.*,
XXXVII.]
"Dna Ioa(nn)a voc(ata) Nanna filia Pieri Ser
Laurentij Paoli uxor Andree Marci Simonis
della Robbia. dos F. 800   58"
[Idem, idem, Libri di Notificazioni, c. 286.]

21. Marriage of Antonia della Robbia

della Robbia
            "Dna Antonia filia Andree Marci della Robbia

Mascalzoni
            uxor Hieronimi Michaelis Ioa(nn)is Mascalzoni   202"
[Idem, idem, c. 238 Libro D 236 Qᵗᵗ S. Gio', 1485.]

22. Marriage of Giovanni della Robbia.

della Robbia
            "Gio' di Andrea della Robbia consumò
            matrimonio con

Bartoli
            Mᵃ tomᵃ fig'ᵃ di Carlo di Geri Bartoli con dote di
            f. 600 l'anno 1503   176"
[Idem, idem, Lib. di Notif., c. 288.]

23. Marriage of Maria della Robbia

della Robbia Fantini

"Mª Maria fig^{ia} di Andrea della Robbia moglie di
Tom^{so} di Marco Fantini Tintore di seta   60"

[Idem, idem, c. 289, Lib. di Notif. 1515 e 1516.]

1515   "Tom^{so} di Marco fantini
Maria di Andrea della Robbia"
[Ancisa, N. N., 232.]

24. Marriages of Luca di Andrea della Robbia.

1524   "Luca di Andrea della Robbia
Agnoletta (di Pietropaolo Falconieri)"
[Idem, 179.]

1528   "Luca di Andrea di Marco della Robbia
Bartol^a di Leonardo di Tomasso Altoviti."
[Zibaldone di Ferd. del Migliore, Cod. cart. sec. XVII segnato
Magliab. Cl. XXVI, Cod. 133, c. 273.   Notif. anno 1528.]

25. Marriage of Girolamo della Robbia

1543   "Girolamo d'And^a di Marco della Robbia stà
in francia Luisa di Piero Mattei.
[Idem, c. 307, Notif., anno 1543.]

26. Death of Andrea della Robbia's mother.
"Maggio 1444
La moglie di marcho dj simone delarobbia morj adj 14 di Magio
Recata ī sanpiero Maggiore"
[A. di S. Ufficio della Grascia.   Libro dei Morti, Cod. Cartapecora,
1438-1448, c. 58.]

27. Death of Andrea's father.
"Adj 17 di dicembre (1448)
Marcho di simone della robbia lan(aiol)o
pp^o di sto piero maggior di cataro"
[Idem, c. 106^t.]

28. Death of Andrea della Robbia.
"Agosto MDXXV
Andrea di Pagolo (error for Marco) della Robbia
Adi 5. Recato in s^{to} p^o m^a (Sancto Piero Maggiore)"
[A. di S. Arte dei Medici e Speziali.   Libro dei Morti G, 1521-1530,
segnato Arti 6, Cod. 249, c. 4; also in Ufficio della Grascia, Libro dei
Morti, 1506-1560, c. 216^t.]

29. Death of Andrea's brother Simone.
" + MDXXj
Simone di dom^{co} (error for Marco) della robia
Riposto in S^o anbrugio   dj 10"
[A. di S., Ufficio della grascia, Libro dei Morti, 1506-1560, c. 393.]

30. Death of Andrea's son Piero.

" + MCCCCLXXXXIj
Uno figluolo dandrea dallarobia
Riposto in san p° maggiore adj p° detto (gennaio)."
[A. d. S., Ufficio della Grascia, Libro dei Morti, 1457-1506, c. 238.']

31. Andrea's daughter Margherita is Suora Agnolina in the Convent of S. Lucia.

208. "Suora Agnolina d'Andrea de la Robbia venne alla Religione d'anni
16 e 62 anni visse in questo Mon°. Questa Madre era sana, di
buono ingegno, leggeva bene, et sedici anni stette cantora, e molto si
dilettava delle divine laude in coro, e della lettione della s'ᵃ scrittura,
parlava volentieri delle cose spirituale, e si rallegrava dell' honor di
Dio, e del profitto spirituale del Mon°, e della salute dell' anime. Era
devota, humile, e dispregiata di se stessa, e fuggiva gli honori, stava
volentieri solitaria, e molto si dilettava della cella. Nell' ultimo della
vita sua si infermò di febbre cõtinua con enfiagione grande di
stomaco e di corpo, et haveva pene grande sopportò cõ tanta patientia
che dava edificatione et esempio grande a' Medici, e a' tutte le suore,
e quando gli pareva megliorare si contristava, e diceva non vorrei
tornare a' drieto, perche mi par ogn' hora mille di andare dal mio
celeste sposo al quale sono stata giurata 62 anni, e quando era nella
maggior' pene si voltava con devotione e fervore a' Dio, e diceva
signor' mio se non son tante queste pene datemene pur dell' altre,
perche mi cõtento di patire piu assai che nõ patisco, e con gravita,
e molta devotione ricevette li st' sacramenti, con buon conoscimento
in sin' all' ultimo, e si riposo in pace la seconda festa de lo spõ s'ᵒ
a di 22 di Maggio 1564. Ha havuto le 30 Messe — —"
[Archivio di San Marco da Un Frammento di Una Cronaca del Monastero di Santa Lucia, Cod. Cart. del Sec. XVI c. 88.]

32. His daughter Caterina is Suora Speranza in the same convent.

211. "Suora speranza d'Andrea della robbia venne alla religione d'anni
16 e 69 anni visse in questo mon°. Questa ven''ᵃ. (veneranda) Madre
era di buon cervello, e bonissimo ingegno, faceva molte oratione, e
frequentava e s'' sacramenti. Leggeva assai le scritture sãte, e si
dilettava delle divine laude. Era humile e dispregiatrice di se stessa.
Lavorava bene. Leggeva bene in coro. Scrisse dua graduali, e dua
antiphonarj pel coro. Et finalmente essendo vecchio di 84 ãni si
ĩfermo di hidropico, e si corruppe la sua carne con grande enfiagione,
in tal modo ch haveva quindici piaghe nel corpo suo cõ pene grandis-
sime, le quale sopportava con tanta patientia, et humilita, che com-
moveva a' lacrime chi la vedeva e udiva parlare. Era la p' (prima

i.e. la più vecchia) Madre del monº, e veramente ha lasciato un grande esemplo di perfettissima patientia, et humilta, cō la quale devotamente, e cō gran' sūmissione, continamente si racc"ª (raccomandava) a Dio, cō grande affetto, e lacrime, e veramēte il suo fine è statto laudabile notabilmente e di grande odore di bonta. E ricevuti li s". sacramēti si riposò nel sigᵗ. a di 7 d'Aprile 1565. Ha havuto le Messe di sā Gregorio — — —— "

[Idem, 88'.]

33. Andrea's provision for his daughter Margherita (Suora Agnolina).

"Andrea della Robbia de dare f 58 lj dº l 5 . 12 p(er) limosina duna sua figliuola chiamata Margherita hora dcā sᵗ Agnolina p.ch. cosi p(ro)misse al Mon"ᵗᵒ (Monasterio) cioe f 84 dj sug¹º(suggello) ch(risto)-fanó la sopdcā soma — f 58 l 5 s 12"

"Andrea di cōtro de havere a di 7 di Maggio 1502 f octāta quattro di suggello p(er) staiora 14 di terra posta nel popolo di san Cristofano a nuovolj luogo dcó lolmartello delle quale vera circa staiora 3 vignata furono stimate f 60 di suggello la qual vigna dcó Andrea decte (dette) p(er) limosina della Margherita sua figliuola al psēte (presente) vocata sᵗ Agnolina somáo a f lj–f 58 l 5 s 12"

[Archivio di Stato, Monastero di Sᵗ Lucia, Libro Debitori e Creditori A, 1512-1538, segnato Corp. Sopp. III Cod. 40, c. 38.]

34. Payments made for Caterina (Suora Speranza).

1542 "Luca cōtra scripto de dare hoggi qº di 21 l 210 equalj se li sono rēdutj qº di sopradcō et p(er)luj a Thomaso di lionardo altovitj dixe p(er) fare la dota alla Nānina figliuola di dcō Luca di ādrea della robbia–fj 30"

"Luca di andrea della robbia de havere hoggi qº di 15 di settēbre 1541 Δ(scudi) 18 lj dº di l 7 p(er) Δ equalj ciha prefattj ī 3 partite p(er)le manj di sᵗ speranza sua sorella la quale li havutj di piu maseritie vēdute — fj 18 E de havere dcō adi 26 dottobre l 35 dcē cōtantj sᵗ sperāza sorella del sopra dcō ——— fj 5 E de havere dcō adi 28 di génaio 1541 l 49 dcē cōtantj dcā sᵗ sperāza — fj 7"

[Idem, c. 84.]

35. Andrea revised the list of matriculates of the Arte de'Maestri di Pietra e di Legnami.

"Andreas Marci Simonis della robbia Intaglator recognovit matriculam dicti luce Simonis Marci eius avi della robbia die XVI Septembris 1458"

[A. di S. Arte de'Maestri di Pietra e di Legnami, Libro dei Matricolati; segnato Arti 11, Cod. 2, c. 110ᵗ.]

36. Andrea's admonition, 1498.

"Ricordo di Ciptadini amuniti parte da' signori, e parte
dagli Otto della Balìa, che furono di Maggio, e Giugno
1498. e' qua' Ciptadini erano, perchè facievano fede al
Papa Alessandro Sesto, che fra Girolamo predichava
buona dottrina, perchè andavano a udire le sue prediche,
e perchè gli erano da 300. e que' Ciptadini che lo feciono
ardere amunirono questi Ciptadini

(Here follows list of citizens)

Questi furono amuniti per dette chagioni addì 19
di Giugno 1498 per anni dua, e dipoi vinciere el
partito per le 44 fave, e prima

(Here follow 16 names and then)

Andrea di Marcho della Robbia   per la minore"
  [G. Cambi, *Istoria di Firenze*, II, 131.]

36ᵃ. "Fam. della Robbia.

Andrea fu uno dei più galanti seguaci di fra
Girolamo Savanarola e segue che avendo prese le
armi in sua difesa durante la battaglia ch'ebbe
luogo a S. Marco per il suo arresto fu per sentenza
de' 19 giugno 1498 privato per due anni dell'abilità
ad ogni pubblico officio."
  [Bibl. Naz., Schedario Passerini No. 198ᵇⁱˢ, Ms. Sec XIX.]

37. Passport for Andrea to go to Rome, July 26, 1506.

"Universis et singulis ad quos presentes p(er)venerint Saltem(Salutem)
cum dilectus filius Andreas dela rubia ad nos venturus sit pro nõ nullis
rebus atque operibus per eum nrõ nõie(nomine) factis nos cupientes eidem
andree tutum et securũ iter ubique patere et in locis p(er) que iter facturus
est cum benignitate et humanitate tractarj devotione vrãm (vestram) ac
vrm (vestrum) singlos(singulos) hortamur in dñõ subditis vero nrīs (nos-
tris) et gentiũ armigerarum capitanis atque ductoribus expresse precipiendo
mandamus et eũdem andream cum rebus op(er)ibusque hmõi (huismodi)
nec nõ valisijs et salcivulis suis p(er) civitates terras passus pontes et alia
loca qlibet tamen nrã q vestra asque ullo reali p(er)sonali jmpedimẽto aut

datij passagij aut cuiusuis alterius jndicti vel jndicendi oneris solutione pro
nrã et ap(osto)lice sedis reverentia jre transire redireque p(er)mittatis
eique descorta et salvo conducto si opus fuerit et enquirēdum duxerit ita
benigne provideatis ut vrã (vestra) exinde devotio apud nos et hanc sanctam
sedem predictam possitis īmerito cōmendari pntibus (presentibus) ad nēm
(nostrem) benem placitum valituris: Datum Rome XXVj Julij millesiō
quĩgentesīo sexto pontis (pontificatis) nrē anno tertio:—"

[Archivio Segreto del Vaticano, Brev. Julj II, Tomo III, Anno 1506,
segnato Armadio XXXIX Cod. 24, c. 360, 360'; Milanesi, *Misc.*, XIII,
segn. 34 III P, c. 217.]

38-39. Della Robbias eligible for the Grand Council of 1525.

38. "Die XXVIIj mensis novēbris 1525
Johan(n)is et ⎰frēs et filij andre marci della robbia
Luca   ⎱scultoris in civitate florentia volens
venire ad magistratum dicte artis et describi
inter alios matricolatos propterea promiserunt etc
juraverunt etc obligantes etc rogantes etc
  Debent solvere florenos sex sig" pro qualibet
    eorum"

[Arte dei Medici e degli Speziali, Libro Verde d. mat° per città dell' Arte
d. Med. e spez., segnato Arti 6, Cod. II, c. 22'.]

39. "Nota di tutti i Cittadini Fiorentini descritti, et abili
per il Consiglio maggiore della Città di Firenze qui distinti
per i loro Quartieri e Gonfalonieri, et i Gonfaloni per
Casate, prima per le Maggiori, e doppo per le Minori Arti
copiata da un libretto in quarto del Sig. Francō Rosselli
coperto di Cartapecora che nella costola del med᷾᷾ dice:
  Consiglio Grande del MDXXV.
Quart° S. Gio. Gonf° chiave per le Minori
Giovanni   ⎱
Girolamo   ⎰di Andrea della Robbia"
Luca   ⎰

[Bib. Naz. di Firenze, Memorie di Firenze raccolte da Gaetano Martini
l'anno MDCCXXXV, Cod. Carta, segnato Panciatich. n° 116, Tomo I c.
189.]

40. Accounts of Andrea with the Arte de'Maestri di Pietra e di Leg-
nami.
"Andrea di marcho della robbia de dare
per lanno 1466 soldi dodici   1 – s xii d –
E de dare per lanno 1467   1 – s xii d –
E per lanno 1468 1469   1 1 s iiij°

E per lanno   1470   1471   l ɪ s iiij
E per lanno   1472   73   74   l ɪ s xvj
E per lanno   1475   .   l – s xij
E de dare soldi cinque perchè Rifiutò
    desere festaiuolo lanno 1476   l – s v
E de dare per lanno 1476   l – s xij
E per lanno 1477   l – s xij
E per la sua tassa delanno 1477 1478   l ɪ s iiij
E pel suo torchietto delanno 1478   l – s vj
E pel suo torchietto 1479   l – s vj
E per la sua tassa 1479 1480   l ɪ s iiij
E pell suo torchietto dellano 1480
    81 82 83   l ɪ s iiij
E per la tasa dellano 1481 82 83   l ɪ s xvj
E per la ttassa per lanno dellanno (sic)
    1484   1485   1486   1487   13 . 9 . 0   l ij s viij
            15 . 17

Posto debitore in questo c 291 di soldi uno
denari iij per resto di tutto lanno 1487"

    [Archiv. di Stato, Arte de'Maestri di Pietra e di Legnami. Libro Debitore e Creditori, segnato Arti 11, Cod. 4, c. 11.]

    Documents 40-46 were copied by Sig Giovanni Masi.

    41. Continuation of the same.

"Andrea di marcho di simone della robbia intaglatore deve
    avere

soldi sei piccioli per resto di sua ragione per tuto lanno 1465
chome apare al champione V° c 101   l – s vj
E de avere a di XXIIIj° di dicembre 1468 lire una soldi dieci
antrata di marjotto ciotoli Kamerario c 7   l ɪ s x
E de avere a di ultimo dachosto 1469 soldi xviij perche fu
    del chonsiglo   l – s xviij
E de avere a di ultimo daprile 1471 soldi xviij perche del
    chonsiglio   l – s xviij
E de avere a di ultino di dicembre 1472 soldi xviij perche
    fu del consiglio   l – s xviij
E a di ultino daprile 1473 soldi X perche fu sindacho di
    stefano da sanchasciano Kamerario   l – s x
E a di XXXI° dottobre 1476 soldi cinque a entrata di
    pacholo picchardi chamerario   c 6   l – s v
E de avere soldi XVJ per lui da lucha suo zio per Resto
    della sua inposta pachata posto debi dare allibro spe-
    dale G c 34   l – s xvj

E de avere a di ultimo daprile 1478 soldi XVIIJ perche
fu del chonsiglo   l— s xviij

E a di ultino dachosto 1479 soldi XVIIJ perche fu del chonsiglo mesi IIIJ° passati   l— s xviij

E a di ultimo di dicenbre 1479 lire una soldi X per lui da ser
bastiano nostro notaro posto debi dare allibro Rosso
debitori e chreditori G a. c. 51   l ɪ s x

E de avere a di ultino daprile 1480 soldi X perche fu
sindacho   l— s x

E a di ultino dachosto 1481 soldi XVIIJ perche fu del chonsiglo 4 mesi passati   l— s xviij

E a di XXIIIJ° di febraio 1481 soldi VJ denari VIIJ° Reco
domenicho a entrata di marcho da terra rossa   c 18   l— s vj d viij°

E a die ultino dachosto 1482 soldi XVIIJ perche fu del
chonsiglio IIIJ° mesi passati   l— s xviij

E a di ultino di dicenbre 1483 soldi XVIIJ perche fu del
chonsiglo IIIJ mesi passati   l— s xviij

E per insino a di 8 di novenbre 1482 soldi VJ del torchieto
a entrata di francescho di bartolomeo di berto c 9   l— s vj

E a di 8 di novenbre 1483 soldi VJ del torchieto a entrata
di michele di rinaldo angeni   c 18   l— s vj

E a di utino dagosto 1484 soldi X perche fu sindacho IIIJ°
mesi passati 9—8   l— s x

E de avere a di ultino daprile 1485 soldi XVIIJ perche fu
del chonsiglo e 4 mesi passati   l— s xviij

E a di ultino daprile 1486 soldi XVIIJ perche fu del chonsiglo 4 mesi passati   15   l— s xviij"

                         15.15.9

[Idem, idem, c. xi.]

42.   **Continuation of the same.**

"Andrea di marcho della Robia de dare soldi
uno denari IIJ per Resto di tutto lanno 1487
chome appare in questo c 11   l— s ɪ d iij

E de dare per la sua tassa dellanno 1488
1489 1490 1491 e 1492   l iij s —

E de dare per la sua tassa dellanno 1493 1494   l ɪ s iiij

E per la sua tassa dellanno 1495   l— s xij

E per la ttassa dellanno 1496 1497   6.1.4   l ɪ s iiij

E per lla tassa dellanno 1498 99
     1500 1501 1502 1503   l iij s xij

E per la ttasa delano 1504 soldi sei   l— s vj

E perl ttorchietto delano 1504 soldi sei   l— s vj

In questo
c 416

E de dare per la tassa dellano 1505 6

    7 8 a soldi XII lano   10.11.4   l ij s viij

E per lal torchietto dellanno 1508 soldi vj   l– s vj

E per la tassa dellano 1509 et perl torchietto

di detto ano in tutto   13. 6.4   l– s xviij

Resto   E de dare posto gli debbi avere in questo

c 416 per resto di questo conto   13. 4.4   l l s l d 8"

                            l 14 6 6

[Idem, idem, c. 291.]

    43. Continuation of the same.

"Andrea di marcho della Robia de avere a di ultino di

dicenbre 1487 soldi diciotto perche fu del chosiglio e quattro

    mesi passati   · l– s xviij

E de avere a di ultino di dicenbre 1488 soldi XVIIJ perche

    fu del chonsiglo e 4 mesi passati   l– s xviiɈ

E de avere a di ultino daprile 1490 soldi XVIIJ perche fu

    del chonsiglo e 4 mesi passati   l– s xviij

E de avere a di ultino daprile 1491 soldi XVIIJ perche fu

    del chonsiglo IIIJ° nesi passati finito detto di   · l– s xviij

E de avere a di ultino di dicenbre 1492 soldi XVIIJ perche

    fu del chonsiglo IIIJ mesi passati   l– s xviij

E de avere a di XXX di magio 1495 soldi venti richo pacino

    pel suo acchatto a entrata di chorso di maso nostro

    Kamerario c 30   l l s —

E a di ultimo di dicembre 1496 soldi 18 perche fu del con-

    siglio 4 mesi passati   6.8   l– s xviij

E de avere lire IIIJ sono per resto duna sua ragione allibro

    roso c 148   l iiij s –

E de avere soldi 18 perche fu del chonsiglio adi ultjmo di

    dicembre 1502   l– s xviij

E de avere per lesere stato delo chonsiglio 4 mexi comin-

    ciato a di primo di maggio 1503   l– s xviij

E de avere per essere stato del chonssiglio 4 messi chomin-

    ciatti a di primo di magio 1504   l– s xviij

E de avere addi primo di settenbre 1508 soldi XVIIJ per

    essere istato del nostro chonsiglio   13   2   l– s xviij

E de avere perl torchietto dellanno 1508 antrata di finoxino

    di michele   14.6   l– s vj"

[Idem, idem, c. CCLXXXXJ.]

    44. Continuation of the same.

"Andrea di marcho de la robia de dare pela tasa e

torchietto delanno 1510 11 12 13 14 a soldi diciotto lano

in tutto lire quattro soldi 10   14 s 10

E de dare pe la tasa e torchietto delano 1515 soldi 18   1– s 18

E de dare a di 30 daprile 1515 lire sette soldi diecenove
denari 2 che tanto gli tocha per esere istato nostro
camerario per 4 mesi cioe da di primo di gienaio 1515
chome si vede a loscita sua c 20 a soldi 15 denari 11
per lira   17 s 19 d 2

E de dare pela tasa e torchietto delano 1516 soldi 18 13.7.2 1– s 18

E de dare pela tasa e torchietto delano 1517 soldi 18 14.5.2 1– s 18

E de dare pela ttasa e torchietto delano 1518 soldi 18 15.3.2 1– s 18

E de dare per la ttasa e ttorchietto delano 1519 soldi 18   1– s 18

E de dare per la tassa e torchietto del ano 1520 soldi 18 1– s 18

      Posto debi avere in questo c 505

E de avere a di 8 di novembre 1518 soldi sei tutto e detto
   aentrata di lorenzo bochi camerario   c 16   1– s 6

E de avere soldi 18 sono perche fu del nostro chonsiglio
gienaio febraio marzo e aprile 1519   1– s 18

E de avere a di 8 di novembre 1519 soldi 6 aentrata
di gieri ciofi camerario   c 8   1– s 6

E de avere a di 30 daprile 1520 soldi 18 per esere
istatto chonsigliere 4 mesi passati   1– s 18

E de avere a di novembre 1520 soldi 6 tutto e
detto aentrata di bernardo del maestro gerdo camerario   1– s 6"
   [Idem, idem, c. 416.]

   45.   Continuation of the same.

"Andrea di marcho della Robbia de avere addi primo
di settenbre 1509 soldi XVIIJ per essere istato del nostro
chonsiglio IIIJ° mexi chomiciati addi detto di sopra   1– s xviij

E de avere lire 1 soldi 1 denari VIIJ posto gli debbi dare in
questo c 291 per resto di per el chonto   11 s 1 di viij

E addi VIIJ di novembre 1510 soldi VJ° da entrata di jacopo
di stefano Rosegli nostro kamerario   (c) 26   1– s vj°

E de avere per esere stato del nostro chonsiglio IIIJ° mesi
chominciati addi primo di maggio 1511   1– s xviij d –

E addi 8 di novembre 1511 soldi 6 per il tutto di questo anno
da entrata di andrea di marcho della robia   c 10   1– s vi°   d –

E de avere per esere stato del nostro chonsiglio mesi IIIJ°
chominciati addi primo di settenbre 1512   1– s xviij d –

E addi 8 di novembre 1514 soldi VI a entrata di francescho
de bellacino   1– s vj

E de avere soldi diciotto per esere istato del chonsiglio 4
mesi chominciati a di primo di settenbre 1513   1– s 18   d –

E de avere soldi diciotto per esere istato del chonsiglio 4
mesi chominciati a di primo di settenbre 1514   1— s 18   d —

E de avere lire sette soldi 19 denari 2 per suo servito istato
nostro camerario per 4 mesi chominciati a di primo di
gienaio 1514   17 s 19   d 2

E de avere soldi 18 perche lui e stato del nostro chonsiglio
4 mesi chominciati a di primo di settenbre 1515   1— s 18   d —

E a di 8 novembre 1516 soldi 6 a entrata di andrea ciofi
camerario   15.6.10   c 7   1— s 6

E de avere soldi 18 sono perche fu sindacho a sindichare
lentrata di giovani di cristofano   1— s 18   d —

E de avere soldi 18 perche fu del nostro chonsiglio di
gienaio 1517   1— s 18   d —"

[Idem, idem, c. CCCCXVj.]

46. Continuation of the same.

"Andrea di marcho de lucha
de dare per la ttassa e

Mori a di
4 dagosto
1525

E de dare per la tassa e
ttorchietto delano 1522   23
a soldi 18 lano   l 1 s 16

†Andrea di marcho dela robia de
avere per resto di una sua ragone
in questo c 416 lire due soldi 5
denari 8 e le si vede achonce tutte
le tasse chorse per tutto lano 1520   12 — 5 — 8

E de avere adi 31 di dicenbre 152j
soldi dicotto perche fu del nostro
chonsiglio 4 mesi passati   1 — 18

E de avere a di 8 di novenbre 152j
soldi 6 per suo ttorchietto di detto
ano a entrata di francescho santini
nostro kamerario   c 18   1 — 6

E de avere a di 31 dagosto 1522
soldi 18 per eser istato del nostro
chonsiglio 4 mese passati   1 — 18

E de avere a di 31 dagosto 1523
soldi 18 per eser istato del nostro
chon siglio 4 mese passati   1 — 18

E de avere a di 8 di novenbre 1523
soldi 6 pel suo torchietto antrata
di filipo lorenzi nostro kamerario c 7   1 — 6

E de avere a di 30 daprile 1524
soldi 18 per ser istato del nostro
chonsiglio 4 mesi passati   1 — 18

E de avere soldi 18 per esser
istato sindacho dela nostra arte   1 — 18

E a di 30 daprile soldi 30 sono per

once 6 di pepe e per rimettere a
marioto donzelo 1 1 –

E a di 30 di dicenbre 1524 soldi 18
per ser istato del nostro chonsiglio
4 mesi passati 1 – 1{

E a di 8 di novenbre 1524 soldi 6
antrata di balomeo di baldino
nostro kamerario c. 6 1 – (

[Idem, idem, c. 505 and CCCCV.]

47. Accounts of Andrea with the Compagnia di S. Luca o l'Arte della Pittura.

"MCCCCLXXII

Andrea di mācho della robia ītagliatore de dare
p(er) la grazia fatta adi 17 di giugno 1472
dogni debit° p(er)īsino adi p° di luglio 1472 sol. vj   1 – s 6 –

E de dare p(er) la oferta del dì di s° lucha adi
8 dottobre e p.llo dett° anno 1472 sol. cinque   1 – s 5 –

E de dare p.lla sovēzione deluogho e arte e
p(er) ogni anno sol. sedicj paghando ogni mese
sol. 1° dj 4 e da chomīciare adi p° di luglio 1472   1 – s 16 –

E de dare p.lla ī posta fatta el dì di s° lucha adi 8
dottobre 1472 sol. cinque p(er) paghare e penonj de tronbette

E de dare p.ll (this entry was left unfinished.)

Andrea di marcho della robbja de dare adi 25 dj
novenb(r)e 1482 sol. dieci p(er) partito universale -   1 – s 10 –"

MCCCCLXXII

Andrea di marcho della robia ītagliatore de avere
sol sej paghati p.lla grazia a piero Zucherj k° a
sua entrata c. 17   1 – s 6 –

E de avere adi 8 dottobre 1472 sol. cinque pagho
chotantj p.lla oferta di dett° anno a pièro
zucherj k° a sua entrata c. 16   1 – s 5 –

E de avere sol. cinque dj 4 pagho chontantje
andorono ī chasetta chome alluscitta va fuorj
di sua mano sono p(er) parte della sovenzione dellarte   1 – s 5 dj 4

E de avere insino adi 11 di luglio 1472 sol. uno
dj quatro messi ī chasetta chome alluscitta
andava atorno   1 – s 1 dj 4

E de avere adj 24 daprile sol. due dj 8 pagho

al(1)ib(r)o della sovenzione c. 3 a entrata di Bonaiuto k° l— s.2 dj 8"

1.0.4

[Archiv. di S., Compagnia di S. Luca. Libro Deb. e Cred. 1472-1520, segnato Arti 27, Cod. 2, c. 12ᵗ, 13.]

48. Andrea was Camarlingho of the Compagnia di San Luca in 1472.
The records of the Compagnia di San Luca give an account of the candles offered on the day of S. Maria Candellaia. The four capitani gave candles valued at 4 denari each; the Counsellors and Andrea di Marco della Robbia as Camarlingho offered candles worth 3 denari each, while the thirty-two remaining members gave candles valued at 2 denari each.

[Arch. di Stato., Libro Rosso della Compagnia di San Luca, c. 144ᵗ; Horne, Botticelli, 30, 347 (Doc.); Burl., Mag., Oct., 1915, 5.]

49. Concerning rental of house in the Via Guelfa to Marco and Luca della Robbia 1447.
"Ricōdo chome adj 9 digenaio 1467 cū licētia del chap(ito)lo lucha
dellarobia se dice la īfrascripta chasa īnavillare a vita
di mō frācescha dimācho disimone roghato s(er) domenicho
dant° da fighinj e pagho f dua lā antā(aentrata)
al(1)ib(r)o s(ig.)bb c. 36 ——— l 11 s 4
Marcho di Simone della robia de dare
p(er) avillare duna chasa cū orto posta ī via
guelfa cōdotta p(er) se e suoj figliuolj adj 11 (31?)
(dagosto?) 1446 roghato p(er) jacopo daromena chome
appare ī questo c. 75 pagha lano 1 diecj s. otto
e p(er) resto di detto avillare p(er) tutto ottob(r)e 1461
l 16 s tre ī questo a detta ca(r)ta c 75 — l 16 s 3
Posta allibro rosso S. A c. 264"

- - - - -
- - - - -
- - - - -
- - - - -

[Archiv. del Rev.ᵈᵒ Capitolo di Firenze. Specchio di Livellari, Sᵗᵒ A, 1437-1461, c. 136.]

50. The house in the Via Guelfa, from July 2, 1485 is rented to Andrea della Robbia.
"Via Guelfa + Mcccc°LXXIIIJ°
Marcho et ⎰.frateglj et figluolj di Simone
Lucha ⎱ della robbia deono dare l diecj
et s otto. Sono p(er) avjllare duno anno
īcomīciato adi p° di novēbre 1473 et
finito come seghue. Duna casa con

corte et orto grande didrieto . Posta
in via guelfa nel pplo di scō lorenzo
in firenze con sue mjsure vocabolj
et confinj Come appare alcāpione
del cap(ito)lo c 24 laquale condussono
in avillare adi 11 di .... 1446. Rogato
Ser Jac° di Ser Ant° daromena
E paghano lanno davjallare dette
l diecj et s otto levatj dallo spechio
deglj avjllarj S. A. c 136 ——————— l 10 s 8 dj –
Et deono dare 1 vēti et s sedici p(er)
avjllare dānj dua finiti p(er) tutto
ottobre 1476 —————————— l 20 s 16 dj –
Et deono dare l vētj s sedicj p(er) avillare
danj dua finiti p(er) tutto ottobre 1478 —— l 20 s 16 dj –
Et deono dare l septantadua s 16 p(er)
avillare dannj septe finitj p(er) tutto
octobre 1465 della sopradetta chasa ——— l 172 s 16 dj –
124 16

Nota chome addj 2 di luglio 1485
Simone di Marco
dellarobbia fratello
dandrea della robbia in
p(re)sentia di tutto elcap(ito)lo renuntio
p(er) et sua descendentj p(er) linea
maschulina ·et cedette ogni suo
ragone di livello havessj nella
sopradetta chasa a Andrea della
robbia suo fratello cō licentia et
auctoritate di Messer gorgo datj et M(esser)
Rinierj Ghuiccardinj comissarij elettj
dalcap(ito)lo a questo acto particolare come
di loro cōmissione apparisce p(er) cōtratto
rogato p(er) Ser domenicho dafigline notaio
inveschovado sotto di 20 di gugno
px°(proximo) passato et detto dj 2
di luglio suddettj e dettj cōmissarj
concedettono al detto andrea la
detta chasa riconducēte p(er) se
e p(er) la sua linea maschulina et
dis(cendentj) se p(er) alchuno capo(caso)
lasopradetta chasa fusse schaduta et

ritornata al detto cãplo et p(er)
recognitione della sopradetta casa
dette et pago a S(er) franc° di stefano
distribuitore di detto cap(ito)lo f diecj
lar. doro inoro come appare alla
sua entrata s⁰ n n c 41 et promisse
detto andrea pagare e livello
cõsueto come di tutto apparische
alibr s⁰ c 73"

In margine: l 10 s 8
"Andrea dimarcho della robbia de dare
adj 31 dottobre 1486 l diecj s 8 della
soprascripta casa laquale ricõdusse
p(er) se et p(er) sua linea maschulina adi
dua diluglio 1485 come apare p(er) nota
q di sopra et depagare ogi ano
el medesimo avillare coe l 10 s 8 et
po(pero) si pone debitore detto andrea
sono p(er) uno ãno passato adj 31 dottobre 1486 — l 10 s 8 –
Et de dare l dua s 17 dj 8 p(er) resto davillare
p(er) tutto ottobre 1485 postj marcho et luca
della robbia debbino avere adirinpetto ——— l 2 s 17 dj8
Et de dare l cinquantadua p(er) avillare danj 5
ī comīciatj adi p(er) dinovēbre 1486 et
finitj adj ultimo dottobre 1491 — . — l 52"
[Archiv. del Rev⁰⁰ Capitolo, Libro Maestro Rosso A +, 1474-1490,
c. 263ᵗ, 264.]

    51. Credits on account of house in Via Guelfa.
        "+Mcccc°LXXIIIJ°
    Marcho et ⎫ frateglj et figluolj di simone
    Lucha ⎭ della robbia contrascritti deono avere adi
    26 daprile 1475 l cinque et s undicj
    pagho contãti Simone di marcho
    detto p(er) pte(parte) davjllare
    della casa contrascritta messi
    aentrata s. f.f. c 18 ——————— l 5 s 11 dj
    E deono avere adi 15 di maggio
    1477 l quattro pagho contanti
    Simone sop(ra)detto et p(er) luj messer
    franc° rucellaj p(er) pte davillare
    messi aentrata di ser Dello s. LL. c 40 — l 4 s –

E deono avere adi detto l cīque et
s tredici pagho simone detto et p(er)
luj da pagnago ridolfi p(er) pte
davillare messi aentrata di ser
Dello s. LL. c 40 ———————————— l 5 s 13 d

E deono avē adi 27 di novēbre
1477 f dua larghi dettono posti
aentrata di ser Ant°. s. mm. c 29— l 11 s 6 d

E adi 22 digiug° 1480 l trentasei
aentrata di ser ant° s(segnato)
pp c 29 ———————————— l 36 s –

E adj 28 di Gennaio 1481 l cinque
s 17 pago locha aentrata di
s ant° s qq c 27 ———————————— l 5 s 17 d

E dadj p° dagosto 1482 p(er) insino
adj 30 dj maggio 1483 l venti
s tredicj picciolj alib s rr c 40 — l 20 s 13 d –

E addj 14 dagosto p(er) insino adj 8 di
Gennaio 1484 l undicj s 17 dj 4
p(er) entrata di S franc° st''tt, c. 31 —— l 11 s 17 d 4

E adj 5 dag° 1436 f dua larghi dō
inō p(er) luj dabenedetto ghorj ch di
tantj si trae s 7 spesi ī veschovado
restano l 11 s 17 aentrata S°(segnata)
xx c 29 ———————————— l 11 s 17 –

E adj 23 di gēnaio 1486 l nove s 4
pago simone dellarobbia p(er) uno
resto tocchava adetto simone p(er)
luj damatteo daterra rossa
aentrata S xx c 29 ———————— l 9 s 4 –

E deono avere l dua s 17 dj 8
sono p(er) resto di q° ragone posto andrea della robbia
debba dare aldirinpetto pch(perchè)
ladetta casa dice ī luj come apare
p(er) nota aldirinpetto ——————— l 2 s 17 dj 8

                                              124 16 0

Andrea di marcho dicont° de avere
dadj 27 di settemb 1487 ī sino adj
3 dj marzo 1487 l dicotto s 12
aentrata S° xx c 32 ——————— l 18 s 12 dj
E dadj 31 digēnaio 1488 ī sino adj

29 di mag° 1489 l quĩdicj s 15 dj 8
aentrata S⁴ zz c 32 ——————————   l 15 s 15   8
E dadj 27 di novemb
1489 ĩsino adj 8 dimarzo 1489 l diccj
s 8 aentrata S⁴ 3 a c 39 ————   l 10   8 –"

[Archiv. idem, idem, c. CCLXIIJ-CCLXIV.]

52.   Credits on account of house in the Via Guelfa.
"+yhs MDxxxj°

Andrea di marcho della Robbia dicontro de avere
addj 13 di dicembre 1532 l sei recho filipo della robja
aentratta 18 Cas(sa) c 205   l 6 –
E addj 22 digenaio l dieci s viii recho ridolfo
diac° aentratta 20 Cas(sa) c 210   l 10 . 8 –
E addj 26 daghosto 1534 l x s viij p(er) lui
da mᵃ lisabetta di lucha aentratta 47 a chassa c 257   l 10 . 8 –
R(Richordo) E avere p°(posto) dare allibro n°(nero)
f a c 58 p° detto libro dare (inquesto) c 297   l 14 . 16
                                    l 41 . 12 –"

[Archiv. del Rev.⁶° Capitolo di Firenze. Libro Maestro Rosso E, 1531-
1534, c. LXXVIIj; also, L'Arte, 1918, 192 no. 6.]

53.   Credits to account of house in the Via Guelfa.
"+yhs MDXXXIIIJ°

"Andrea djmarcho dellarobia dj chõtro de avere
addj 5 dj djcenbre 1534 l vij p(er) lui dafilippo
di Gᵃⁱ e p(er) lui dadom⁶° schultore aentratta c 4
a chassa c 191   l 7 s
1535   E addj ij di marzo l xij – p(er) llui daridolfo
dj yac° de mozzi aentratta 36 a c°(chassa) c 284   l 12 s –
E addj detto l v - s x p(er) llui da Lᵗ° altovitj
aentratta c 36 a chassa a c 284   l 5 s 10
E addj 8 di novembre 1537 l sette pago
tommaxo di Lᵗ° altovitj aentratta 76
a chassa a 367   l 7 s –
R   E de avere posto dare allibro pagonaxo sᵗ°
g 38 p° detto libro dare ĩ q°(questo) c 412   l 25 s 5
                                    l 56 .. 15 –"

[Archiv. idem, Libro Maestro Nero F, 1534-1538, c. LVIII; also L'Arte,
1918, 192 no. 7.]

54. Concerning rental of house in the Via Guelfa.

c⁸⁰

"yhs MDXXXXIIIJ°

In margine: l 10 - 8
"Andrea dimarcho dellarobia nrō
livellario duna chasa posta in
via ghuelfa dellaquale ci debba   1550
paghare ogniano lx sviii p(piccioli)
in dj 3 dottobre de dare addj
IJ di novembre 1544 .. .. ..
- - - -
- - - -
- - - -
- - - -   .

Richoncessa alinea agirolamo
dandrea dellarobia a sua linea
maschulina chome in suo chontto
si dice in q° ——————— 371 - - - -"

" +yhs MDXXXXIIIJ°

Andrea dimarcho dellarobia
dichontro de avere - - - -
- - - - -

E addj 21 di gug° 1550
l LVIJ, s 11 dj VIII p
e p(er) luj da gᵐᵒ suo figˡᵒ
e p(er) luj dalfonsso della chasa
camarlingho dell arcivescho-
vado r°(reco) el suo figˡᵒ
chontantti aentrata 111
a c°(cassa) 374   157 s 2.8
E adi 6 daghosto lxiii
s xiiii° dj viii p r°
gᵐᵒ suo figˡᵒ aentrata
112 a c° 378 ——————— 113 s 14.8"

[Archiv. idem, Libro Maestro Rosso H, 1544-1553, c. 30 and c. xxx.]

55. Tax return of Simone di Marco della Robbia 1427.

"Gonfalone chiavj Quartiere S giovanj   (1427)
A di 10 di luglio
Questa e la rechata di Simone dimarcho della
robbia e de figliuolj prestanziatj jn decto
gonfalone jn fiorinj quatro soldj quactordicj
e danarj cinque a oro ——   f 4 sol. 14 dj 5
In prima una chasa dallavoratore cō palchj
sala camera e terreno posta nel pplo
di santa maria dal tartagliese valdarno
disopra contado di firenze nel luogho
del tartagliese nella strada publica
confinata da primo decta strada a ij
via a iij° Niccholo di giovannj
del bellaccio a iiij° Marcho del bello
del bellaccio
Item una chasecta posta dirietro
alla sopradecta chasa che sene
fa la stalla da bestia posta nel
decto pplo e luogho confinata
a j° via a ij° filippo di firenze
del pancia a iij° via a iiij° lerede
di piero terj cogli jnfrascrictj

pezzi di terra cioe
Uno pezo di terra lavoratia di
staiora cinque a grano posto nel
decto pplo luogo decto alla tavolaia
a j° via a ij° Marcho del bello bellaccij
a iij° filippo di firenze del pancia
a iiij° di simone di marcho sopradecto"

(Here follow declarations of 18 other parcels of land in the same vicinity and covering a total area of staiora 48½ all under cultivation except one small parcel which is described as "rovinata e coduta nel fiume darno.")

"Rendono tucte le sopradecte terre ogni anno luno
anno pelatro ristorando

Staia sexanta	di grano
Barilj diecj	di vino
Staia diecj	dorzo
Staia dodicj	di sagina
Staia sej	di miglio
Staia sej	di panicho
libre diecj	di lino grosso

Uno paio di chapponj libre 250 di carne di porco
Serque cinque di uova

Lavora le sopradecte terre soprascricte Marcho di
berto daltartagliese debacj dare fiorinj diēcj — f 10 —
Item abbiamo jn sul decto podere
   uno paio di buoj di stima di f diecj
   una asina di stima ———— di f tre
   cinque porcj grandicellj   } di stima jn tucto
   una troia con secte porcellinj } di f diecj
delle qualj buoj e bestie nabbiamo avere la meta
Item una chasecta posta jn chastello san
giovanj valdarno di sopra luogo decto via di
rachasolj confinata a j° dcā via a ij° rede di
lucha di jacopo a iiij° francescho di lucha a iij°
chiasso la decta chasetta tiene a pigione
francescho di lucha saldj di chastello san
giovanj e debbacj dare di pigione lano fiorino
uno d(oro) ——— f 1 —
Item uno pezo di terra vignata e pte lavoratia
di staiora quatro a grano posto nella corte di
chastello sangiovannj valdarno di sopra loco decto alla
fossa corboli confinato a j° via a ij° e iij° antonio di
girolamo a iiij° checcho di macteo spadaio

Item uno pezo di terra vignata di staiora due a
grano posta nella decta corte loco decto fossato ala
villa a j° e ij° via a iij° e a iiij° Messer palla di nofri degli strozi
Item uno pezuolo di terra che non e se non e macchie
di pruni di meno duno staioro posto nella decta
corte luogho decto nel fondale a j° via a ij° benj
della pieve di chastello san giovanj a iij° e a iiij°
ser Masso di ser piero di ser Masso
E sopradectj tre pezi di terra tiene a ficto da noj
Antonio di conte da chastello san giovannj e danne
di ficto lire sedicj p(icciole) — l 16 —
Item uno podere con chasa da signore e
dallavoratore con terre lavoratie alborate
vignate e con p(er)gole e con alberj fructiferj
e non fructiferj posto nel contado di firenze
nel pplo dj san tomme a baroncellj loco dcō
a baroncellj confinato a j° lerede di francescho
di duccio mellinj via jn mezzo a ij° filippo di
simone e jl fratello fossatello jn mezo a iij°
Maso davizj a iiij° via
Item uno pezo di terra lavoratia e alborata
apartenente al decto podere di staioro uno a
grano posto nel dcō pp loco dcō alcanpuccio
a j° e ij° via a iij° e iiij° lerede di cante p(er)uzi
fossatello jn mezo
Item uno pezo di terra lavoratia apartenente
al dcō podere di staiora uno a grano posto
nel dcō pplo loco decto ritortolo a j° via a ij°
e iij° lerede di cante peruzj fossatello jn mezo
a iiij° lerede dj francescho mellinj fossatello jn mezo
Rende il sopradecto podere luno anno ristorando
laltro

  Staia trenta di grano
  Barilj quaranta di vino
  libre diecj di lino grosso
  fructe f dve
  due paia di chapponi

Serque diecj duova
Lavora il sopradecto podere Bartolo di jacopo
vocato Bartolo delladina
Item una chasa posta nella citta di firenze nel pp
di san piero maggiore nella via che si chiama
via degli albertineglj e riesce nella via di san gilio
confinata da primo via degli albertineglj a ijᵒ dello
spedale di santa maria a iijᵒ dellerede di maso di
Ugho deglialessandrj a iiijᵒ via di san gilio la decta
chasa a tenuta e tiene la meta una Mō Nera
vedova pellamore di dio gia sono annj ventj e
più e maj noncene a data nulla laltra meta
abbiamo apigionata del mese daprile pximo
passato a ugholino di messer giovannj e non
sene a facto pacto niuno credano cene dara
fiorinj tre lanno o circa pero che nō vale
tuctadecta casa fiorinj sessanta — f tre — f iij
Item debbe avere Simone p(ro)prio dalle jnfrascricte
p(er)sone le jnfrasricte quantita cioe da
Corso di giunta tintore che a fallito   lib. XXVIIIJᵒ
Bernardo baldovinj che e nelle stinche — lib. XV —
Mino di borgianj tintore fiorinj tre — f. IIJᵒ —
lone di ser Macteo conciatore   — lib. XIIIJᵒ
Jacopo di antonio di bartolo mal(?)
di val di sieve f octo d(oro) ——   f VIIJ —
Simone di benvenuto schardassare —   lib. V ——
Item deve avere S(er) giovannj di simone p(ro)prio da
Messer francescho di sandro chanbinj p(er) carte fiorinj
quatro lib. cinque sol sedicj piccioli f 4 lib. 5 sol 16
francescho e giustro di cino di cino da citina vecchia
e Mᵃ Bartolomea loro madre fiorinj sexanta danegli
(gliene dà) pella meta volentieri ————— f 60 d(oro)
Mᵒ papera figluola fu di lenzone di simone
ghalighaio e donna del decto S giovannj p(er)
resto di dota fiorinj cento diecj doro — f 110
S(er) Bonacchorso di piero bonacchorsj ———   f 3
Incharichi

> Simone di marcho sopradecto deta dānj — 84
> Mᵃ Margherita donā dello decto simone danj — 65
> Marcho di simone dānj —————— 42
> S(er) giovannj di simone dānj ————— 33
> lucha di simone dānj ——————— 27

M° papera donna del decto S(er) giovanj dãnj — 26
pulisena figluola di S(er) giovãnj nacque adj p° setēbre 1427
Abbiamo a pigione una chasa con
sale palchj camere terreno corte cucina
e volta e pozo nella quale noj abitiamo
dentrovj nostre masseritie posta nel
pp di san piero maggiore nella via di
san gilio confinata a j° via decta a ij° stefano
di salvj a iij° simone di salvj a iiij° rede di
giovãnj di salvj
La decta chasa e dellerede di Giovannj di
Salvj paghianne di pigione fiorinj dicianove
doro lanno ——————————— f XVIIIJ°
Item abbiamo a dare aglinfrascrictj huominj
e p(er)sone le infrascricte quantita di danarj cioe a
Sindachj del ghonfalon(e) delle chiavj —   f xxij
Comune di firenze per prestanzonj —   f xv
lorenzo e Bernardo di benino linaiuolj —   f lxx
Tomas(s)o Bartolj ritagliatore e conp(agni)—f lxx
Macteo rondinegli e conp(agni) ritagliatore — f xxx
Item devono dare a
La ghabella del vino p(er) una p(ro) messa — f xxx
Bernardo de bardj e con(pagni) orafi   — f xv
Pagholo di S(er) giovan(n)j spectiale —   f xviij
Priore risalitj e conp(agni) ritagliatore —   f viij
francescho di pierozo della luna —   f lxj
Item deve avere
M° papera donna del decto s(er) giovannj dellerede
di Benedecto di S(er) francescho del Maestro piero
fiorinj dugento o circa p(er) resto della sua dota
e qualtj sanno (si hanno) a piatire po(pero) sono
in diferenza de qualij na (ne ha) a dare al decto
s(er) giovan(n)j fiorinj cento diecj chome dette di
sopra in questa scrita Se si rischonteran(n)o gli
raporteremo alla vostia Signoria
Item mi tru(ovo) jo giovannj sopradecto tantj
tra li brj e jnbreviature che gli fanno f xxv"

[Arch. di Stato. Archiv. delle Decime, Anno 1427. Quartiere di San Giovanni, Gonfalone Chiavj, segnato No. 59, c. 976-979'; M., *L. d. R.,* XXXII, Doc. 1.]

On the back of c. 981 is written the following:

G° chiavj adj 10 di luglio (1427)

Simone dj marcho dellarobia e figluolj   f 4
f 4 sol 14 dj 5 n° c. 6
    Messo allibro c. 532 R

56. Simone's tax return of 1430.
      "Quartiere S Giovannj
        Gonfalone chiavj
Questa e la rechata di Simone di marcho
dellarobbia e de figluoli e chatastatj In
detto Gonfalone In fiorinj uno —   f 1
In prima una chasa dallavoratore etc, etc - - -
- - - - (Omitted portions are repetitions)
- - - -

      Incharichi

	Simone dimarcho sopradecto deta dannj	87
Mō	Margherita donna del decto Simoni — danj	68
	Marcho di simone deta dannj —	42
Ser	Giovannj di simone deta dannj —	36
	Lucha di simone deta dannj —	30
Mō	Antonia donna del decto marcho deta dannj	30

filippo figluolo del decto Marcho di mesi due e mezo"
[Archiv. delle Decime, Q^re San Gio. Chiavi, filza 386, c. 734.]

57. Simone's tax return of 1433.
      "Gonfalone chiavj Quart° s Johī
Questa e la rechata di Simone di Marcho della
robbia e de figluoli chatastatj In decto Gonfalone
In soldi sedicj e dj tre a oro
In prima una chasa dallavoratore etc etc - - - - - -
- - - - - -
- - - - - -

      Incharichi

	Simone di marcho sopradetto	danj —	89
Mō	Margherita sua donna	danj —	70
	Marcho di simone — — — — —	danj —	46
Mō	Antonia sua donna — — —	danj —	20
	Checcha figluola del dcō marcho —	danj —	1½
	Jacopo figluolo del dcō marcho —	danj —	1½
Ser	Giovannj di simone — — ·	danj —	39
Mō	Nanna sua donna — —	danj —	19
	Lucha di simone — —	danj —	33

Tegnano a pigione una chasa laquale e dellerede
di simone di salvi di filippo posta nel pp di
sanpiero maggiore di firenze nella via di sangilio

nellaquale habitano paghianne lanno di pigione
f dicanove doro ———   f 19 — doro
- - -
- - -
- - -
- - -

Truovasi Marcho di simone debito(re) In sulla
bottega dove e conpagno con Agnolo di ser
Martino lanaiuolo per saldo facto fiorinj ottanta
quatro et soldj quatordicj a f —   f lxxxiiij sxiiij a f—"
    (Omitted portions are repetitions)
On the back of the declaration is written
      Ge chiavj
    Simone di marcho dellarobia s 16 dj 3
    Richordo adj 31 dj mag(gio)"
[Idem, idem, filza 479, c. 583.]

  58. Tax return of Andrea's father Marco di Simone, 1442.
      "Q. S. Giovanj G. chiavj

Marcho di
Simone delarobia
  c 290

    Dinanzi davoj Signorj uficialj della conservatione et......(a
word written and canceled illegible) aumentatione delle nuova gravezza della citta di firenze si rapporta le substanze et benj dj
    Marcho di simone di Marcho della robbia lanaiuolo aprestanziato
nella presente distribuzione della cinquina nel gonfalone delle chiavj
In f uno soldj nove dj uno aoro — —   fɪ s 9 dj ɪ
- - - - - -
- - - - - -
- - - - - -
      Incharichj
    Tengho una chasa apigione p mio habitare Insieme cõlucha mio
fratello posta nelpp di Sanpiero Maggiore laquale e dantonio ditadeo
deglj albizj et dane lano f vẽtj doro f 20
      Bocche
Marcho decto . . . .   danj 56
Mõ antonia sua dona —   danj 32
andrea suo figluolo   —   danj 7
checcha sua figla   —   danj 11
Simone suo figlõ   —   danj 4
pagholo suo figlõ   —   danj 2"

[Archiv. d. Stato, Portata al Catasto di Marco di Simone della Robbia dell' anno 1442, segnato Archiv. delle Decime, Quartiere San Giovanni, Gonf. Chiavi, filza 627, c. 332.]

59. Tax return of Ser Giovanni di Simone, 1442.
S(er) Giovanj di Simone
di Marcho delarobia
    c 256
        "Q s. Giovanj G. chiavj
Dinanzj davoj Signorj uficialj della conservatione et aumentatione della nuova graveza della citta di firenze si raporta le sustanze e benj di
S(er) Giovanj disimone dimarcho ^{della robbia} (above the line in original) notaio fiorentino aprestanziato nella presente distribuzione della cinquina nel gonfalone delle chiavj In f uno sol. nove et dj uno aoro
— f 1 s 9 dj 1 f —
- - - - - -
- - - - - -
       Incharichj
Tengho una chasa apigione p mio abitare dalorenzo ditaddeo diristoro posta nel pplo di santa maria In campo dirimpecto allospedale delle donne di santa maria nuova dellaquale pagho lano f sedicj doro et uno recho(?) — —
       Bocche
S(er) Giovanj decto danj 48
Mō chosa sua donā danj - - - - -"
[Archiv. idem, Portata al Catasto di Ser Giovanj di Simone di Marcho delarobia dell'anno 1442, segnato Archiv, Quart. e Gonf. detti, filza 627, c. 22.]

60. Tax return of Ser Giovanni, 1446.
        "Quartiere s giovanj. G. chiavj
       Substanze et Incharichj dj
S(er) Giovanj di simone dimarcho della robbia notaio fior° etc etc
- - -
- - -
       Bocche
S(er) Giovanj decto —   danj — 53
Mō chosa sua donna . — danj — 30
francescho suo nipote — danj —   4
On back of last page   R° Ser giovannj adi 26 (di febraio)"
[Archivio idem, Portata al catasto di Ser Giovanni della Robbia dell' anno 1446, segnato Archiv. Quart. e Gonf. detti, filza 681, c. 102.]

61. Tax return of Marco di Simone, 1446.

"Quart S Giovannj G. chiavj

Sustanze īcharichj dj

Marcho di simone di marcho della robbia More usino (intended perhaps for usual word "usato") a dj decini s 15 °′° dj dispiacente f 1° s 2 dj 6 oro dj chatasto f 1° p(er)¹⁸⁷²° chonposizione diceva ī simone dj marcho dela robia e ne figliolj

- - - -   * above the line in original

- - -

Incharichj

Tengho apigione una chasa posta nelpolo dj Sanpiero Magiore nela via alchanto alabrigha da figluolj e rede dj pagholo di ser giovannj speziale alangiolo da prima via e sechondo ser giovannj Mencj a ⅓ dofo da firenzuola donne (i.e ne do) loro lanno dj pigione f 13 s 6 dj 8 oro

Bocche

Marcho dj Simone detto	dannj 62
Mõ giema mia donna —	dannj 36
ceccha Mia figluola —	dannj 16
Andrea Mio figluolo —	dannj 11
Simo Mio figluolo —	dannj 9
pagholo Mio figluolo —	dannj 7
Margherita Mia figlola —	dannj 4

O adare alchomune p(er) Mia graveza f 30"

On back of last page R° Marcho adi 28 (febbraio)

[Archiv. idem, Portata al Catasto di Marco della Robbia dell'anno 1446, segnato Archiv. Quart. e Gonf. detti, filza 681, c. 409.]

62. Tax return of the heirs of Marco di Simone, 1451.

"Quartiere sco giovannj g° chiavj

Sostanze de

figluolj e rede dimarcho di simone dellarobbia prestāziatj in nome di marcho loro padre in g° chiavj

Disse el primo chatasto in simone di marcho loro avolo f 1 s —

Ebbono di decina 1447 in nome di marcho loro padre f 1 s 1 dj 6 a oro

furono sgravati nel primo sgravo   s 1j dj vj

restorono in —   f — s 19 d —

ebbono gratia e furono chonpòstj in s 1j per gravezza e per ricrescimento

restano al presente in —   f — s 4 —

Una meza chasa etc

Una chasa dalavoratore etc

Una chasetta etc

19 pezzj di terra etc.

della detta rendita ne tocha loro la terza parte elaltra
alucha disimone della robbia loro zio elaltra allaredita
giacente di ser giovannj loro zio

- - - -

- - - -

- - - -

Tre pezi di terra posti nel pplo di sanmartino aputorno cho suo vocabolj
e confinj chome chiaramente si mostra per la scritta dandrea di rinaldo
sceglitore in chuj diceva nel primo chatasto nelquartiere di santa m' novella g° lionrosso laquale terra rimase a mona mea donna del detto andrea
chella prese per sua dote laquale la detta mona mea dono allamargherita
figluola di marcho della robbia detto e circha anj dua charta per mano di
ser iachopo da romena tenevala a fitto nel primo chatasto domenicho di
chele chalinj per istaia 32 di grano ogj rende meno

    grano   staia 32

la detta terra lavora ogj amigo antonio diachopo chiamato chappello rende
in parte staia 24 di grano e debbono dare ognāno a detta m' mea lire otto
mentre chella vive.

               Beni alienatj

Una chasa posta nelpopolo di sanpiero maggiore nella via deglj albertineglj
chōfinata da p° e secondo via da $\frac{1}{3}$ bartolomeo deglialexandrj da $\frac{1}{4}$ via
venduta antonio di chorso della rena per luj o per chj e nominasse adj 6
daghosto 1451 per pregio di f quarāta charta per mano di ser piero dicharlo
sarto

la detta chasa era scritta nel primo chatasto in Simone della robbia e
affittavasi per f 3 lanō

           Boche

Andrea	deta danj 15	}	
Simone	deta danj 14		
Pagholo	deta danj 12	}	tuttj figluolj di detto
Francescho	deta danj 8		Marcho di Simone della robbia
Margherita	deta danj 7	}	"

[Archiv. delle Decime, Quartiere San Giovanni, Chiavi, filza 717, a. 222.]
NOTE.—For the Taxation of the heirs of Marco for 1457 see my *Luca della
Robbia,* XXXVI-XXXVII.

63. Tax return of Andrea della Robbia, 1470.
"Archivio delle Decime Q° S Giovanni chiave
Andrea di marcho di simone dellarobbia chio nel primo
chatasto dissi in simone di marcho e nel valsente del
51 in filglioli di marcho nel 58 in filglioli di marcho

detto nela decima presente in figlioli detti in detto
gonfalone

Sustanze

Duna chasa pro non divisa chon lucha mio zio e simone
mio fratello da p° via da second° berto di rondone da
terzo beni di sca M° delfiore da quarto piero sassetti e
la detta chasa chonpramo da lippo di biagio da peretola
per pregio di f. 220 - - - - - -

Dun podere posto altartiglia e pro non diviso chon sopradetti - - - - -

Dun podere pro non diviso chon sopradetti posto a san
tomaso a baroncielli tutti confinati chome gli hanno detto
lucha di simone - - - - - -

Dun pezzo di terra vingniata di staiora quattro - - - - -.

- - - - posto nel popolo di san christofano annuovoli - - -·

- - - - - - (bought 18 September 1468)

Dun pezzo di terra vingniata di staiora 4 luogho detto
gondilagi popolo santa M° a peretola - - - - (bought 5 April 1468)

Dun pezzo di terra posto in detto luogho di staiora dieci
o circha parte vingniata e parte lavorati (bought 9 April
1468 for fi. 34)

Incarichi

O addare ongni anno al cam° (camerario) di sca m°
delfiore (here follow a word or two illegible) di lib 10 soldi 8 si pagha
davillaro della sopradetta chasa

Lucha di simone dellarobbia mio zio mi domanda buona somma
di danari della quale 10 ne fussi debitore chome lui dicie
mi rimarebbe picchola chosa et pero mi vi rachomando

E trovomi chon bocche

Andrea detto deta danni	33	f. 200
Nanna mia donna deta danni	21	f. 200
Antonia mia figliola deta danni	3	f. 200
Marcho mio figliolo deta danni	2	f. 200
Giovanni mio figliolo deta danni	1	f. 200"

[Portata al Catasto di Andrea della Robbia, Anno 1470. Archiv. delle
Decime Q″ S. Giovanni, Gonf. Chiavi, filza 927 c. 52; Gaye, I, 186-187;
Cr., 304; M., *L. d. R.*, XXXVII.]

64. Andrea's Tax return of 1481.

"A quarttiere sangiovannj chonfalone chiavi
Andrea di marcho dellarobbia ebbe di catasto lanno 1470

in detto nome	f ——
ebbe detto	f 1.3.7.5

Una partte di casa nel chonfalone delliondoro in
via ghuelfa un terzo mi tocho nella divisa con lucha
mio zio e con simone mio fratello da p° via second°
piero sasetti 3 capittolo di santa m* del fiore 4 lucha
di simone comperola marcho mio padre e lucha mio
zio dallippo di biagio daperettola lanno 1446 costo
f 220 cartta p(er) ser iacopo da romena tenghola a mjo
uso p(er) abitazione f ——

Una quartta casa per non divisa con lucha di simone
mio zio e con simone mio fratello nel popolo di santo m*
altarttagliese da p° via second° strada 3.4 nicholo e
giovannj bellacj

La quartta partte di dicannove pezi di terra per
non divisj con luca e simone come di sopra posti
alltartigliese da p° via second° marcho di bello bellacj
3 filippo del panca 4 loro medesimj lutjmo (?) da second°
3.4 piero di biagio daltarttagliese

Un pezo di tera per non diviso con lucha e simone
come di sopra comperato da firenze di zelone lanno
1468 costo f viiij s x cartta p(er) ser andrea dacampi
e di sopradettj terrenj inoggi buona partte innarno
come si puo vedere lavora dettj terrenj chimentj di
marcho rendono p(er) la partte mia

f 80 — 9 — o

ghrano	staiora —————	15 —	
carne	libbre 50 ———	50	—
uova	serque una	— 1	—
capponi	paia ———————		

Un podere per non diviso con lucha e simone come
di sopra con casa daoste e dallavorattore nel popolo
di santommaso a baroncellj da p° via second° piero
mellinj 3 filippo di simone fossattello in mezo 4 lerede
di tommaso davizi

Due pezi di tterra per non divisj con lucha e simone
dettj e con detto podere da p° via second° 3 lerede di
conte peruzi fossattello in mezo 4 piero mellinj lavora
lucha di franc° garlonj rende p(er) mja partte f 76 — 2 — 2

ghrano staiora	st(aia)	7
vino ————	b(arili)	6
capponi ————	p(aia)	—
uova ————	ser(que)	1 —

lavoransi dette terre con um bue di l xxxiiii tocamj p(er) ¼ 18 s 10 - 10
Un poderetto nel popolo di san gorgo aruballa sanza

casa da signiore con cinque pezuoli di terra con detto
podere chon 3 pezi anno p(er) confino da p° second"
via 3 papi di gerj de bardi 4 chiesa di sangorgo
aruballa coglialltri due pezi confina da p° via second°
chiesa di sangorgo 3 chiesa di sanlorenzo amontj sone 4
piero ghuaschonj et 5 fossatto comperossi da m°
nanna donna di zanobi ficozi 1469 cartta p(er) ser
paolo paoli p(er) f 375 di sugello lavoralo ant° diromolo
cō un bue di l xxxvj rendemj mja partte —

ghrano	———————	st(aia) 35
vino	———————	b(arili) 8
olio	———————	b(arili) 7
carne di porcho	——	ll(libbre) 102
uova	———————	ser(que) 5
capponi	———————	p(aia) 1

Frutto di piu ragioni   l 2 (lire 2)   412 — 19 — 9

Due pezi di tera di staiora dieci in circha partte
vigniata e partte no posta a perettola in ghondilagi da
p° via second° dant° vocato farfa 3 zanobj calzolaio
4 via comperatto da simone di bencivennj scarfa p(er) f settanta
di sugello cartta p(er) ser girolamo pascholinj lanno 1468 rendono
in partte

       vino barillj ——————— b 12 —
       ghrano ——————— st 4 —

Un pezo di vignia nel popolo di san christofano annuovolj
da p° second° via 3 munistero di santa aghata 4 benj della
comp° di castello 5 guljano dantonjo e fratellj comperata
da m° zanobja e m° lisa sirocchie e figluoli furono di
giovannj di lorenzo dannuovoli comperata adi 18 di
settembre 1468 costorono f xxxv cartta p(er) ser piero da
campi rendemj in partte

       vino ——————— b(arili) 8

      Incarichi

Da dare ogni anno al capittolo di santa M°
delfiore p(er) lavvilaro della casa dove abitto l 2 s 12

      Bocche

Andrea	etta danni	44
M° nana sua donna e sta p(er) fare		
el fanciullo di dj in dj (i.e. di giorno in giorno)	etta anj	31
Antonia mio fioliuola anj	13 a di dota insulmonte	
Marcho mio fioliuolo ———————	11	f 600

Giovanni mio fioluolo ———	9	
Paocholo mio fioluolo ———	8	
Lalisabetta mia fioliuola ———	7	non a (non ha) di dota nulla
Lucha mio fioluolo ——	6	
Francescho mio fioluolo ———	4	

Somã la prima faccia del valsente —   f 412 — 19 — 9

Somã la faccia disopra   f 139 — 0 — 0

        551 — 19 — 9

Abattj p(er) 5 percento p(er) la conservagione de benj   f 27 — 12 —

        524 — 7 — 9

Somã del valsente netto f 524 — 7 — 9 a 7 percento

fa di Entratura   f 36 — 15

Abattesj f 4.18 di valsēte p(er) la ¼ parte di l 11 s 8

duno livello pachano al capitolo di sãta mᵉ del fiore

della casa dove abitono fanno di Entratura(?) s 7 di Entratura(?)

dalentrata ———————   f 36 — 8

Avanzagli f 36 — 8 tochagli p(er) la schala di gravezza f dua 5 dieci dj

            undicij — f 2 — 10 — 11 oro

Arbitrio s diecj di f larghi   s 10"

[Portata al Catasto, anno 1481, di Andrea della Robbia, Archiv. delle Decime, Qᵗᵉ S. Giovanni, Conf. Chiavi, filza 100, c. 137.]

65. Andrea's Tax Return of 1498—actually made about Apr. 1, 1495.

"Andrea di marcho di simone della Robbia Q di sangiovani

G chiavi disse la gravezza della scala dellanno 1481 in andrea detto

Una casa per mio abitare posto nel popolo disanlorenzo

luogho detto via ghuelfa nel gonfalone delione doro che da pᵒ

via da sᵒ eredi di berto legnaiuolo da tᵒ capitolo di santa maria

delfiore da qᵒ govanni tessitor di panni lini o conperato un

pezzuolo di terra cioè di campo che confina chollorto della detta

casa e per crescere lorto dallato drieto alla casa confina collorto

di detta casa e con detto capitolo in dua lati costo ff ottanta

larghi doro per ff 40 lo staioro che furono staiora dua sotto di

15 di settembre 1492 roghato ser Guntino di lorenzo di guntino rende

vino barili 4 lanno ———————   f 1 — 16

E piu una casa posta in detto popolo allato a quella abito

murata in sulla via prima compera della terra era orto di detta

casa chio abito laquale al presente apigionata confinata da pᵒ

via da sᵒ andrea sopradetto da tᵒ govanni tessitor di panni

lini da qᵒ beni di santa maria delfiore tiella a pig(i)one

baldo di giovanni di berto da careggi per preg(i)o di ff quattordici

e mezzo larghi doro exun pacha fu roghato ser bastiano forci della
alloghagone ———————————— ff 19 — 7 — 10
Un podere posto nel popolo di san gorgo aruballa con casa
dalavoratore diviso in cinque pezzi di terra E prima tre
pezzi insieme da p° via da s° papi di Geri de bardi da t° via
da q° detto papi E piu dua pezzuoli di terra spiccati da
quegli tre sono staiora quattro on circha da p° via da s°
la chiesa di sangorgo da t° antonio di piero Ghuasconi da q°
chiesa dimonte isone ed è in tutto staiora dicotto ulivata vingniata
e affruttata lavorasi con uno bue di ff nove lavorato meo di
zanobi berni rende in parte

Grano	staia	30	
vino	barilj	6	
olio	barilj	5	
fichi sechi	staia	4	
carne	libre	100	
capponj	paia	1	
uova	serque	5	f 24 — 3 — 6

E piu tre pezzi di terra vingniata posta nel popolo di
sacristofano anuovoli luogho detto gondilagi confinata da
p° e s° via da t° ser diecaiuti prete insalorenzo da q°
lorenzo di Giuliano dant° da qui°(quinto) âtonio sta alla
torre lavorale alpresente miglor di romolo sta a castello e
de staiora quattordi(ci) rende lanno in parte barilj 15 —   f 9 — 16
E piu conperai un pezuol di terra per murare una casa posto
nel popolo di salorenzo luogho detto via mozza che va a santa
caterina la quale conperai dal capitolo di santa m° delfiore
per preg(i)o di ff quaranta larghi doro lo staioro che costo in
tutto ff quarantacinque e mezzo larghi côfinata da p° e s° e
t° beni della detta chiesa da q° via alquale fu braccia venti-
quattro in sulla via e ba(braccia) settantazette indrieto a canna
di tera sotto di 6 di marzo 1492 roghato ser alesandro braccesi
la quale terra si vende come si vedra nellaltra faccia ne benj
alienatj —   f ——

                                    53·3·4
         benj alienatj
Un quarto podere per non diviso con simone dellarobbia mio
fratello posto nel popolo di santomaso a baroncelgli e nel pievier
diripoli si vende a domenico mellinj ebine (that is ne ebbi)
ff cento sessanta larghi inoro cioe del quarto podere confinato
·in questo modo cioe de p° via da s° domenico mellinj deto
da t° bastiano covoni da q° via da qui° fossato da sesto e
1/7 (settimo) eredi dallessandro peruzzi roghato ser ant° di ser

niccolo ferrinj sotto di 30 daghosto 1486

E piu o alienão pezzi tre di terra posta nel popolo di santa m*
altartilglese confinata in questo modo cioe da p° via da s° borro
da t° benj della detta chiesa da q° andrea bellacci da qui°
ristoro ser ristorj lequali terre furono istimate staiora venticinque
conperolle tinoro bellaccj costerolgli ff settanta larghi inoro
nettj roghato ser lorenzo di vivaldo sotto di 15 di settenbre 1492 di firenze

E piu o alienato un pezzo di terra posta nel popolo di sanlorenzo
luogho detto via mezza che va a santa caterina laquale conperai
dal capitolo di santa m* del fiore per preg(i)o di ff quaranta
larghi doro lo staioro confinata da p° e s° e t° beni di detta chiesa
da q° via alquale fu ba(braccia) 24 insulla via e bracc(i)a
77 indrieto a canna di terra sotto di sei di marzo 1492 roghato
ser allessandro braccesi la quale terra si vende a baldo di
govannj di berto da careggi per preg(i)o di ff sessanta cinque
larghi inoro tolse per murare chasa rogha ser quntino di
lorenzo di guntino

Somm* la Entratura di questa scrittura chome nella prima
faccia si vede f cinquanta cinque s iij dj iiii° aoro di sugello cioe —

$$f\ 55 - 3 - 4$$

Sono f quaranta cinque s xviiii° dj vj aoro di sugello
Tochagli p(er) dex* (dexima) f quattro s xij aoro sugello —

$$f\ 4 - 12\ \text{sugello}$$

Adi 24 di marzo 1524 abbatesi f 1 s 12 d 4 p(er) una
casa ridotta p(er) suo habitare p(er) partito degli uficialj
delmonte roghato ser Lo(Lorenzo) arutj sotto detto dj
in filza n° 208 resta ——— $$f\ 2 - 19 - 8$$

Al 32 (1532) in lucha dand* di simone della robbia
e altri G* (Gonfalone) detto n° 470 p(er) a/x (decima) di
f dua s xviiij dj vii larghi di grossi in soma di
f 4.15.4 di a/x ——— $$f\ 2 - 19 - 8"$$

[Archivio di Stato, Archivio delle Decime, Q^(te) di San Gio. Gonf. Chiave,
filza 120, c. 88; Pini, Scrittura di artisti italiani, sec. XIV-XVII; Cr., 308-
309.]

66.   Registration entry of will of Andrea della Robbia.
Documents:

1. (At the top of page: Ser Giuliano di Ser Domenico da
   Ripa)
"Andreas Marci Simonis della Robbia condedit
testamentum die 14 Septembris 1522. Heredes instituit Johannem Lucam et Jeroni-
mum eius filios.   lib 3-15
Die 31 Januarij 1529 (modern reckoning

1530) solvit Johanni marie de Corbi-
nellis camerario c. 4 lib. tres cum o/4
(quarto) Johannes Andree della Robbia."   lib. 3–15

[Archivio di Stato, Archivio Notarile Appendice, Registro di Testamenti Santa Maria Novella, N° VIII, segnato Cod. 89 c. 98; Milanesi, *Misc.*, 39 III P., c. 23; R. G. M., *Am. Jour. Arch.*, XXIV(1920), 140.]

67. Will of Andrea della Robbia, 1522.

"+yhs

In dnj no(min)e ame(n) anno dnj jncarnationis
1522 Jndict. X et die 4 settembris actū
florētie jn p(o)p(o)lo scī laurentij florētie et jn
sagrestia ecc(lesi)e scj marcj de florētia
p(rese)ntibus jbid venerabilibus viris

frā paulus johīs de cavalcantis de prato ⎰ omnibus fratribus
frā pacifico filippi de gualteritis   ⎱ conventus scj marcj
frā nicholaio mariotti de sexto   ⎰ florētie testibus
frā bart° pauli de finis   ⎱ ad jnfrascripta omnia
frā johannes s(er) lionardi de florētia   ⎰ et singula vocatis
frā angelo petrj de beninis   ⎱ h(ab)itis et
frā francisco johīs de dinis   ⎰ rogatis proprio hore
                                          ⎱ infrascripti testatoris

Cum nihil sit certius morte nihilque jncertius hora
eius hi(n)c est q(uod) prudens vir andreas marcj
simonis della robbia plj scj lavrᴵᴵ florētie sanus
p(er) dei gratiam sensu mente jntellectu et corpore
volens dum mens salubre est posteris de suis p(ro)vi-
dere nolens jntestatos decedere sed de suis bonis
p(ro)videre p(er) hoc suum nu(n)cupatum testamētū quod
dictitur sine scriptis de bonis suis deposuit fecit
et ordinavit jn hu(n)c qui sequitur modū et formā
viz.
Jn primis q(ui)de(m) animam suam om(n)jpotentj
deo eiusque gloriose matrj marie semp(er) vir-
ginj et toti celeste curie paradisi humilter et
devote racommandavit corporis autem suj sepultu-
ram elegit jn sepulcro suorum p(re)dicessorum sito jn
eccᴵᵉ scj petrj maioris de florētia et circa eius
funus fierj voluit q(uo)d et quantum videbitur
jnfrascriptis suis heredibus
Item jure legati reliquit et legavit ope(re) scē marie
del fiore de florētia nove sagristie nuovi op(er)i mu-
rorum jn totum sechundum ord(inamenta) comunis

Marginal notes (left column):

Test Andree Marcj della robbia 1522 4 7 bre (N°) 177

Sūt codicillas T mano mei

Mixi ad op-(er)am

data fides ut patet

est revocatus manu s(er)-johīs petrj de borghesis

p(re)dicte lib. Tres f.p.

(This was a registration tax as wills were registered at the opera.)

Item amore dei et p(ro) rimedio anime sue voluit et reliquit q(uod) infra otto dies p(roxi)m(o)s futuros post mortem dcj testatoris q(uod) in ecc¹ˣ scj marcj celebrentur misse scj gregorj et p(ro) elimosina teneantur dare infrascripti sui heredes flor.

unum aurj lar. in auro

Item relequit sorori sperantie et sorori angeline et cuilibet earum p(ro) rimedio anime sue flor. decem aurj l(arghos) in auro et ultra rasciam et pannum condecentes p(ro) uno vestitu p(ro) quolibet earum

Item relequit amore dei (two words written and cancelled) marie sue filie pannum p(ro) una cioppa (cappa) et unum strigatorium tempore mortis d(i)c(t)j testatoris et ultra p(re)d(i)c(t)a eidem relequit quolibet anno quousque vixerit flor. novem lar. in aur° et stinta eius vita na(tura)lj presens legatus evanescat

+yhs m˙ (head of 2nd page)

Item relequit jure legati d(omi)ne nannine p(ro) usu sue dotis (these four words written and cancelled) sue uxorj (text mutilated—missing word must be *uxorj*) dotes suas quas dixit fuisse et esse flor. ottingentos quos h(ab)uit jn chontantibus a co(mun)i flor(entie) jam s(un)t annj quinquaginta et considerans bene merita ipsius dne nannine eidem relequit et legavit usum fructum integrum pdij(praedii) dcī testatoris positi jn pplo scī giorgij aruballa infra suos confines cum o(mn)ibus suis pertinentiis et cum usu omnium masseritiarum et bestiaminarum et bonorum mobilium existantium sup(er) dictis bonis tempore mortis dcī testatoris et ultra predicta reditum jn domo dcī testatoris inf(r)a assignate jn portione infrascriptj hieronimj et usum camere cum omnibus suis fulcimētis tam de lignamine q(uam) p(ro) usu lettiere lettuccj et cum lettis fornitis p(ro) omni tempore et p(ro)ut verioris retineat et retinet ipse testator ac et(iam) usum o(mn)ium dcē dnē pannorum lintorum et lannorum p(ro)usu suj dorsj quousque viderit. Et presens legatus voluit durare quousque nō petierit dotas suas et liberaret dotam ab honere satisdandj et fidem p(re)standj decit-

andj(?) et faciendj ad arbitrio bonj virj et a quacumque con-
fectione jnventarj qui intendet et vult ipãm terram ad
restitutionem bonorum p(re)d(i)c(t)orum tam mobilium
quam jmobilium prout erunt et que et nõ essent usu con-
sumpta
Item reliquit a dcē dnē panna et strigam p(ro) bruno (i.e.
lutto) faciend° p(er) dcū testatore(m)
Item autem in o(mn)ibus suis bonis suos heredes universales
                                                      jnstituit
fecit et esse voluit johannem lucam et hieronimum suos
filios l(egiti)mos et nat(ura)les equis portionibus
et volens evitare scandala que solent saepe orirj in divisionibus
bonorum et dividet domos jn portione dcj luce de bonis
jmobili(bu)s jure legati
reliquit et posuit unam domum cum suis habitationibus et
p(er)tinentiis
positam in p(o)p(o)lo scj lavr'' florētie et jn via que dicitur la
via Guelfa cuj a p° dcā via a ij palatium dnē magda-
lene olim petrj de sassettis a iij jnfrascripta domus posita
jn portione dcī hieronimi a 4 bona cap(itol)j scē marie del
fiore de florētia p(ro) tanto quanto est p(er) latitudinem domus
p(re)dcē una cum orto et vinea que est ī orto dcē domus
p(ro) tanto quanto capiet latitudo domus p(re)decte proce-
dentem per altitudinam prout traet paries dividens domum
p(re)dcām a domo infrascripti Hieronimj cum omnibus pertinentiis domus predicte et que domus et vinea est libera dcī
testatoris et cum honere q(uod) dcūs lucas nõ possit aliquid
repetere ab heredibus dcī testatoris de his que hodie est in mani-
bus dcī testatoris et hoc quod domus ip(s)a est cum
melioris conditionis jnfrascripto domo - - - - - jn portione
vero dcī hieronimj de bonis jmobiliis jure legatj reliquit posuit
et esse volvit unam aliam domum cum suis habitationibus et
p(er)tinentiis et finimentis positam juxta
sup(ra)scriptam domum muro comuni mediante una
cum una stantia infrascripte domus assignata jnfrascripto
johni que est post cucinam domus jnfrascripti johīs
denominata lanticucina
               +yhs M°(head of 3rd page)
jn qua anticucina est furnus et truogolj reservato tamen
arti victreriarie p(ro) faciendo unum anditum ad ortum p(ro)
domo dcī infrascriptj johīs bracchia duo cum dimideo alterius
bracchi juxta parietem dividendum domum datam
dcō infrascripto johāni et domum

andree venitianj in quibus bracchijs duobus com dimideo teneatur dcūs johēs fierj facere suis sumptibus unum parietem
dividendum dcūm andronem fiendj residuum dcē stantie
dcē antiquoqúina (anticucina) Et in dicta portione
domus date dcō hieronimo voluit venire totum ortum qui
fuit comprehensus a linea ortus datj dcō luce usque ad
lineam ortus rettam p(ro)ut trahet linea retta
dcī parietis fiendj p(er) dcū johēm ad cordam adeo q(uod)
ortus dcī hieronimj erit p(ro) tanto quanto capiet domus sua
sub sua dominatione et et(iam) p(ro) tanto quanto capiet
jnfrascripta domus data dcō jnfrascripto johī restens jn portione dcī hieronimj posuit totam integram vineam que est dcī
testatoris libera jnfrascriptorum ortorum
et jn capit' ortus d(i)c(t)arum domorum ī portione supradcī
luce infra versus viam dictā mozzam adeo q(uod) tota
vinea que rimanet nō data dcō luce jn sua portione
restet et sit jn portione dcī hieronimj cum honere solvendo cap(ito)lo ecc'(ecelesie) flor. lib. quinque et sol. 4 quolibet anno p(ro) livello debito p(ro) dcā domo
et hoc p(ro) raguaglio eius jn quo et de quo ipse hieronimus est creditor dcī testatoris quam voluit p(er) eum
pati possi et cuj domus a p' via p(re)dcā et a ij' domus dcī luce
a iij domus jnfrascripti johīs a 4° cap(ito)lum flor""
In portione vero partis dcī johīs de bonis jmobilibus jure legati
reliquit et posuit unam aliam
domum positam juxta dcām domum datam dcō hieronimo
cum suis habitationībus excepta dcā antiquoquina data supra-
dcō hieronimo duobus bracchijs cum
dimideo p(ro) faciend' dcūm andronē et cum
toto residuo ortus rimanentis a dcā dirittura procedenti
a dicto muro faciendj in dcīs duobus bracchijs cum
dimideo supra versus viam p(re)dcām et usque
ad sepem qua sepes rimaneat et sit
jn portione dcī hieronimj cuj domus a p' via a ij dcā sepes
a iij domus dcī hieronimj a iiij dcū andreas venetianj et cum
honere solvendj anno quolibet cap(ito)lo ecclesie florētiē lib.
quinque et sol. quatuor p(ro) suo livello
Declarans q(ud) puteus in quoquina (cucina) sit in comuni
cum jnfrascriptis hieronimo et johāni
Et licet etc
                    +yhs M'(head of 4th page)
Cassans etc Ego julianus olim s(er) dmcj julianj de ripa
                    civis florēt. rogans etc''

[Archivio di Stato, Rogiti di Ser Giuliano di Domenico da Ripa, Filza di Testamenti 1490-1546, segnato Notai G. 532 No. 177; R. G. M., *A. J. A.* XXIV (1920), 136-145.]

68. Codicil to Andrea's Will. 1523.

"Jn dej no(min)e amē anno dnī jncarnationis mille quingento vigentesimo sechondo jndict vj et die

Codicilli andree Marcj della robia 1522 18 Feb. (N°) 183

xviij mensis februarij 1522 (old style) actum jn p(o)p(o)lo scī laur" florētie et jn domo jnfrascripti codicillatoris presentibus

fratre bartilozo johīs de cavalcantibus	fratribus	omnibus testibus
fratre damiano marcj de beninis	scj marcj	ad infrascripta
	florētie	oīa et sin-
johī leonardj de manischalcis	civibus	gula proprio
Marcello leonardj de vernacis	florētie	hore jnfra-
Franc° julianj de bonis		scripti codi-
		cillatoris vocatis

Mixi ad op(er)am

Cum ambulatorio sit voluntas usque ad mortem hīc est q(uod) prudens vir Andreas marcj simonis della robbia

h(ab)itis et roga-
tis

p(o)p(o)lo scj laur" flor. sanus p(er) dei gratiam mente sensu et intellectu et corpore languens renumptians et recordans q(uod) alias dcūs andreas mano mej notarj infra-scripti sub die xiiij(?) mensis settemb(ris) proxime preterite v(e)l alio die veriorj suum condedit testamētum jn quo p(ro) hoc simil(it)er disposuit inter alia que jn eo continentur post dcūm infrascriptum testamētum mutata sue volontate cira jn-frascriptum quodam in eo continentur hac particulari disposi-tione de bonis suis p(er) has presentes codicillos disposuit et ordinavit et fecit jn solitū modū et formā
Jn primis renumtians q(uod) jn dcō suo testamēto reliquit marie sue filie anno quolibet quousque vixerit flor. novem lar. jn auro mutata sua voluntate ut jnfra voluit et declaravit q(uod) eidem marie
debeantur dcī floreni novem lar. jn avr° quousque*

*nō pettierit dcā maria cum viro suo et nō ultra hic debeantur q(uod) viro suo mortuo et evanescat p(rese)ns le-gatus

[ipē (ipse) vixerit durabit vita naturalis tomasij marcj fantinj virj et maritj dcē dnē marie et nō ultra vita dcī tomasiij etiam postquam vixerit ipā dnā maria sive non huiusmodj legatus evanescat] (all in brackets was cancelled after death of Tomaso Fantini, an asterisk (*) was put after quousque and marginal note is to be read.) Et voluit q(uod) ad solvendum dcōs flor. novem teneantur quilibet dcōrum suorum heredum jn dcō testamēto institutos(?)

p(ro) flor. tribus et nō ultra et voluit q(uod) dcā maria nō
possit illos patere nisi a quolibet dcōrum pred(i)c(t)orum
heredum p(r)out patet et nō possit illos consequi nisi
sup(er)scriptis bonis cuiuslibet d(i)c(t)orum suorum heredum et obumatorum (for successorum?) in portione sint ex
bonis testatoris p(ro) parte tangenti cuilibet suorum heredum
(Head of 2d page)
Item renumtians jnstituisse suos heredes
lucam johēm et hieronimum suos filios et eis divisisse et
cuilibet eorum dedisse certam portionem suorum
jmmobilium p(ro)ut jn testamēto et jn portione hieronimj fuisse cum domo data hieronimo unam stantiam denomina-
tam anticucina que est jn domo data dcō johani
Et voluit q(uod) johēs teneatur facere
unum andronem juxta murum dividend(um) domum
datam dcō johani et domum andree venitianj bracchior(um)
·duor(um) cum dimideo cum muro fiendo denovo p(ro) divi-
dendo anticucinam a d(i)c(t)o androne et p(r)out jn testamēto latius apparet mutata sua voluntate voluit q(uod) dcā
antiquoquina restet jntegra dcō johī et q(uod) dcūs johēs
teneatur facere hostium pro intrando jn orto juxta dcūm murum andree venitianj et nō maioris latitudinis bracchior(um)
duor(um) cum dimideo adeo q(uod) hostium p(re)d(i)ctum
possit capere jntegram viottolam
dcī ortus existantis semper colupna de lateribus que est supra
angolo viottole prope vineam domus jn portione ortus dcī
hieronimj et residuum ortus restantis
juxta dictam colunnam et versus viam mozzam restet et sit
dcō johī usque ad viottolam sepis que sepes cum viottola
existente juxta sepem et ortum dcī johis usque ad
domum d(i)ctam sit dcī hieronimj Et ad tollendum
pasculum declaravit quod integra sepes p(re)dcā p(ro)tanto
quanto capeat ortus dcī johīs et viottola juxta dcām
sepem et ortum dcī johīs sit et veneat jn portione dcī
hieronimj
Et loco dcē antiquoquine posuit et venire voluit unam
stantiolam que est jn domo data dcō johāni et respondit
cum fenestra jn lodia dcī hieronimj in qua hodie sit
paries cum palatio existanti sup(ra) ea et cum tetto et
sit afondamentibus usque ad celum Et teneatur
dcūs hieronimus facere intraturam jn dcā stantiola jn

androni domus dcī hieronimj et introitus intrantis

jn dcā stantiola debeant renumtiarj

Declarandum p(er) hos p(rese)ntes codicillos

q(uod) paries existens dimideo juxta domum datam

hieronimo et domū datam johī dividet, domos afunda-

mentis usque ad celum

Cassans anti etc confirmans etc

Et ha(n)s etc

Ego julianus s(er) dmcj de ripa notarius florent. rogans etc"

[Archivio idem, Filza idem No. 183; R. G. M., *A. J. A.* xxiv (1920),
163-144.]

69. Revocation of Andrea's Will.

"1524 jndict(ione) 12 et die tertio mensis junij

actū flor"ᵃ ī arte magistrorum (lapidum et legna) p(rese)nti-

bus Cante Michaellis cantis p(ro)visore dicte artis

Revocatio Test' Michaelle pieri cini d(e) lucherellis cive flor. p(opo)li scī

laur"ᶦ d(e) flⁱᵃ jobatiste aloisij ant' d(e)guidottis cive flor.

p(opo)li scī marcj d(e) flor. Tomasus d(omini)cj filippi d(e)

rinucis cive flor. p(opo)li sce Margherite d(e) flor.

franc° soldj batiste chappucceris cive flor. p(opo)li dcī

dom"° ol(im) lari andree lari cive flor. habitante ī castro vici

vallis else (Castel Vico Vald'elsa)

testibus ad infrascripta o(mn)ia p(ro)p(ri)o hore infra-

scripti andree d(e) robbia vocatis habitis et roghatis etc

Cum sit q(uod) andreas ol(im) marci d(e)robbia civis flor. jā

sunt duo anni p(reteri)te elapsi vel circha p(r)out vidi

recordari manu s(er) julianj s(er) Domc' d(e)ripa notari flor.

v(e)l alterius notari flor"ⁱᵃ' suū condedit test"ᵐ in q(u)o et

p(ro)q(u)o in est etc p(ro)ut asseruit fecit et ordinavit

q(uo)dā legatū et seu voluit et alia de quibus postea dissit

se multotiens penituisse et continue penitere attento

notaro q(uod) test"ᵐ p(re)dcūm de facto et absque p(re)-

meditatione aliqua condedit et ordinavit : et adeo ītendens

dcūm test"ᵐ et o(mn)ia ī eo contenta de presente revocare

ad hac ut aliud aliter et alio m(od)o maturo consiglio et

consulte suo loco et tempore condere ordinare et p(er)ficere .

possit et valeat : que p(ro)p(ter) dcūs suprascriptus andreas

testator constitutus ī presentia et ī conspecto mei jp'(jo-

hannis petri) notari infrascripti test"ᵐ suprascriptum dissit

asseruit et confessus fuit et dicit asserit continere test"ᵐ

p(re)dcūm de q(u)o s(upra) p(er) eū p(re)dcūm testatorem

et manu dcī s(er) juliani d(e) ripa seu alterius cujusque notari

rogantis se iterum atque iterum sepi sepis sepisime penituisse et
penitere fecisse et condedisse test^m de q(u)o supra et o(mn)ia
contenta ī eo p(ro)p(ter)ea et omnia meliori m(od)o in q(u)o
potuit test^m p(re)dcūm et o(mn)ia ī eo contenta irritavit et
revocavit cassavit et anullavit et irritat revocat cassatet anull-
lat : et p(ro) irrito casso revocato et anullato haberj voluit et
vult ī o(mn)ibus p(er) eū o(mn)ia pariter et ac si p(er)eū
factū conditū et ordinatū nō esset Rogans etc"

[Archivio di Stato, Rogiti di s(er) Giovanpiero Borghesi, Protocolli
1519-1524, segnato Noti, B. 2202, c. 537; R. G. M., *A. J. A.* xxiv (1920),
145.]

70.   Petition of Giovanni della Robbia for his third of Andrea's estate,
1529.

" +yhs
M.D. XXVIIIJ Jndictione 2ª de mense Julij

- - - -

- - - -

- - - -

Item postea dictis anno indictione dìe(xxviiij) et loco et
coram dictis s(upra)s(crip)tis testibus etc
Pateat omnibus evidenter qualiter johannis q(uondam) andree
marci della robbia de florentia Asserens et affirmans
dictū Andreā eius patrem mortuū esse et decessisse
ab intestato jam sunt annj tres prox(imi) elapsj et ultra
relictis post se dicto johanne et hyer^{mo} et luca eius
filiis le(giti)mis et naturalibus et nullis alijs relictis
habentibus eos excludere ab h(e)r(ed)i(t)ate vel
successione dicti andree eorū p(at)ris aut et(iam)
eis et aliqua parte concurrere Et sciens et cognoscens
p(re)fatus johannis h(e)r(ed)i(t)atem, dicti andree eius
q(uondam) p(at)ris eidem pro tertia parte ab intestato fuisse
et esse et et(iam) delata(m) illamque for(e) et esse sibj
portius utile(m) et lucrosa(m) qua(m) dannosa(m) jdeo
h(e)r(ed)i(t)atem predicta(m) sibi delata(m) p(er)-
tinente(m) et pro omnj alia parte
et portione etc Adivit et o(m)nj mel(iori) mō(do) etc
Asserens et Protestans et Rogans etc"

[Archiv. d. S., Rogiti di Ser Matteo da Falgano, Protocolli 1527-1530,
segnato Notai M. 300, c. 297ᵗ; R. G. M., *L'Arte*, XXII(1919) 111; M.,
G. d. R., XXII.]

II. CATALOGUE OF MONUMENTS

ANDREA DELLA ROBBIA

1470-1480

ANDREA DELLA ROBBIA

1470-1480

1 MADONNA OF THE IMPRUNETA TYPE. Berlin. Herr Minister W. von Dirksen Collection. Round-headed relief. H., 0.44m.; W., 0.29m. Photo., Private.

This Madonna (Fig. 1), perhaps one of Andrea's earliest works, was inspired by Luca's Madonnas on the frieze of the baldachino which protects the altar of the Madonna at Impruneta. Andrea has given a nimbus to both Mother and Child, has added nimbed cherub heads and indicated

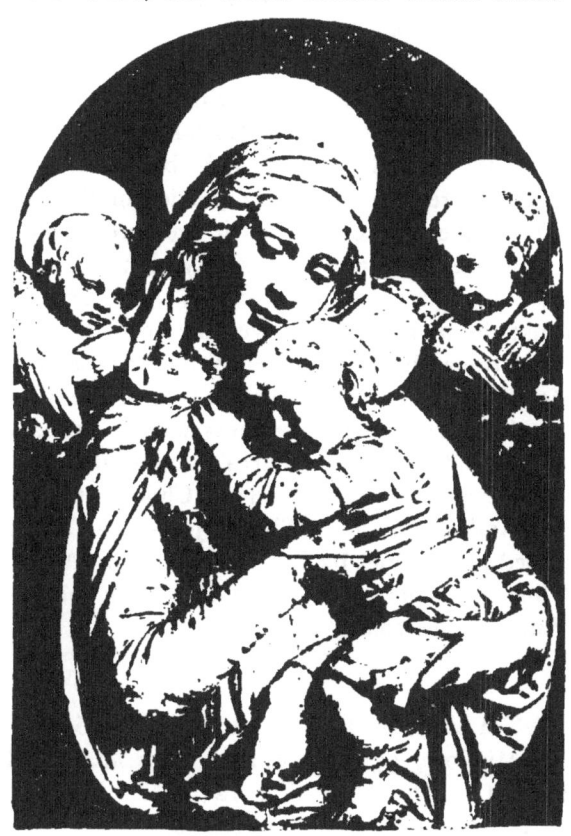

FIG. 1.—MADONNA OF THE IMPRUNETA TYPE.

clouds. He has also modified the type and indicated the eyes in his characteristic manner.

Bibl. :
> B., *Fl. Bild.*, 130; *Fl. Sc.*, 91; *Münchn. Jahrb.*, I (1906) 32; M., *L. D. R.*, 236.

2 SEATED MADONNA WITH DRAPED CHILD BLESSING. Florence. S. Gaetano. H., 1.25m.; W., 0.80m. Photos., Alinari, No. 2427; Brogi, No. 4896. Casts, Cantagalli, 407; Lelli, 436.

The church formerly known as S. Michele Berteldi, de'Bertelli, de'Diavoli, a Piazza Padella, or agli Antinori, transformed and rebuilt, came under Cosimo I to be known as S. Gaetano. A subterranean chapel, reached from No. 1 Via degli Agli, is now reserved to the Compagnia di S. Michele Berteldi. In this dimly lighted chapel is preserved one of Andrea della Robbia's earliest and noblest Madonnas (Fig. 2).

It is rightly attributed to Andrea della Robbia, although it exhibits strongly the influence of Luca. The frame with the garland of fruit, rising upward without the conventional vases, is Luca-like in its simplicity, but is made of plaster. In the central relief the light blue background, scattered throughout with clouds, reminds us of the Justice in the Cluny Museum. The symbols of the Father and of the Spirit are here, as in the Madonna of the Architects, but the absence of haloes may be noted—a rare omission in Andrea's works, though common in Luca's. We note also many of Luca's mannerisms; the mantle drawn over the head, the ruffle about the neck, the cord and buttons, the twisted linen girdle, the manner of colouring the eyes except for the yellow irises. But the type of the Virgin's face, of the chair on which she is seated, her bare knees and the swaddling clothes of the Child may be paralleled only in Andrea's compositions. The pose of the Madonna, in three-quarter profile, and the Child seated to the left, are also indications of Andrea's design. The subject—the Child in the act of blessing—is one used many times by Luca as well as by Andrea della Robbia. The swaddling garments worn by the Child link this relief with the *bambini* of the Innocenti Hospital.

Bibl. :
> B., *Denk.*, 73, Taf. 243; Burl., 56-57, 107; C-M., 76, 111, 207 no. 14; Cr., 134; Del Migliore, 437-453; Foratti, *Rass. d'Arte*, XIX (1919), 30; Fov., 102; M., *D. R. A.*, 30, Fig. 12; R., *D. R.*, 172; *Sc. Fl*, III, 160; Richa, III, 191-230; S., 111, Abb. 120.

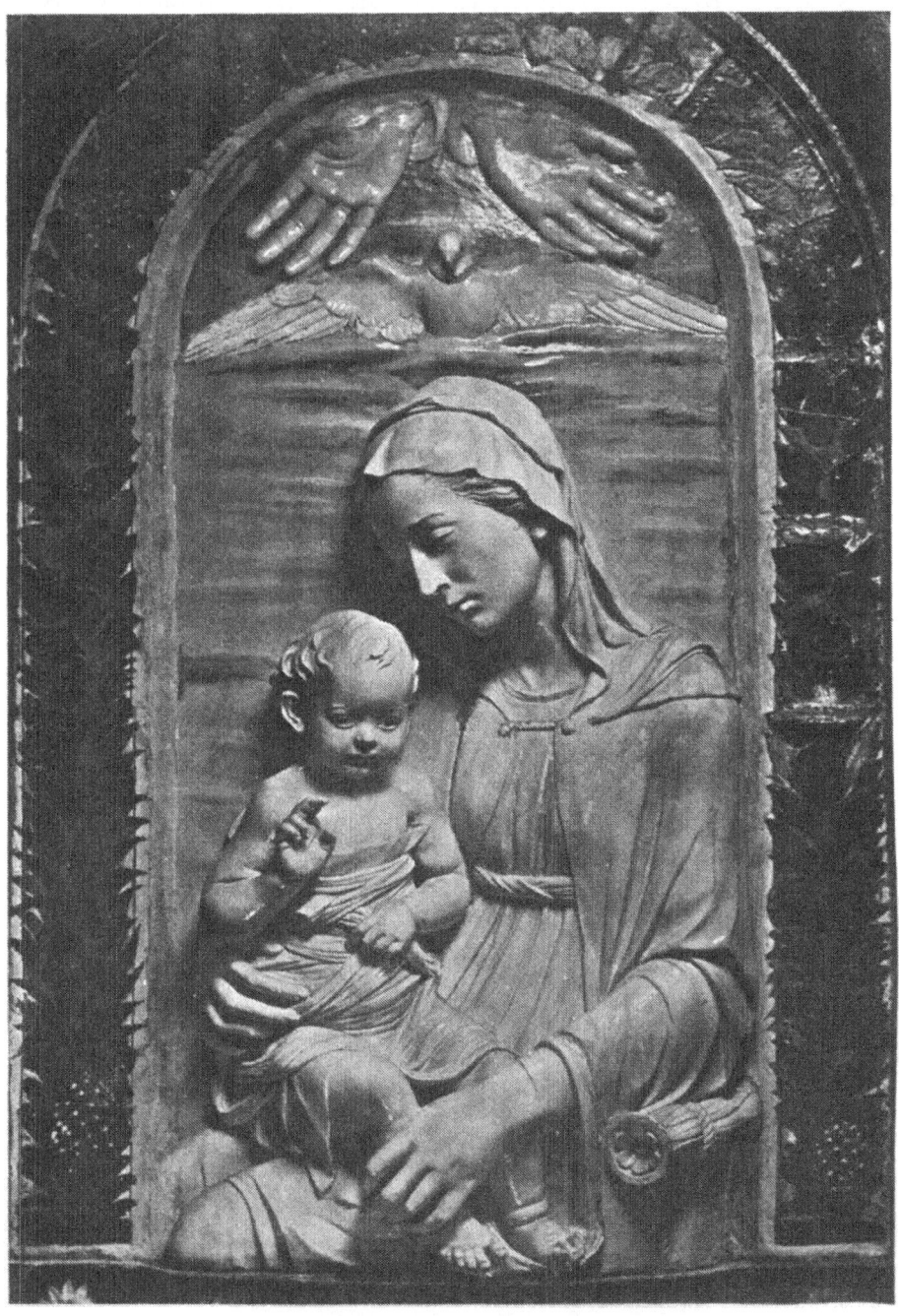

FIG. 2.—THE S. GAETANO MADONNA.

3 SAME SUBJECT. Newport, R. I., Mrs. O. H. P. Belmont Collection. H., 0.95m.; W., 0.55m. Photo., Private.

This fine relief (Fig. 3), was formerly in the collection of M. Émile Gavet, Paris. The subject, the seated Madonna with the draped Child blessing, is the same as that at S. Gaetano, but the differences of treatment make of it a variant rather than a replica. The Trinity is less symbolically expressed. Instead of the symbolic hands alone the crowned head of God the Father appears with outstretched arms rising from the clouds, sur-

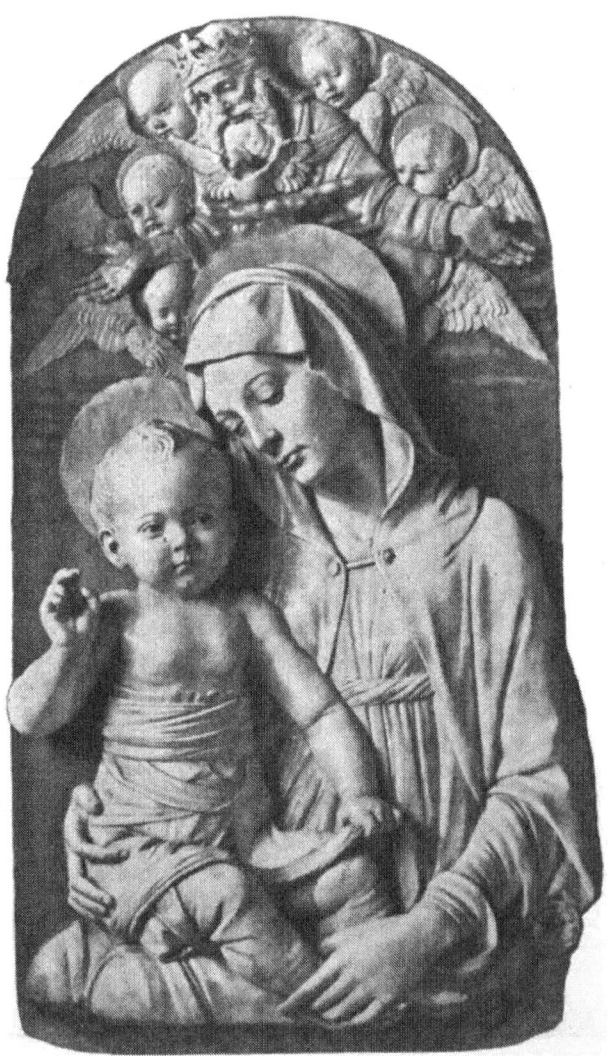

FIG. 3.—THE BELMONT MADONNA.

rounded by six nimbed cherub heads, like a translation of the earlier relief. The Dove, with a small nimbus, is thrown slightly into profile, to harmonize with the pose of the Father and of the Madonna. The Madonna and Child are provided each with a nimbus. Their poses and the details of their costumes are not directly copied from those of the S. Gaetano Madonna, but are slightly varied. The chair, which in the earlier relief exhibited one of its sides carved like the pulvinus of an Ionic capital, is here more summarily expressed. Only the rosette in front is visible. The use of colour is also slightly different. The sky is a darker blue, and the clouds reduced in number. The colouring of the eyes with dark pupils and dark irises does not differ from that in the S. Gaetano relief. The border of the Virgin's mantle and her girdle were once ornamented with gold.

Bibl.:
C-M., 281 no. 474 note; M., *D. R. A.*, 30, Fig. 11; Molinier, *Cat. Gavet*, 3, Pl. 1.

4 SEATED MADONNA WITH NUDE CHILD HOLDING A BIRD. Florence, S. Egidio. H., 0.90m.; W., 0.50m. Photo., Alinari, No. 2195.

The Hospital of S. Maria Nuova was founded in 1287 on land purchased from the Frati di S. Egidio, whose church is still connected with the Hospital. For this church in 1442 Luca della Robbia had made the marble ciborio now at Peretola, and the Gallery of the hospital formerly contained fine reliefs by Luca and Andrea, now transferred to the Museo Nazionale. In 1464 the hospital appears to have been overcrowded and special appropriations were made for extra-mural annexes for those afflicted with contagious diseases, especially the plague. It is quite possible that this Madonna (Fig. 4) was set up as a thank offering by some one who had been cured.

As a type it is certainly to be classed with Andrea's early Madonnas. It shows the mantle with the same triangular fold above the forehead, clasped with an oval brooch not unlike that which Luca had used at S. Pierino; the linen girdle; the bared knees; the chair terminating in a scroll and decorated in front with a rosette. In type this Madonna is to be classed with the Annunziata in the Niccolini altarpiece at La Verna. The Child, in every detail except pose and motive, is the counterpart of the Child of the Madonna of the Architects (1475). Overhead in the midst of plastic clouds is the Holy Dove.

The motive of this relief, the Child holding a bird, is of considerable antiquity. It was not uncommon in the XIV century and became very popular during the entire period of Andrea's artistic career, as may be seen by comparing this relief with those of the same subject at Rickmansworth, at Stia, at Viterbo—not to speak of many school reproductions. In the blue of the background Andrea has reached a hue to which he long adhered.

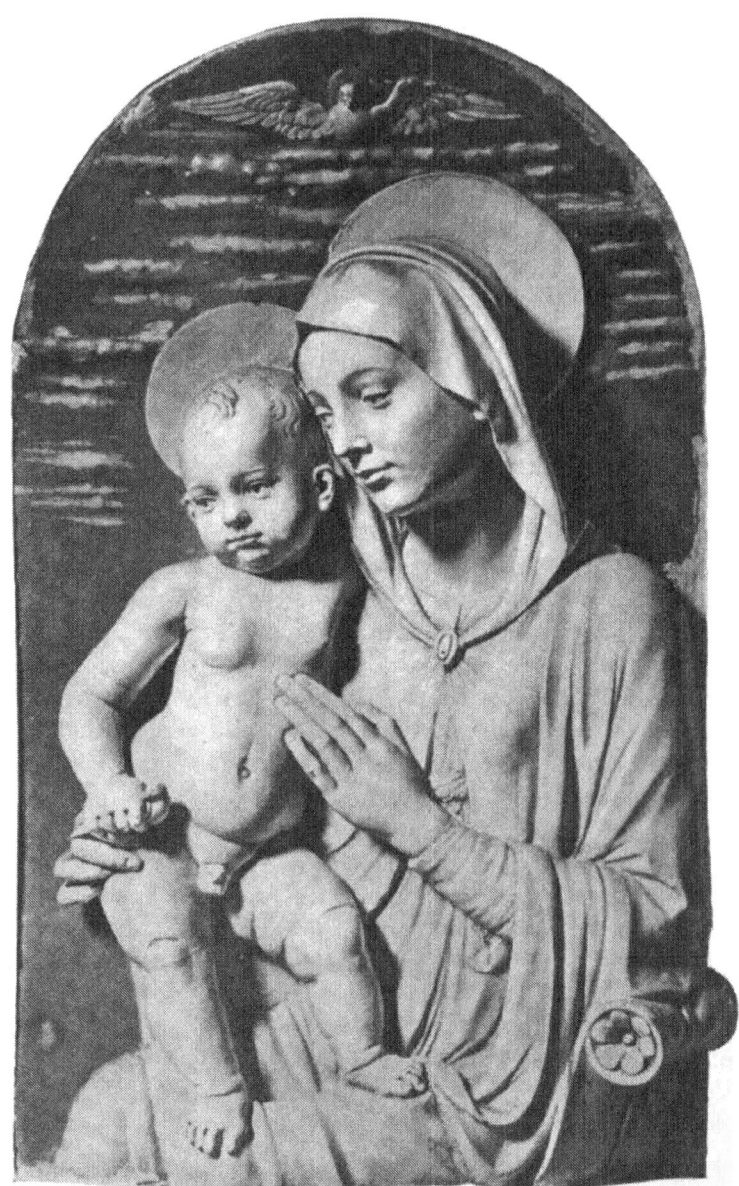

FIG. 4.—THE S. EGIDIO MADONNA.

For the pupils of the Madonnas' eyes he uses a copper lustre, and for the irises a gray blue.

Bibl.:

B., *Kf.*, 16, 24; *Ital. Bildh. Ren.*, 84; *Denk.*, 82, Taf. 253; *W. d. K.*, 8, Taf. 34; Burl., 56, 107; C-M., 106, 207 No. 13; Cr., 195-196, 325; M., *D. R. A.*, 35, Fig. 13; R., *D. R.*, 202; *Sc. Fl.*, III, 174, 184; S., 111; V., VI, 580, Fig. 381.

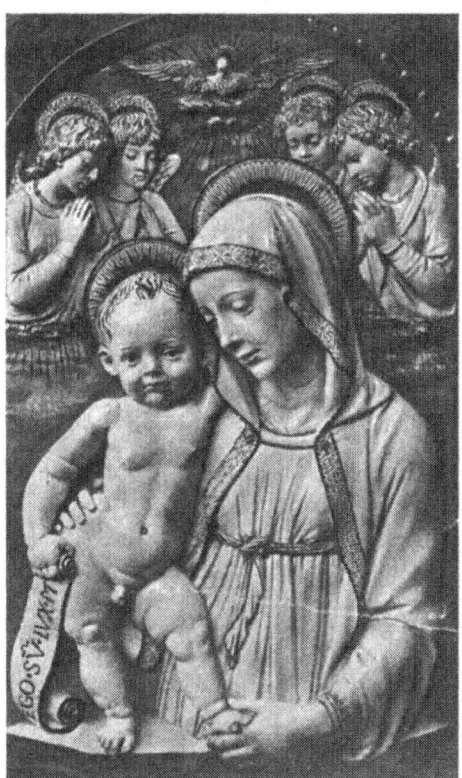

FIG. 5.—THE SIMON MADONNA.

5 MADONNA WITH NUDE, STANDING CHILD HOLDING A SCROLL; FOUR ANGELS. Berlin. Kaiser-Friedrich Museum, No. 99 (I, 4997). Round-headed relief. H., 0.80m.; W., 0.49m. Photo., Museum.

This relief (Fig. 5) formerly in the Seillière (Paris), Heckscher (Berlin), and James Simon (Berlin) collections was acquired by the Museum in 1904.

The subject, the Madonna with the Child bearing a scroll inscribed EGO ◆ SVM ◆ LVX ◆ M(VNDI), had inspired several of Luca's Madonnas (Altman, Via dell'Angelo, Innocenti, Urbino, Bronze Doors), but was not popular with Andrea. It occurs again only once; in a relief in the collection of Mr. Paul Chalfin, New York. Adoring angels were introduced by Andrea into Adoration scenes, Coronations, Assumptions, Crucifixions, but seldom as here and in the Varamista altarpiece into simpler representations of the Madonna. The Dove, the clouds, the type of the Madonna, the pose of the Child link this relief with the Madonna and Child with a Bird, in S. Egidio, and with others of Andrea's early Madonnas. The elaborate gilding appears to be modern, and as a restoration is only partially successful.

Bibl.:

B., *Denk.* 83 Taf. **256**; Foratti, *Rass. d'Arte,* XIX(1919); Katalog d. Samml. J. Simon, No. 25; Schottmüller, No. **99**; S., 112, Abb. **121**; Seillière Cat., 13 No. 1; Tschudi 83, 226, Taf. **60**; V., VI, 580, Fig. **387**.

6 FOUNDLINGS IN SWADDLING CLOTHES. Florence. Ospedale di S. Maria degli Innocenti. Diam., 1m. Photo., Alinari, 3168-3178; Brogi, 4759, 12610-12612, 12919-12925, 4697-4706. Casts, Cantagalli, 291, 301; Ginori, 252-263; Lelli, 408 (4 subjects).

The façade of the Innocenti Hospital, as designed by Brunelleschi in 1420, exhibited a raised porch or arcade of nine arches limited on the north and south by closed walls, each containing a door and window and framed by colossal pilasters. The wall to the north blocked the passage from the open Piazza della Annunziata to the Via della Colonna; and, although it was ordered removed in 1495, remained a closed wall until 1599 and 1600. The wall to the south was extended under Brunelleschi's successor Francesco della Luna at some time between 1427 and 1440. This extension, condemned on aesthetic grounds by Brunelleschi's biographer Manetti in 1480, remained unchanged as late as 1819—as we may judge from the frontispiece of Bruni's *Storia dell'Ospedale degl'Innocenti*—possibly as late as 1842 to 1845 when the Hospital underwent restoration. This later change consisted in making an arched opening in the space immediately south of the raised porch and transferring the door to the last and southernmost compartment.

Brunelleschi had designed that the spandrels of the arches of the raised porch should be filled with tondi or medallion frames which might contain sculptural decoration (Fig. 6). These circular frames seem to have remained unfilled for some years, as we may infer from the documents published by Fabriczy from the *Libri della fabrica della muraglia*, which form a record of the building from 1419 to 1451 and make no mention of the now famous sculptured *bambini*. These were added at a later date, but at precisely what time is more difficult to determine. That Andrea della Robbia is the author of them, as Vasari asserts, is universally admitted. The generally accepted date, 1463-1466, is based upon Cavallucci's state-

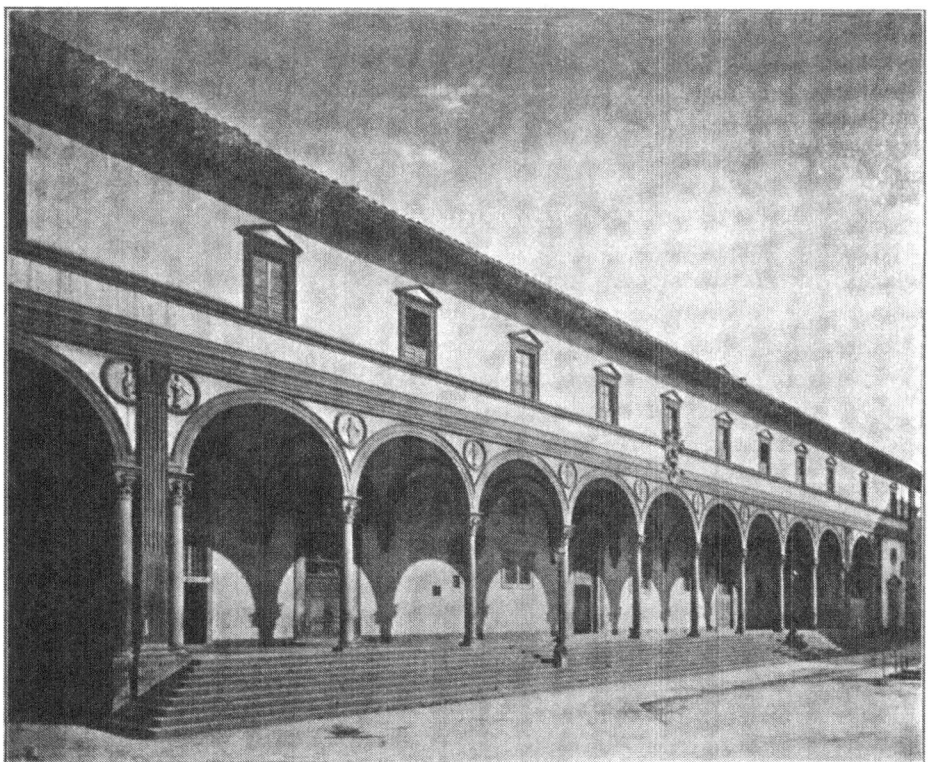

FIG. 6.—THE INNOCENTI HOSPITAL.

ment that in the year 1466 the hospital was bankrupt and by 1483 many foundlings died for want of food. I do not know from what source Cavallucci obtained this information. The hospital was under the protection of and obtained its resources chiefly from the Arte di Por Santa Maria, better known as the Arte della Seta. We are told by Benedetto Dei (Cronaca 22-44) that in 1472 this guild of silk merchants controlled eighty-four workshops, including sixteen thousand operatives and superior workmen in the city of Florence and its immediate vicinity. That they devoted much care to this hospital, would appear from its continued development. In 1485 the hospital was enlarged. According to Bruni, in April 1444 it contained two hundred and sixty foundlings, and by 1511 the little family had grown to 1200. Del Migliore in 1684 gives the number of foundlings and their caretakers as between 3000 and 4000. The decoration of the hospital might well have occurred in the seventies or eighties when the resources of the Arte della Seta were in its most flourishing condition.

One who stands upon the Piazza in front of the hospital can count fourteen bambini, of which four are modern reproductions, made at the Ginori factory at Doccia in 1845. These four decorate the arch of 1599-1600 over the Via della Colonna, and the arch of 1842-1845 immediately to the south of the raised porch. They repeat the design of the first and last medallion in Andrea's series and in fact repeat themselves. They may be readily distinguished from the originals: (1) by the background, which in Andrea's medallions is composed by sectors which radiate from the figure to the circumference, whereas in the Ginori reproductions (Figs. 17, 18) a portion of the background follows the outline of the figure; (2) by the glaze, which in the modern medallions is more vitreous in character, and, being subjected to more sudden heat, has a crackled surface; (3) by the colours, which show more red in the violets, and a different shade of blue. The eyes of the Ginori reproductions show a dark line for the lower lashes, which does not occur in the originals. Cavallucci and Molinier, Bode, and Venturi unfortunately publish the Ginori reproductions as originals.

The original ten (Figs. 7-16) are composed as follows: At each end is a truncated terminal medallion containing a *bambino* with the outer arm bent, and the other extended in the direction of the remaining medallions. In all the completely round medallions both arms are extended, as if appealing for mercy. There is little variety in character or expression. All evince the same temperament. It is the swaddling bands that vary and the colours of the wrappers which alternate regularly from violet in one medallion to blue in the next—except in the last pair where both are violet.

If we compare these *bambini* with Luca's *putti* which serve as supporters of the arms of the Arte della Seta on Or San Michele, we can readily detect the change from Luca's representations of child life. Luca's are more plastic, more alive; Andrea's, while full of charm, are posed with view to decoration. Even so slight a detail as the colouring of the eyes is not without significance. In spite of the fact that his medallion was to be set high above the ground, Luca marked the irises of the eyes of these winged putti with the same blue with which he delighted to paint the eyes of the Virgin. Andrea almost never painted the iris blue and here seems to have massed pupil and iris together as was frequently done by his followers.

If one should compare these bambini with the heads of cherubs with

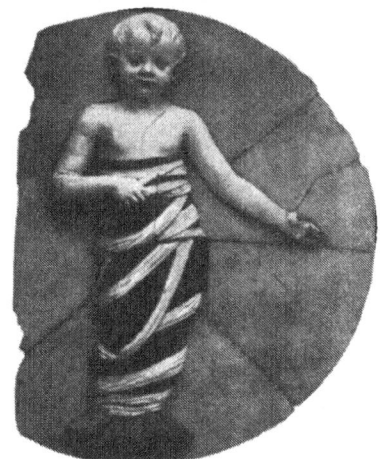

FIG. 7.—FOUNDLING.

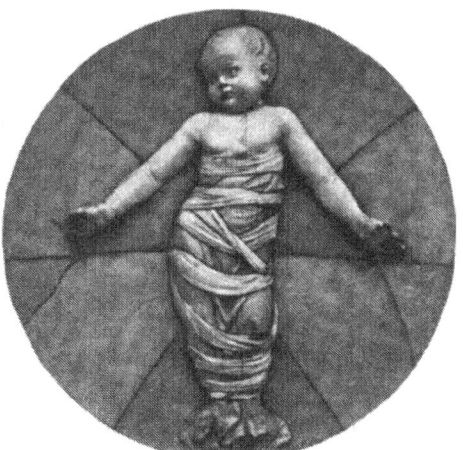

FIG. 8.—FOUNDLING.

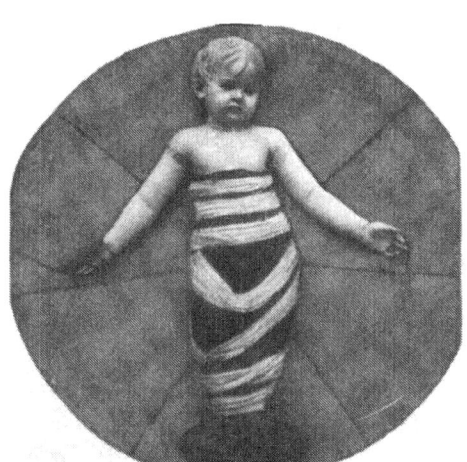

FIG. 9.—FOUNDLING.

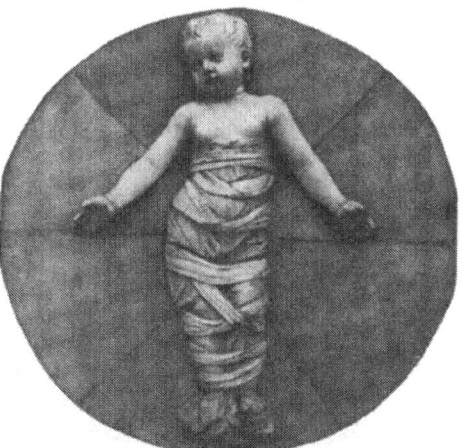

FIG. 10.—FOUNDLING.

which Andrea decorated the frames of his reliefs, or with his representations of the Christ Child, it is not easy to find the exact place in the series to which they belong. It is simpler to compare them with two specific examples of the Christ Child both clad as here in swaddling clothes. One of these is found in S. Gaetano in the chapel of the Berteldi. This relief is undoubtedly an early Andrea, retaining much of Luca's dignity. The other relief is in Newport, R. I., in the Belmont (formerly Gavet) collection. Here in the upper portion of the background God the Father, the Dove, and a halo of cherubs are figured somewhat a in the La Verna Adoration altarpiece. These reliefs we have assigned to the decade 1470-1480 during which period the Innocenti bambini were probably set in place.

Documents :   [Copied by Mr. Rufus G. Mather.]

Aloghagione
deglocchi archi-
trave e cornice

I.   "Mcccc° xxiiij°

Ricordo che adi 6 di maggio p(er) gloperai dello spedale fu aloghato a albizo dipiero et a betto dantonio scarpellatorj

tutto il detto
lavorio an(n)o i
dettj albizo e
betto cōpiuto
e murato alquale
glop(er)ai an(n)o
posto il pregio
questo dj 24
dap(ri)le 1425
chome apare al
quaderno b c 163
i quale pregio
e questo
p(er) ciascuno
occhio f 2
del bia (braccia)
dellacornice
l s s 4 e a cōcio
a ragione de
dettj i questo
c 90
e posto cācello
questa allogha-
gione

cioe a ciascuno di loro la meta p(er) diviso dello ifrascritto lavorio cōgli ifrascritti pattj e modj cioe

A albizo cīque ochi dicōcio iquali stano a mettere fra glarchi del cōcio che sono sopra il porticho dello spedale cioe I|5| occhj hanō andare verso e dalato della casa dellavoratore delorto e la meta d(e)llarchitrave e della cornice del
[cōcio

ha andare i sulle colonē quadre e i su dettj archi cioe la parte della prima colonā quadra che(ch'è) dalla parte della casa delsopradecto lavoratore i sino al mezo deglarchi sopradettj
[cioe

i sino almezo e i sulmezo del quīto archo del detto porticho et A betto dantonio laltra meta del sopradetto lavorio cioe 5
[occhj

e architrave e cornice hanō andare dalmezo del quīto archo
[i sino

alla colona quadra ultima che(ch'è) verso santa Rip(ar)ata ilquale lavorio a astare ala propia forma e modo che quello
[dalbizo

El detto lavorio cioe glocchi tondj e scorniciatj e beligli
[(belli)

chome sara il modello e la forma dara loro filippo di ser brunelescho e debbono essere ciascuno dettj occhi grādj di giro
[p(er)

modo che tocchino il giro deglarchi e disopra larchitrave

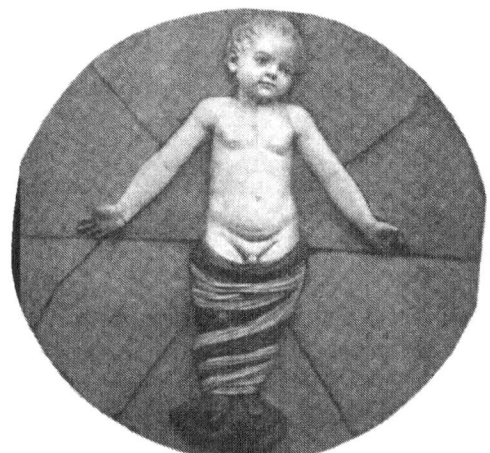

FIG. 11.—FOUNDLING.

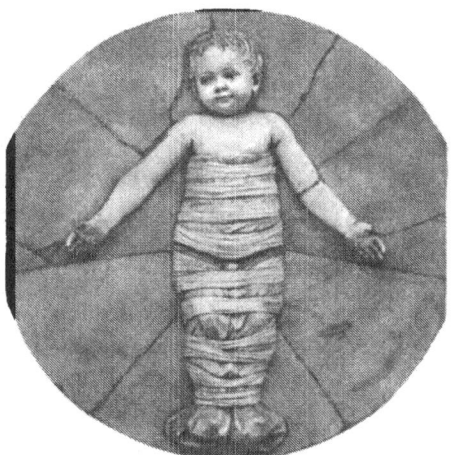

FIG. 12.—FOUNDLING.

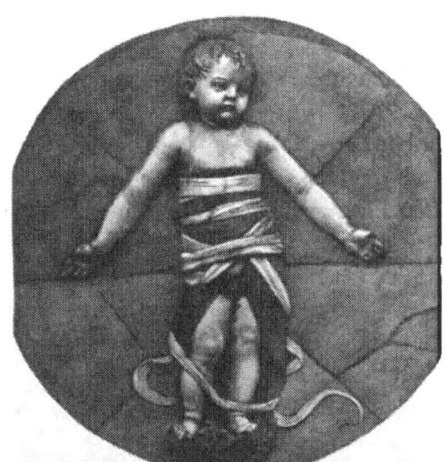

FIG. 13.—FOUNDLING.

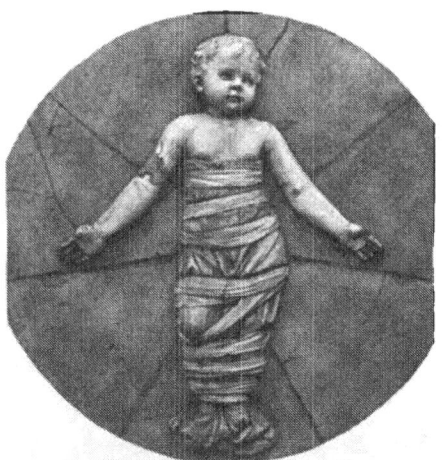

FIG. 14.—FOUNDLING.

El sopradetto architrave debbe essere alto ¼ di braccio
[elargho p(er)
loverso del suo giacere cioe q(u)ella parte che posa ī sul
[colmo
deglarchi 2/3 di braccio ella cornice che va sopra il detto
[architrave
debbe essere alta 1¾ di braccio e scorniciata ebbella secōdo il
modano del detto filippo
I lquale lavorio debbe essere tutto di salda grossa e buona
petrina e bene lavoratj e nettj e bene pulitj
Et tutto il detto lavorio debbono dare fatto cioe ciascuno la
[sua
parte a tutte loro spese di pietre e dognaltra cosa e posto
elavorato a pie dello spedale p(er) di qui adj 15 daghosto
[1424 e debbe
essere tutto recipiēte a uso dj buono maestro e a chiarigione
deglop(er)ai
Et dj poi il debbono murare cioe ciascuno la parte sua de
dettj occhi e architrave e cornice e porlo su e cōmetegli bene
a tutte loro spese salvo che dj calcina o piōlo (piuolo) o fera-
mēto a quello tenpo e quādo sara dj piacere de dettj o p(er)ai
e ī caso nollo ponesino su al tenpo parra a dettj op(er)ai il
possono fare murare e pollo a tutte spese e danō de dettj
[maestrj
Et del detto lavorio e cōcio debbono avere quello prezo e
[pregio
che parra e sara deliberato p(er) luficio de dettj op(er)ai
[nelquale
uficio e dettj albizo e betto liberamente si rimettono chome
[dj
tutto apare al quaderno dellop(er)a s͏ͭᵒ b c. 3
　　　nota posto il detto pregio chome apare qua in margine"
　　　[Archivio dello Spedale degl' Innocenti, Libro Deb. e
　　　Cred. della Muraglia segnato B, 1421-1435, c. 177ᵗ.]

2.　　　"Mccccxxxviiij°　　　　　　　　"Mccccxxxviiij°
Pesello di . . . . . dipintore deve dare　Pesello di . . . . . dipintore de avere
adi 18 di magio 1 iiii° p(er) noj da　adi 18 di magio 1 q(u)atro e qualj
nicholo morj camᵒ posto debe　sono p(er) dipintura delarme delarte
avere alquaderno s͏ͭᵒ d c. 59—1 4 s —"　al quaderno giallo s͏ͭᵒ e c 7 —　　1 4 s
　　　　　　　　　　　　　posto la muraglia deba dare ī questo c 65"
　　　　　　　　　　　　　　[Archivio idem, Libro di Muraglie,
　　　　　　　　　　　　　　1439-1450, c. 10ᵗ e 11.]

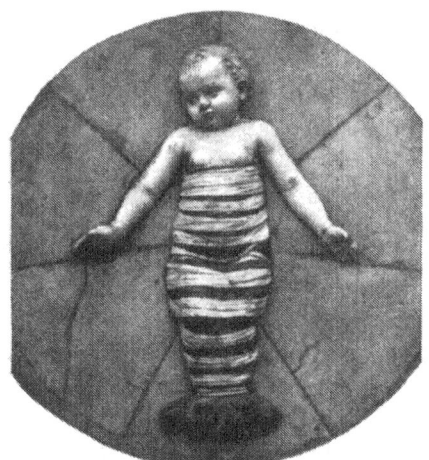

FIG. 15.—FOUNDLING.

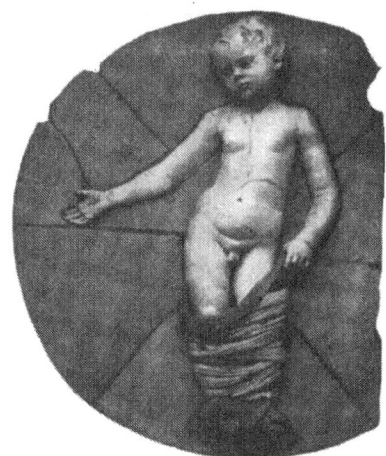

FIG. 16.—FOUNDLING.

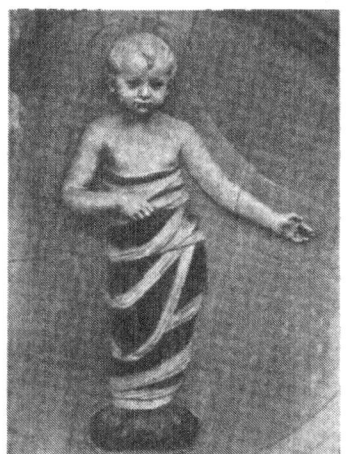

FIG. 17.—GINORI REPRODUCTION.

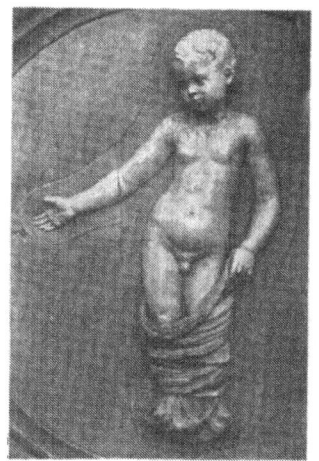

FIG. 18.—GINORI REPRODUCTION.

3.   "Mcccc°xxxviiii°   "Mccccxxxviiii°

Lopera di san m° delfiore deve   Lopera di santa maria delfiore
dare adi 22 dachosto 1 dodicj porto   de avere adi .... di magio
ghualterone proveditore di detta   p(er) marmo bianc° e rosso p(er)
opera p(er) noj gli pagho nicholo   fare larme delarte cioe a p"(parte)
morj cam° posto debbj avere   nelafacia delospedale p(er)
al quaderno d c. 63 —   1 12 s –"   tutto dachordo choloro e

          franc° delaluna ne fa

          mezano — —   f 1 12 s—

          posto lamuraglia debe dare

          ī questo c 65 (this note by a different

[Idem, idem c 22° e 23.]   hand)
Bibl.:

    Arte della Seta, *Libri della Muraglia*, A-E; B.J., 63; B-C., 411; B.,
    Denk., 81-82, Taf. **248-249**; *Kf.*, 16, 24; *W. d. R.*, 8, Taf. **29-32**;
    Bruni, I, 5, VIII; Burckh., 430; Burl., 55, 108; C-M., 80-91, 98-102;
    208 no. 19; Cr., **152-154**, 326; D. D., 30 Abb. **44**; Fabr., *A. S. A.*,
    IV(1891), 291-300 (Doc.); *J. k. p. K.*, XXVIII(1907), Beih., 56-58
    (Doc.); *Br.*, 250-259, 252-283; *Misc. d'Arte*, 1903, 210-211 (Doc.);
    Fov., 99-100, Fig. 85; Geym., I, 7-10; II, 3; Michel, IV, 121; del
    Migliore, 307-316; R., *D. R.*, **154-156**; *Sc. Fl.*, III, **146-149**; Richa,
    VIII, 125-126; von Rumohr, II, 295 note; S., 113, Abb. **125-126**;
    Vas., II, 180; V., VI, 583-594, Figs. **499-501**; *Z. f. C. K.*, XX(1885),
    21.

7 MADONNA OF THE ARCHITECTS. 1475. Florence. Museo
Nazionale, No. 74. Round-headed relief. H., 1.34m.; W., 96m.
Photos., Alinari, No. 2761; Brogi, Nos. 4448, 9469. Casts, Canta-
galli, 289, 375; Lelli, 415.

On the fourth of March, 1475 (Old style, 1474), the consuls of the Arte
dei Maestri di Pietra e di Legname authorized a payment of ten large
florins for an image of the Madonna which they had commissioned Andrea
della Robbia to make to replace the antiquated Madonna in their audience
chamber. For many years Luca della Robbia had been a member of this
guild, but was beginning to feel the weight of years and on that account
in 1471 had declined to serve as its consul. His nephew Andrea was admitted a member of the guild on the sixteenth of September, 1458, and between the years 1469 to 1525, the year of his death he served more than
thirty times as a member of the council, three times as syndic and once as
treasurer.

In the Museo Nazionale there is a Madonna in a frame adorned with the square, the axe, the mallet and trowel, emblems which Luca della Robbia had combined with rare skill in the medallion of the Stone Cutters and Wood Carvers on the exterior of Or San Michele. There can be little doubt therefore that we have in this relief (Fig. 19) the Madonna ordered

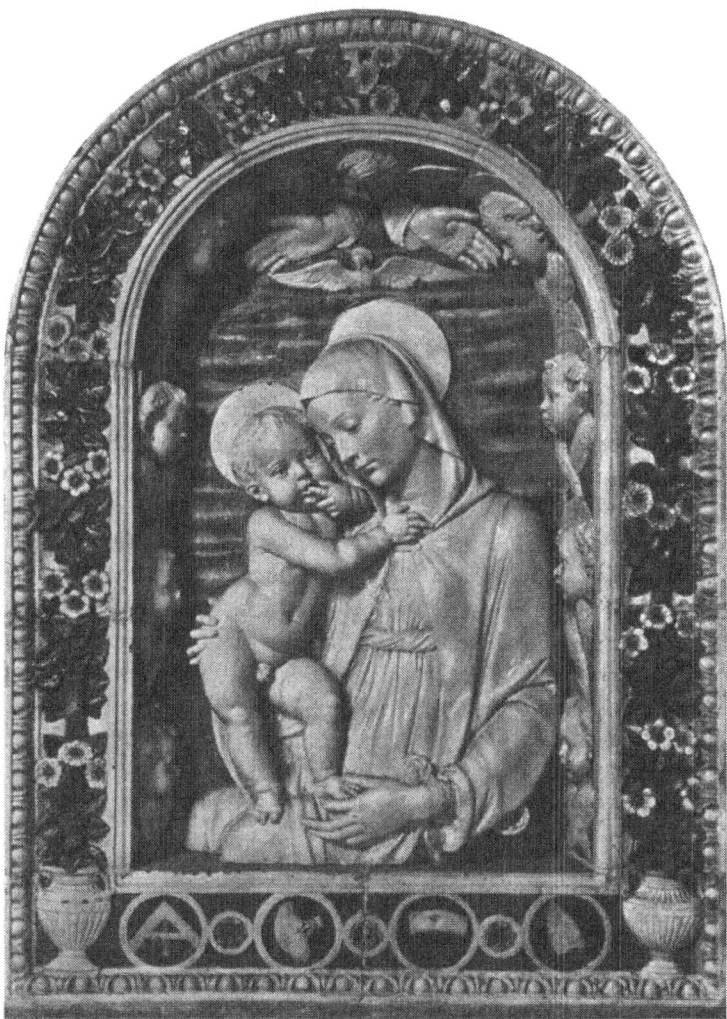

FIG. 19.—MADONNA OF THE ARCHITECTS.

of Andrea della Robbia in 1475. In the sixteenth century the guilds suffered great transformations. Probably then the Madonna passed into other hands. It had been in the offices of the Dogana in the Palazzo Buontalenti when in 1865 it passed into the Museo Nazionale.

The garland of single and double roses rising from chanelled vases does not exhibit the variety of Luca's floral frame for the Via dell'Agnolo lunette, nor is it as conventional as is usual with Andrea's garlands. Although somewhat monotonously conceived and flat in modelling, it was successful enough for Andrea to have repeated it in the frames for the tabernacle in S. Simone, the tondo the Foulc collection, the Salviati stemma at S. Giovanni Valdarno, the Cintola altarpiece at La Verna and other monuments. The frame forms a niche, the inner sides and top of which are decorated with nine nimbed cherub heads. Thus one of Andrea's favorite motives is found in connection with his earliest dated Madonna.

The subject of the relief might be described as the Madonna of the Apple were it not for the fact that no apple is in evidence. Luca della Robbia in the Madonna of the Apple in the Berlin Museum, and in the Cappuccini tondo in the Museo Nazionale, had represented the Christ Child as holding an apple in one hand while drawing the other hand to his mouth—a symbol that the Christ shared with all human beings the taste of the fruit of the tree of knowledge of good and evil. Andrea, with less attention to significance, omits the apple but retains the finger in the mouth, a gesture that suggests to Marcel Reymond a child with the toothache! Andrea and his patrons were so pleased with this motive that he repeated it several times: in lunettes at Prato Cathedral, in the Opera del Duomo (both 1489), and in altarpieces at Prato and Gradara Rocca.

In modelling and composition Andrea follows his uncle in draping the Madonna's mantle over her head, in fastening it with a cord, in the twisted linen girdle and other details, but he introduces new motives in seating her upon a folding chair, exhibiting her bare knees to view, and in placing over the heads of the group the symbols of God the Father (outstretched hands) and of the Holy Spirit (Dove). Unlike Luca he spreads blue gray, black shadowed clouds all over the background, and gives the Madonna's eyes dark blue brows and yellow irises.

Document:—[Revised by Mr. Rufus G. Mather.]
"In dei Nomine Amen anno domini MCCCCLXXIIII
    Inditione VIII et die V mensis Marzii
Consules   ⎱ et corpus artis et qui dictam artem
Consiliarij   ⎰ representant in sufficienti numero
congregati in dicta arte secundum ordinem dicte artis
deliberaverunt
Che considerato che nelaudienzia di decta arte è
una imagine di nostra donna la quale per antiquità
è mancato et semdo in simil forma ne segue piutosto
caricho alarte che no. Et però avendo e nostri Signori
Consoli allogato ad Andrea di marco delarobbia a fare

una immagine dinostra donna in decto luogho apta et
capiente (or this word may be recipiente) alluogho et allonore
di decta arte che da ora s'intenda stanziato per decta
cagione insino nellasomma di fiorini dieci larghi
e quali si debbino et possino pagare add Andrea per
decta cagione per qualunche camerario di decta arte,
et mancandovi che' Consoli che pe' tempi saranno possino
stanziare insino allontero pagamento."

[Deliberazioni dell' Arte de' Maestri di Pietra e di Legnami, Archivio
di stato di Firenze, Arti 11, Cod. 3, c. 27.]

Bibl.:
Burl., 111; C-M., 108, 215 No. 60; Cr., 181, 325; Fov., 102; M.,
R. H., 25-26; Mesnil, *Misc. d'Arte*, 1903, 208-210(Doc.); Michel,
IV, 124; R., *D. R.*, 166-167; *Sc. Fl.*, III, 157; S., 111, Abb. 118;
Supino, 451 No. 74.

8 MADONNA, CHILD AND SAINTS. Berlin. Kaiser-Friedrich-
Museum, No. 98 (I, 147). Altarpiece. H., 1.78m.; W., 1.83m.
Photo., Berlin Museum.

Purchased in England in 1885. Originally in a private chapel at Varramista near Pisa.

The central relief (Fig. 20) exhibits the Madonna in full figure seated
on clouds, and holding a nude Child who stands on her lap. Her nimbus
and hair were gilded, and gold ornament is still found on her kerchief,
girdle, sleeves, and border of mantle. Her eyes show dark blue brows
and lashes, and light yellow irises. The Child, also nimbed, throws his
left arm about his mother's neck and with the right plays with her kerchief,
a motive which occurs with variations in many of Andrea's Madonnas.
Above are four adoring angels, emerging from clouds. On either side,
standing upon the ground (though white in colour), are S. Francesco to
the left, holding a cross and pointing to his wounded side, and S. Cosma
holding a green palm and an apothecary's box. S. Francesco is represented
as sympathetically as in the statues of S. Francesco at Assisi and at La
Verna. His cross recalls that held by Faith in Luca's medallion in the
Heilbronner Galleries. S. Cosma balances the composition, being here represented as equal in importance to S. Francesco. The borders of his collar
and mantle are charmingly decorated with gold. He reflects the dignity
of the Pazzi chapel Apostles.

The frame also indicates an early period in Andrea's career. The pilasters decorated with painted garlands recalls Luca's tomb of Benozzo Federighi and his Pescia altarpiece, but this type of decoration was too unconventional to find a fixed place in Andrea's repertoire. He ornamented predellas in this fashion, but never again the pilasters of an altarpiece.

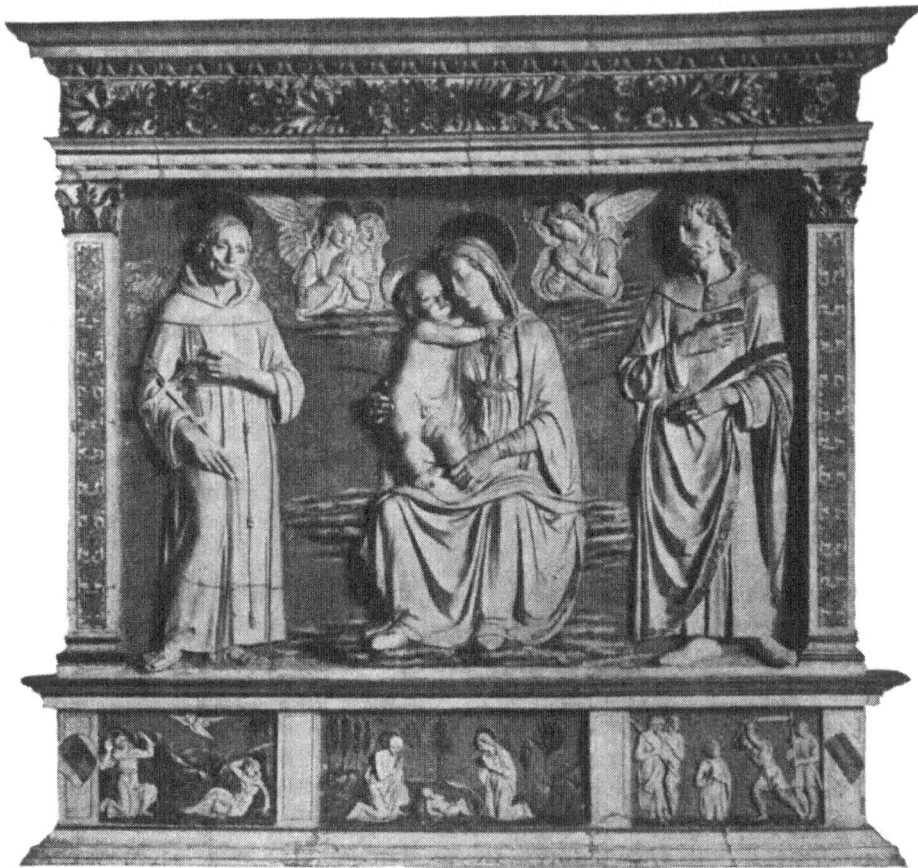

FIG. 20.—THE SASSETTI ALTARPIECE.

The capitals of the pilasters represent a fixed form which he repeated in the Canigiani and in the Assisi altarpieces. The frieze shows the influence of Luca's preference for lilies and white roses, as in the S. Pierino and the Via dell'Agnolo lunettes, composed in naturalistic not conventional bunches, and diverging from the centre to left and right, as in the Federighi tomb, the Impruneta tabernacle and the Pescia altarpiece.

The predella contains three polychromatic scenes: (1) S. Francesco receiving the stigmata. It is represented more simply than in the Canigiani, the Assisi, and S. Fiora altarpieces. (2) The Nativity or Adoration of the

Child by S. Giuseppe and S. Maria. (3) The martyrdom of S. Cosma. These three scenes are directly related to the figures of the central relief. They are separated from each other by upright bands or pilasters almost devoid of decoration. Those at either extremity contain the Sassetti arms: Argent, a bend azure fimbriated or. It is not difficult to guess which member of the Sassetti family erected this altarpiece, when we recall that Francesco di Tommaso Sassetti who was a Prior in 1460 and renovated the Sassetti Chapel at S. Trinità in 1486, had a son Cosimo who was probably named after Cosimo de'Medici Pater Patriae, who died in 1464. It is not unlikely that Cosimo Sassetti was born in this decade since he became a Prior in 1503, 1523, 1524 and 1527. This altarpiece might well be a thank offering for his birth and the association of SS. Francesco and Cosma be explicable as the patron saints of the donor and his son.

Bibl.:
Amtl. Ber., 1886, XXXV; B., *J. k. p. K.*, VII(1886), 206-210, Taf. **206**; *It. Pl.*, 93-94; *Denk.*, 83-84, Taf. **257**; *W. D. R.*, Taf. **36**; B-Tsch., No. 118; C., s.v. Sassetti; Cr., 163 note 1, 186, 325; D. D., 33, Abb. **48**; M., *R. H.*, 14, **15**; Michel, IV, 124; Pr., **842-843**; R., *D. R.*, **204-205**; *Sc. Fl.*, III, **175-176**; Schott., 42-43, No. **98**(I, 147); V., VI, 589, Fig. **396**; W., 173.

9 MADONNA WITH NUDE, STANDING CHILD. Florence. Museo Nazionale, No. 52. H., 0.53m.; with console, 0.80m. Photos., Alinari, 2726; Brogi, 9483.

This relief (Fig. 21) came to the Museum on June 12, 1867, from the monastery of S. Giovanni Battista at Desole or Dedolo. It is a slightly modified copy, in half figure, of the Varramista Madonna in the Berlin Museum.

The console on which it rests is a product of Giovanni's atelier. A similar console, perhaps a modern copy, is in the Museum at Toledo, Ohio.

Bibl.:
Burl., 110; Cr., 339; R., *D. R.*, 203; *Sc. Fl.*, III, 174; Supino, 448 No. 52.

10 STATUE OF S. FRANCESCO. Assisi. S. Maria degli Angeli, Cappella di S. Francesco. H., 1.25 mm. Photo., Alinari, 20017.

This statue (Fig. 22) has been much overpainted, the cross red, the garments a dark brown. But fractures in the painting disclose the fact that

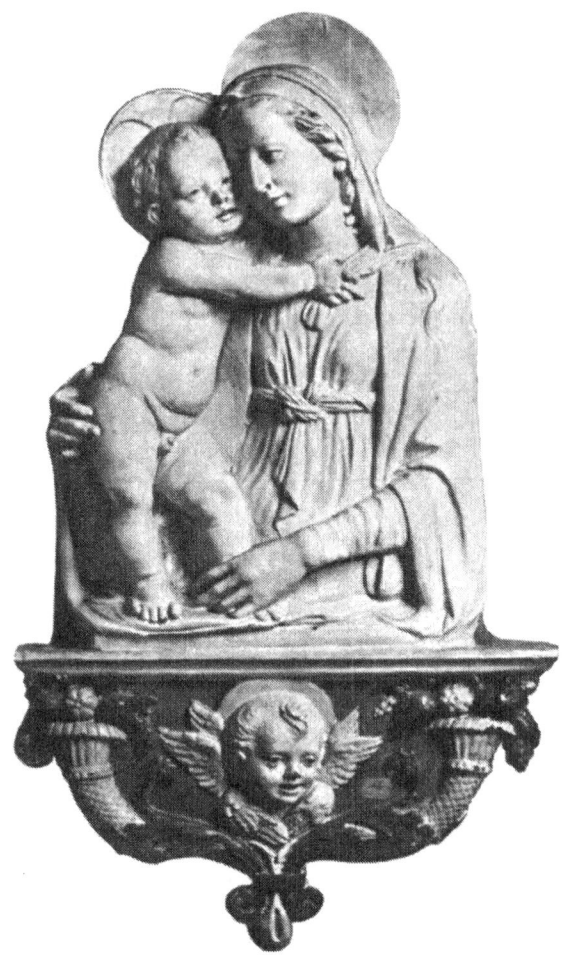

FIG. 21.—MADONNA, FLORENCE.

this was applied over a white glaze. This overpainting has been recently
removed (1921). The statue was probably painted after the controversy
between the Osservanti and the Convenzionali concerning the colour of
the Franciscan habit. It is not far removed in date from the triptych in
the Cappella di S. Giuseppe, and in technique as well as in sentiment may
be classed with the S. Francesco at La Verna.

Bibl. :
Cr., 177, 325; S., 122, Abb. **134**.

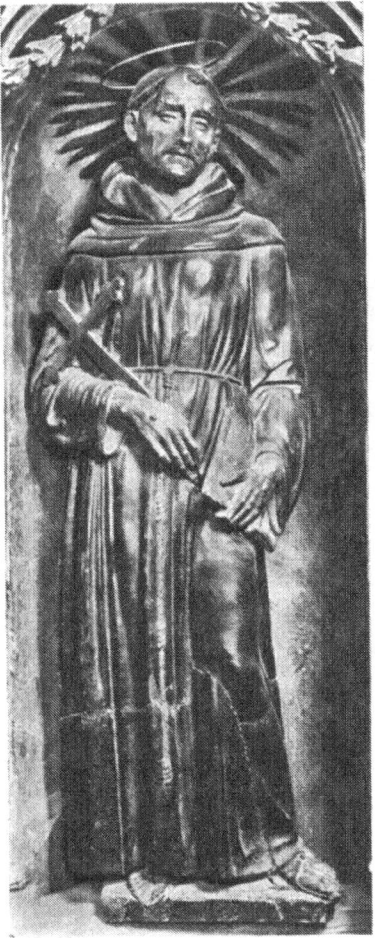

FIG. 22.—S. FRANCESCO, ASSISI.

11 MEDALLION BUST OF A YOUTH. New York. Metropolitan
Museum. Diam., .055m. Photo., Private.

This fine head (Fig. 23), formerly in the collection of Count G. Stroga-
noff, Rome, then in that of Henry G. Marquand, New York, was acquired
by the Metropolitan Museum in 1903. The frame consists of a somewhat
concave wreath of pine cones alternating with quinces and oranges arranged
in single file, as was the case at S. Giovanni in Valdarno with the stemma of
Antonio di Lorenzo Buondelmonti (Fig. 136). Like many of Luca's tondi
the outer moulding is decorated with an egg and dart. The head turned
three quarters to the left is not far removed in type from the medallion

bust of a youth in the Kaiser-Friedrich Museum, Berlin, which recalls the decorative heads on Luca's bronze doors in the cathedral of Florence. Face and hair are glazed white, eyebrows and lashes blue, pupils violet brown, irises yellow. The tunic is a mottled violet, over which is a light

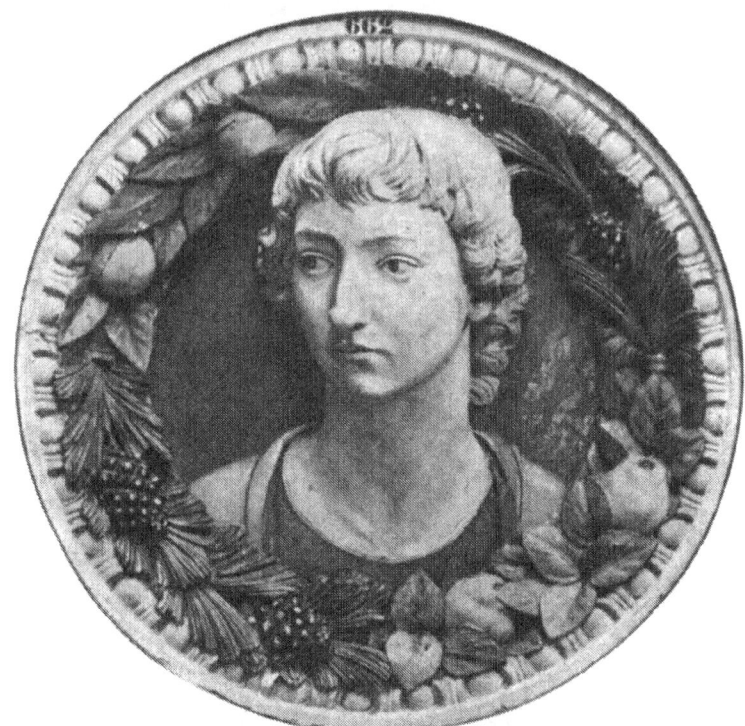

FIG. 23.—BUST OF A YOUTH. METROPOLITAN MUSEUM.

blue mantle lined green. Who the youth may be cannot be definitely determined. On the bronze doors busts of this general type are called prophets, though probably modelled after the features of some young Florentines. This head is closer to Luca's than the somewhat similar medallions in the Liechtenstein, Lehman and Simonetti collections.

Bibl.:
Breck, 40-42; Cr., 349; M., *Cat. of Marquand Coll.*, No. 1199; *D. R. A.*, 89, Fig. 37; *L. D. R.*, 205-206.

12 MEDALLION BUST OF A YOUTH. Berlin. Kaiser-Friedrich Museum, No. 75 (I, 2183). Diam., 0.555m. Photo., Berlin Museum.

This fine medallion (Fig. 24) from the Torrigiani collection came into the possession of the Berlin Museum in 1894. Dr. Bode considers it a portrait; Miss Cruttwell, a S. Ansano or some other Boy-Saint. Though finer in quality than the medallion busts of youths in the Metropolitan Museum and the Liechtenstein Gallery it should be classed with them as products of the same atelier. Here the background is a pale blue, as is

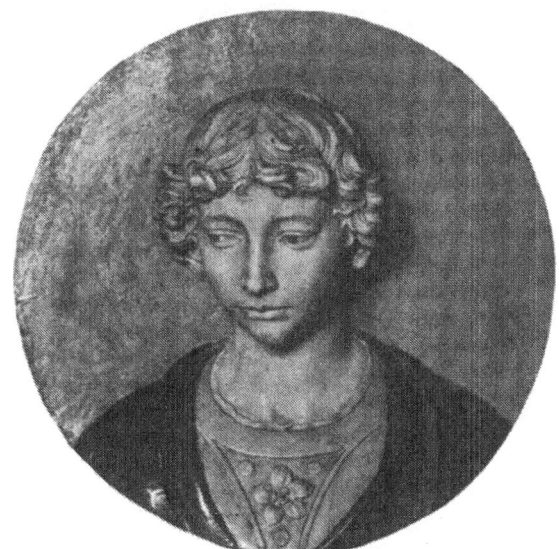

FIG. 24.—BUST OF A YOUTH. BERLIN.

also the robe or breastplate, the mantle is violet with reverse of green. The eyes have yellow irises; the eyebrows, lashes and pupils are violet. The guiding hand of Luca della Robbia is so evident in the execution of this bust that it might well be attributed to Luca himself. Originally it was probably surrounded by a fruit frame.

Bibl.:
B., *J. K. p. K.*, XXI (1900), 30-32; *Denkm.*, 78-79, Taf. **229**; *Fl. Bildh.*, 161-162, Abb. **88**; *Fl. Sc.*, 110-111, Pl. **51**; *Mus.*, II, 69, Taf. **138**; Cr., 89, 323; *D. D.*, 21, Abb. **29**; M., *D. R. A.*, 89, Fig. **37**; *L. D. R.*, **205-206**; Schottmüller, 33-35, No. **75** (I, 2183); S., 89, Abb. **100**; V., VI, **572**.

13 MEDALLION BUST OF A YOUTH. Vienna, Liechtenstein Gallery. Diam., 0.36m. Photo., Liechtenstein Gallery.

This fine medallion (Fig. 25) was formerly in the Antinori collection in the Via dei Serragli, Florence. It is a variant of the Berlin Museum and the Metropolitan Museum medallions representing the same subject, but is more plastic and somewhat later in date. The eyebrows are blue, the irises copper coloured. The simple tunic is green and the mantle a robin's egg blue lined violet, and held together by a brooch in the form of a rose. In

FIG. 25.—BUST OF A YOUTH. LIECHTENSTEIN GALLERY.

spite of its complex character the wreath appears to have been constructed in only three sections; in the composition of fruit and flowers the triplex system prevails, but without the ribbons which Andrea usually employed to subdivide his wreaths into a series of distinct bunches. He also abandoned the use of exterior framing mouldings of architectural character. The egg and dart, here retained within the wreath, was destined also to be abandoned.

Bibl. :
B., *J. k. p. K.*, XXI (1900) 31; *Fl. Bildh.*, 162; *Fl. Sc.*, 110-111; Cr., 327; Demaison, *Les Arts*, 1908, No. 84, 1-4; M., *D. R. A.*, 89; *L. D. R.*, 206.

14   MEDALLION BUST OF A YOUTH. New York, Philip Lehman Collection. Diam., 0.51.

This medallion, formerly in the Spitzer, then in the Rudolph Kann Collection, is to be classed with the Metropolitan Museum and the Liechtenstein

Gallery medallions with similar portrait busts. The egg and dart moulding of the frame is here omitted and the wreath is more summarily treated, consisting of a single file of pine cones and leaves. The head, set against a dark blue ground, is turned to the right in three-quarter view. The tunic is blue and the mantle violet. The type of head is not unlike that of the S. Michele from Faenza, now in the Vieweg Collection at Braunschweig.

Bibl. :
Rudolph Kann, *Objets d'Art,* I, pl. 1; Spitzer Cat., No. 1291; M., *D. R. A.,* 89; *L. D. R.,* 206.

15 MEDALLION BUST OF A YOUTH. Rome, Simonetti Gallery. Diam., 0.80.

Some years ago I saw at Simonetti's, Rome, a medallion bust of a youth. The frame consisted of a wreath in high relief composed of grapes, pomegranates, lemons, pinecones, quinces, artichokes, zucche—recalling the frame of the Liechtenstein medallion. The youth wore a light blue mantle; the background also was light blue.

Bibl. :
M., *D. R. A.,* 89; *L. D. R.,* 206.

16 MEDALLION BUST OF A LAUREATE. New York, Bardini Sale of 1918. Diam., 0.43m.

This bust (Fig. 26) was withdrawn from the Bardini sale in London in 1902 and sold in New York in 1918. When sold in New York it was set in a fruit garland. It is to be classed with the preceding medallion busts of a youth. It represents a victor or one who has made some notable achievement. He is crowned with laurel, his hair is quite plastic, his eyes have blue brows and yellow irises, the ribbons of his laurel crown fall in waving lines. He wears a blue tunic almost entirely concealed by a mantle, violet lined green.

Bibl. :
Bardini Sale of 1902, *Cat.,* 511, pl. 21; Bardini Sale of 1918, *Cat.,* 367.

17 MEDALLION OF A LAUREATE. Paris. Louvre (formerly numbered G. 754. No number in 1908). Diam., 0.40m.

From the Campana Collection. Inferior replica or copy of the preceding. The very light blue tunic is covered by a green mantle. The eyes have yellow irises.

Bibl. :
C-M., 448.

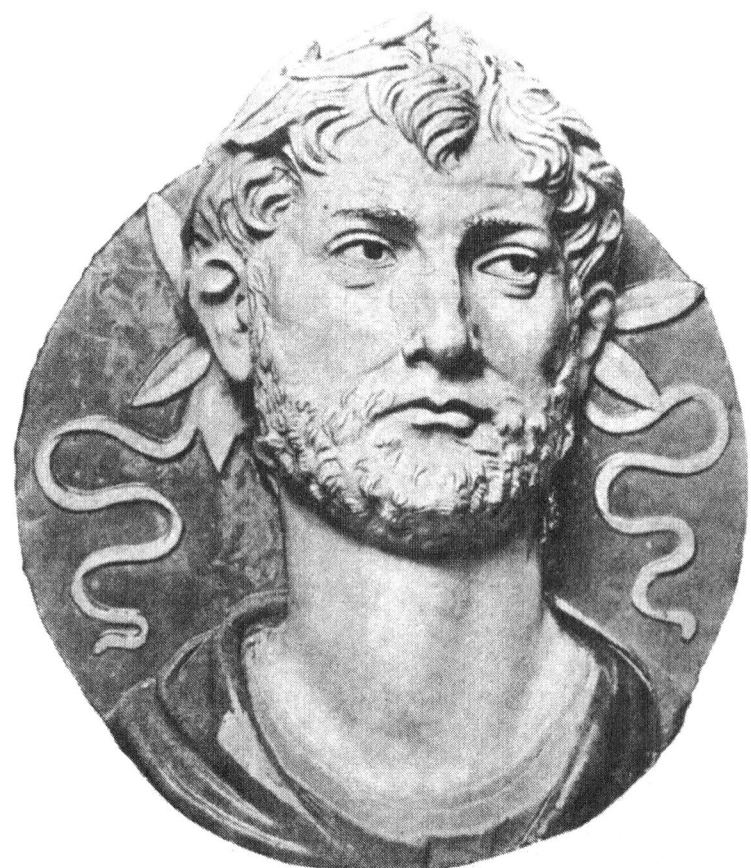

Fig. 26.—Bust of a Laureate.

18 MEDALLION OF THE EMPEROR ANTONINUS. Turin. Museo Civico. Diam., 0.70m.

Within a garland of pine cones, arranged in triplex bunches separated by blue ribbons and bordered by architectural mouldings, is a broken medallion representing the Emperor Antoninus crowned with laurel bound by fluttering ribbons. Cloak was light blue lined yellow. The eyes had blue brows, lashes and pupils, and yellow irises. Inscribed (A)NTONINVS .

From this designation we may infer that the preceding busts of *laureati* represent ancient Romans, though not necessarily Emperors.

19 MEDALLION OF A WARRIOR. Pesaro. Museo Ateneo Pesarese. Diam., 0.50m. Photo., Private.

A portrait of a condottiere (Fig. 27). Helmet, face, neck, and breastplate are glazed white. Over the shoulders is a green cloak lined violet. Background blue. The decoration of the helmet is reminiscent of Luca

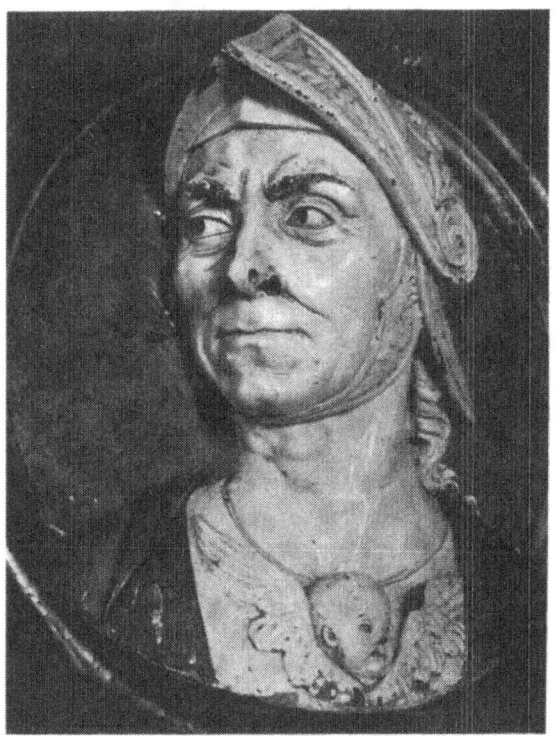

FIG. 27.—BUST OF A WARRIOR.

della Robbia's designs, the cloak and the colouring of the eyes—blue brows and lashes, with hazel irises—indicate a fairly early period in Andrea's work. The cherub head on the breastplate symbolizes the Christian profession of the warrior.

Bibl. :
Anselmi, *A. S. A.*, VIII(1895), **442**; Burl., 69; Cr., 230, 330.

20 BUST OF A BOY. Florence, Museo Nazionale, No. 75. H., 0.33m. Photo., Brogi, 9467; Casts, Cantagalli, 273; Lelli, 416.

This charming bust of a boy (Fig. 28) has been called a boy Christ, but probably had no religious significance. It is certainly not a S. Giovannino, who invariably wears the hair cloth. Its resemblance to the armorial bearers of the stemma of the Arte della Seta on Or San Michele suggests

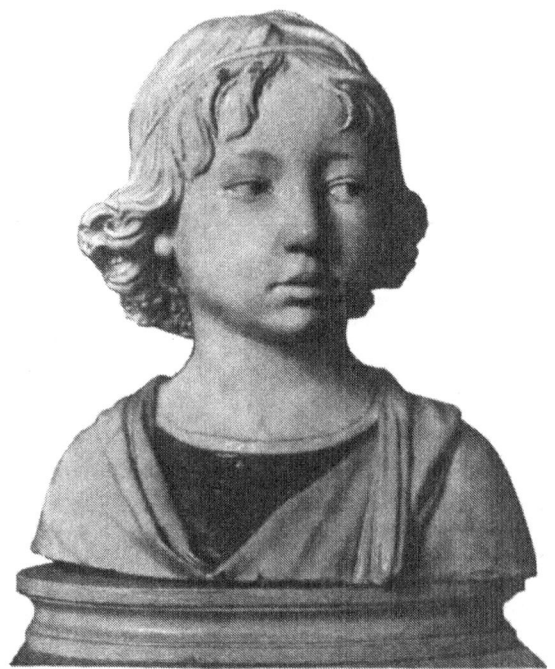

FIG. 28.—BUST OF A BOY. FLORENCE.

the authorship of Luca della Robbia, but its relationship to the medallions with heads of youths makes it more probable that it should be called an early work of Andrea's. The treatment of the eyes shows some uncertainty. The eyebrows seem originally to have been indicated in violet and then done over in robin's egg blue. The irises are yellow as Luca might have painted them, but the pupils are copper coloured—an indication of Andrea's handiwork. The green tunic and its ornamentation and the fine blue mantle are closely related to those of the medallion with bust of a youth in the Berlin Museum.

Bibl. :
B., *J. k. p. K.*, XXI (1900), 32; *Denkm.*, 79, Taf. **228**; *Fl. Bildh.*, 216, Abb. **118**; *Fl. Sc.*, 147, pl. **65**; *Mus.*, II, 71, Taf. **137**; Burl., **111**;

C-M., 113, 219, No. 82 note; Cr., 155; 325; M., *L. D. R.*, 231-232; R., *D. R.*, 259, 276; *Sc. Fl.*, IV, 64; S., 123, Abb. 136; Supino, 452 No. 75.

21 STEMMA OF THE GINORI FAMILY. New York City. Collection of Mr. Thomas F. Ryan. Photo., from Bardini Catalogue.

Formerly in the collection of M. Maurice, Kann, then in that of Sigismond Bardac, this fine stemma passed into the collection of Mr. Thomas F. Ryan. On a pointed, oval shield (Fig. 29) are displayed the arms of

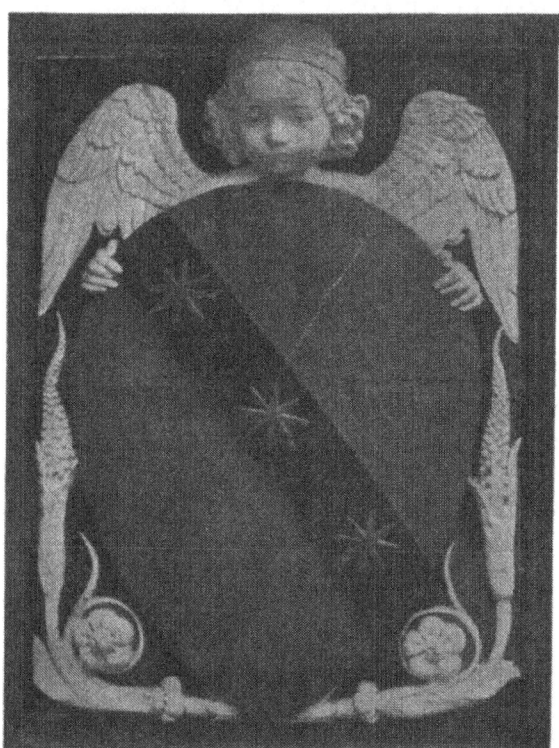

FIG. 29.—STEMMA OF THE GNORI FAMILY.

the Ginori: Azure, a band or charged with three eight-pointed estoiles of the first.

The charming winged putto who supports the shield resembles the bust of a boy in the Museo Nazionale, No. 75. The seeded scroll ornament at the base of the shield suggests the decoration of the consoles of Luca's Cantoria. The background is mottled violet in imitation of porphyry.

This stemma may have been made for Gino di Francesco Ginori, a Prior of Florence in 1471. Andrea della Robbia's atelier supplied coats of arms for Gino di Giulano Ginori, Vicario at S. Giovanni in Valdarno in 1489 and 1490, and for Alessandro di Gino, Podestà and Commissario at Castiglione Fiorentino in 1507.

Bibl.:
Cat. Maurice Kann, No. 200; Cat. Sigsmond Bardac, No. 30; C., s.v. Ginori; M., *A. in A.*, 1914, 242-246; *L. D. R.*, 233-234; *R. H.*, 45-46, Fig. 43; P., 460-462.

22 MEDALLION BUST OF A LADY. Florence. Museo Nazionale No. 73. Diam., 0.45m. Photo., Brogi, 9468; Cast, Cantagalli, 325.

This medallion (Fig. 30), possibly by Andrea himself, portrays a lady from some aristocratic family. The double chaplet of pearls about her

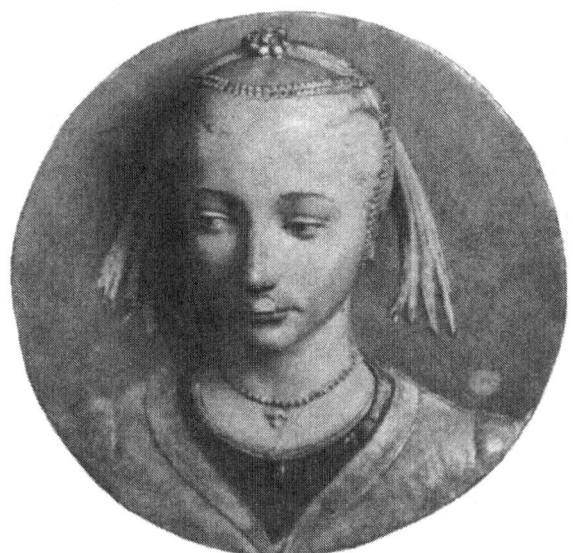

FIG. 30.—BUST OF A LADY.

head, the stiff headdress with its large brooch, and the necklace of pearls with its pendant, as well as her delicate features, indicate her high station. Mino da Fiesole, who seems to have had some influence on Andrea's style, appears to have been inspired by the same lady when he fashioned the Madonna of the Salutati altarpiece in the cathedral at Fiesole. Her green robe and light blue mantle, as well as her eyes with their violet brows, lashes and pupils, and their copper-coloured irises show this relief to be closely related to the Bust of a Boy in the Museo Nazionale. An inferior variant of this medallion is in the collection Thiers of the Louvre.   (See Blanc, *Coll. Thiers,* 12-13, pl. 4.)

Bibl. :

B., *J. k. k. k.,* XXI (1900), 32; *Denkm.,* 79, Taf. 228; *Fl. Bildh.,* 188, Abb. 82; *Fl. Sc.,* 111; *Mus.,* II, 72; Burl., III; Cr., 339; M., *L. D. R.,* 234-236, Fig. 152; S., 89, Abb. 101; Supino, 451 no. 73; V., VI, 578 note. 1.

23 TERRA-COTTA FRIEZE AND CORNICE. c. 1475. Faenza. S. Michele Arcangelo. Photo., Private.

The church of S. Michele Arcangelo at Faenza has an exterior cornice and ornamental terra-cotta frieze (Fig. 31), unglazed, which I am inclined to consider one of Andrea della Robbia's early works. The channelled

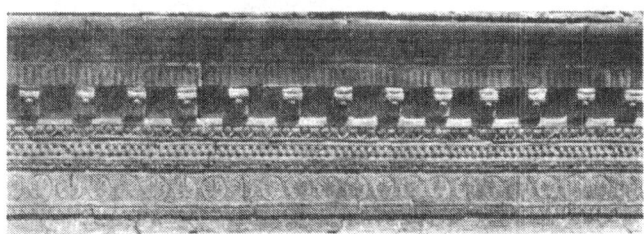

FIG. 31.—ARCHITECTURAL DECORATION. FAENZA.

corona, the corinthian consoles, with the intervening rosettes, not to mention the egg and dart, dentils, and bead and reel mouldings, are such as Andrea was accustomed to see in his uncle's work—in the Cantoria, and the tabernacle at Peretola and Impruneta. But the frieze with the more conventional palmettes suggests Mino da Fiesole's altarpiece at Fiesole and Andrea della Robbia's pilaster decorations at La Verna, Assisi, Prato, and Gradara Rocca. The pattern between the palmettes, of floral origin but resembling a thunderbolt, was used by Andrea in the altarpiece of the Cappella Canigiani in S. Croce.

The date of the church is preserved by a glazed terra-cotta medallion now in the Cluny Museum, No. 2807. It displays the Monogram of Christ and is inscribed *Nicolaus de Ragnolis ad honorem Dei et S. Michaelis fecit fieri Anno D. 1475.* This medallion originally decorated the architrave of the principal entrance of the church.

Bibl. :
Messeri-Calzi, 519-520.

24 LUNETTE OF S. MICHELE ARCANGELO. Braunschweig. Collection of Frau Vieweg. H., 0.79m.; W., 1.57m. Photo., Mazzoni, Faenza.

This lunette (Fig. 32) once decorated the entrance portal of the suppressed church of S. Michele Arcangelo at Faenza. It was sold in 1872 by Count Benevento Pasalini dall'Onda to the antiquarian Cav. Ortensio Vitalini, and in 1875 by the art dealer Angiolini of Bologna to Herr Heinrich Vieweg of Braunschweig.

Anselmo Anselmi asserts that it was set in place in 1475. He cites no

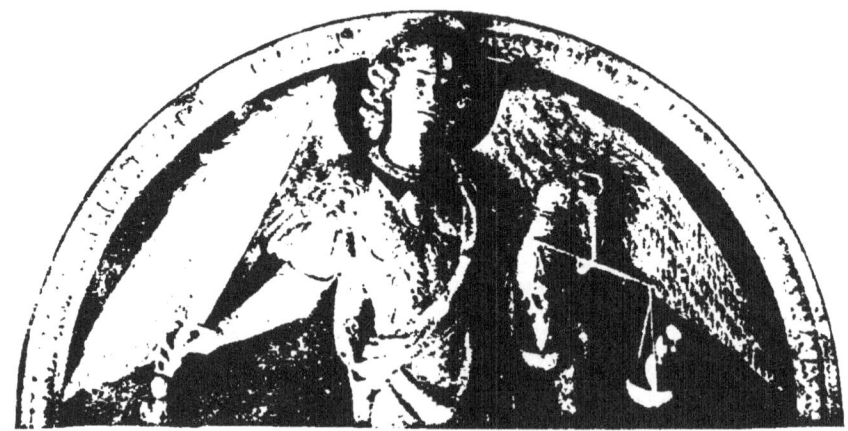

FIG. 32.—LUNETTE OF S. MICHELE.

documents; hence I am inclined to think he has borrowed the date from the Faentine medallion now in the Cluny Museum (No. 2807), which once decorated the same church, but did not issue from the Robbia school. Malagola dates the lunette 1477, but he again borrows the date from that of the Manfredi medallions of the Cathedral. It is probable, however, that this lunette was executed during this decade.

S. Michele is here represented in his capacity as Lord of Souls. He carries the sword, and the scales in which souls, here portrayed as a diminutive man and woman, are weighed. Once again did Andrea represent, in simple fashion, S. Michele as weigher of souls—in the predella of the altarpiece in S. Maria in Grado, Arezzo—, but the Vieweg S. Michele is far more beautiful. The decoration of the breastplate is such as Andrea might have learned from his uncle Luca's Resurrection lunette in the cathedral or from the Fortitude in the Portogallo chapel. Andrea used it again in his grand Resurrection relief in S. Bernardino at Aquila. The manner of representing the wings and the treatment of the drapery are Luca-like, as are also the eyes with their grey blue irises and violet brows and lashes.

Bibl. :

Anselmi, *A. S. A.*, VIII(1895), 444; B., *Kf.*, 26; *Denkm.*, 85, Taf. 252; Burl., 75; C-M., 263, No. 368; Cr., 159, 325; Malagola, 103; Messeri-Calzi, 519-520, 558; Michel, IV, 122; R., *Sc. Fl.*, III, 163; *D. R.*, 179-180; S., 116-117, Abb. 129; V., VI, 583-584.

25 ALTARPIECE. S. FRANCESCO RECEIVING THE STIG-
MATA; TOBIAS AND THE ANGEL. Florence. S. Croce, Cappella Vieri-Canigiani. H., 1.86m.; W., 2.40m. Photos., Alinari, No.
2190; Brogi, Nos. 12126-12128. Casts, Cantagalli, 408(detail);
Lelli, 433(detail).

In a chapel opening into the cloister of S. Croce, founded by the Con-
fraternità della Capanna, later belonging to the Baldi, and now to the Vieri-
Canigiani families, is one of Andrea's early altarpieces (Fig. 33). It was
designed as a ciborio, the depository for the sacred host being closed by a
sportello with a painting.

The patron saint of the confraternity, S. Bartolommeo, is represented in
a lunette against a blue, fluted background. The entablature beneath the
lunette is supported by spirally fluted columns recalling those of Luca's
tabernacle of the Madonna at Impruneta. They rest on a low base the
ornamentation of which is analogous to the interior frieze of S. Michele at
Faenza. To the left of the ciborio is S. Francesco, attended by Frate Leo,
receiving the stigmata, a subject which Andrea repeated at Assisi, S. Fiora
and elsewhere. Christ appears in the heavens like a seraph. The rocky
hill of La Verna is dark blue to contrast with the green trees. The monastery is represented with the utmost simplicity. To the right is a group
of Tobias and the Angel. Tobias is unexpectedly provided with a halo,
as if he were a saint, and his legs are ill proportioned; but his head and that
of the Archangel have all the charm of Andrea's early works. We find
the same subject somewhat differently treated at Prato and at S. Fiora.
As a composition, however, we can hardly believe that Andrea set a group
like this, with its large figures against a plain blue ground, to balance
the scene to the left with its smaller figures and polychromatic mountain scenery. The subject of S. Francesco receiving the stigmata is likely
to have suggested itself for an altarpiece designed for a Franciscan brother-
hood, but it is also likely to have been balanced, as at Assisi, by a cognate
and similarly constructed scene, such as S. Girolamo in the Desert. Tobias
and the Angel is a beautiful group in itself, and an early product of Andrea's
own hand, but it seems to be present in this altarpiece through the desire
of some one other than the artist himself. S. Raffaello, with his outstretched wings is a fit counterpart to the S. Michele from Faenza or the
Annunciation Angel at LaVerna. His costume, with the diaconal stoles

crossed upon his heart, betokens Andrea's design. He carries a pyxis in which is contained the heart and liver and gall of the fish (Tobit, V-VI), and is accompanied by a dog. The eyes of both figures have blue brows, lashes, and pupils, and yellow irises.

The frame exhibits an entablature with a fruit frieze not yet convention-

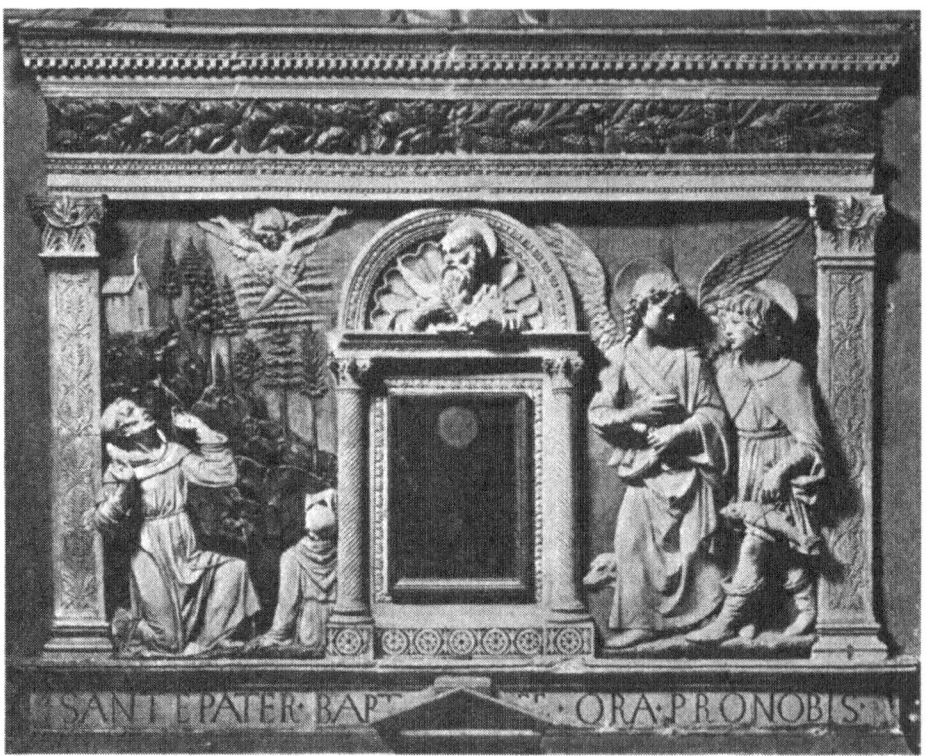

FIG. 33.—THE VIERI-CANIGIANI ALTARPIECE.

alized into Andrea's customary forms, although the light coloured fruits are all set to the left and the dark pine cones to the right. The pilasters are decorated with palmettes like those of the Adoration altarpiece at La Verna, and the base bears an inscription, with lettering and punctuation marks similar to those at La Verna, reading

SANTE PATER ✦ BARTOLOMEE ✦ ORA PRO NOBIS ✦

At either end of the base in monochrome are kneeling brothers of this Franciscan confraternity.

Bibl. :

B., *A. S. A.*, II(1889), 3; *Ital. Bildh. Ren.*, 84; C-M., 207 No. 12; Cr., 183, 341; Michel, IV, 124; R., *Sc. Fl.*, III, 148, 151.

26 BUST OF S. BARTOLOMMEO. Paris. E. Gavet Collection (in 1897). H., 0.47m.; W., 0.65m. Photo., Private.

This bust (Fig. 34) was in the Gavet sale of 1897. Compare the bust of S. Bartolommeo in the altarpiece in the Cappella Vieri-Canigiani at S. Croce, where he is represented holding a knife.

Glazed white, but the eyes have blue brows, lashes and pupils, and yellow irises.

Bibl.:

Gavet Collection, *Cat.*, No. 190, Pl. **190.**

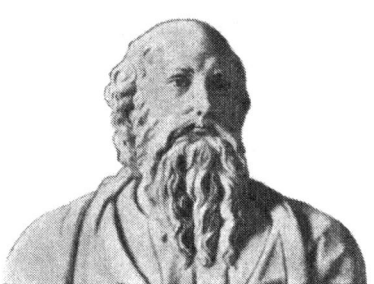

FIG. 34.—S. BARTOLOMMEO.

27 ALTARPIECE. (1) S. FRANCESCO RECEIVES THE STIG-MATA. (2) CORONATION OF VIRGIN. (3) S. GIROLAMO IN THE DESERT. Assisi. S. Maria degli Angeli, Cappella di S. Giuseppe. H., 2.18m.; W., 2.36m. Photo., Alinari, No. 4837.

Luca della Robbia's only altarpiece, in the episcopal palace at Pescia, was composed in three sections, like a triptych. Andrea follows the same arrangement here (Fig. 35). In the panel to the left he represents S. Francesco receiving the stigmata. The composition is very similar to that in the Cappella Canigiani, but finer in execution. The clouds seen behind the trees give greater depth to the picture; the Christ in the sky is less like a winged cherub head; the rocky hillside is more naturalistically coloured; the roof, doors and windows of the little church are here clearly defined by colour. In the copy of this altarpiece at S. Fiora this scene is less sharply modelled, but in the church of the Cappuccini at Barga it was rendered more elaborately. The Coronation of the Virgin recalls the famous altarpiece in the Osservanza, Siena. The seven angels with pipes and the one with a curved horn are here less beautiful; the principal group is more equally balanced; the cherubs who uphold the cloud thrones more adequate to the task. This scene was elaborated later by Andrea for the Coronation and Resurrection relief at Aquila. The S. Girolamo in penitence in a dark rocky landscape balances well the S. Francesco relief; the lion faithfully watches over the haggard saint.

In the predella is: (1) an Annunciation, with a charming S. Gabriele

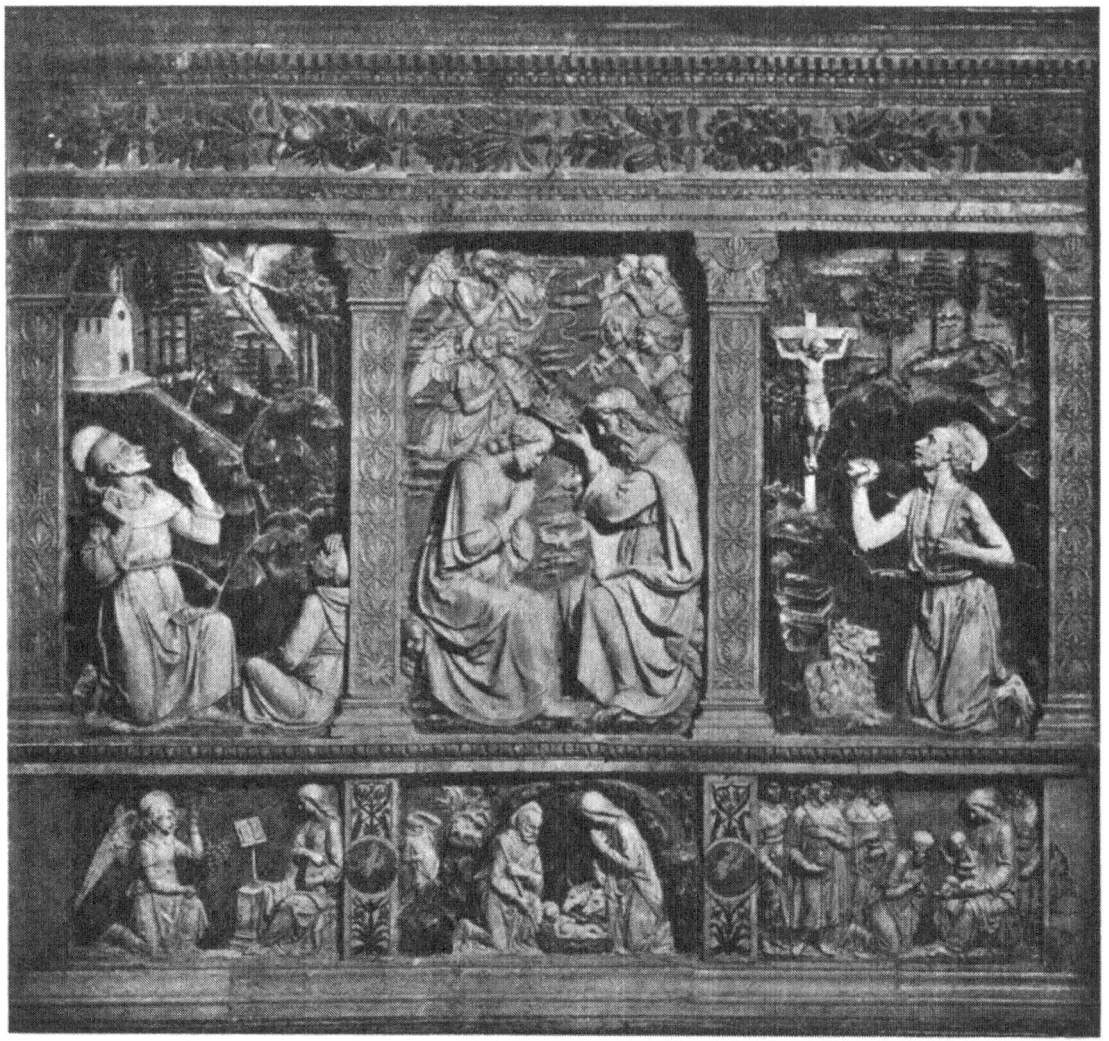

FIG. 35.—THE BAGLIONI ALTARPIECE. ASSISI.

kneeling, pointing upward, holding a lily branch to the Virgin who is seated on a bench before a lectern; (2) a Presepio of the cave type including the Annunciation to the Shepherds; and (3) the Adoration of the Magi, in which besides the Holy Family and the three wise men are three attendants one of whom is an African. The terminal predella pilasters contained vases of roses, similar to those in the predella of the Coronation altarpiece at Siena; the central pilasters are decorated with floral ornament enclosing medallions with the arms of Braccio II Baglioni: Azure a griffin argent with fish tail vert, holding a sword.

This altarpiece appears to have been removed from some other location when the cornice mouldings were cut short; the polychromatic fruit frieze was stupidly set (two of the bunches to the right of the centre being upside down); and one of the pilasters (last to right) set upside down. It may be noticed that while the first pilaster to the left contains seven palmettes, the other three have eight. A similar irregularity, as well as similar design occurs in the pilasters of the Adoration altarpiece at La Verna.

Bibl.:

B., *Kf.*, 26; *It. Bildh. Ren.*, 84; Burl., 72, 112; C., s.v. Baglioni; C-M., 225 No. 122; Cr., 182-183, 325; M., *R. H.*, 28, 30; Michel, IV, 124 Fig. 91; R., *D. R.*, 162-163; *Sc. Fl.*, III, 154-155; S., 105, Abb. 108.

28   STEMMA OF BISHOP FEDERICO MANFREDI. 1477. Faenza, Duomo, S. Pietro. Photo., Private.

The Cathedral of Faenza, designed by Giuliano da Maiano to occupy the site of an earlier church, was built for Bishop Federico Manfredi in 1474. On the sixteenth of November, 1477, the Bishop, who had been serving as Lieutenant General of State and incurred the odium of the people, was driven from the city and suffered severe financial loss. As a testimonial of his benefactions to the Cathedral he had arranged three medallions containing his coat of arms, one to be set in the vault over the high altar, the other two in the vaults which cover the transepts. As the latter two are incomplete, we may reasonably suppose that these medallions were being executed when the Bishop met his unfortunate fate.

1. The central medallion (Fig. 36).

The Manfredi arms, on a tournament shield, display quarterings of argent and azure, here surmounted by a Capo di Francia consisting of three golden fleurs-de-lys on a field of azure. The complex supporter of the shield, called a caprone, looks like a camel seated beside a violet flame or fire, carrying a sack on his back, his head covered with a helmet, the crest of which consists of the head of a white goat with golden (yellow) horns. From the top of the helmet radiate mantlings of violet, white and green. Behind the goat's head is a scroll, not inscribed. The arms and supporter are set against a blue fluted disk framed with a garland of fruit.

The frame is broad and the fruit garland modelled in rather flat masses.

Its composition is conventional.　Each bunch, containing three pieces of fruit and arranged to form a triangle, is held together by a ribbon and is not merged in the mass, as in Luca della Robbia's garlands.　It was baked in eight sections, each containing two bunches of similar fruit.　The sec-

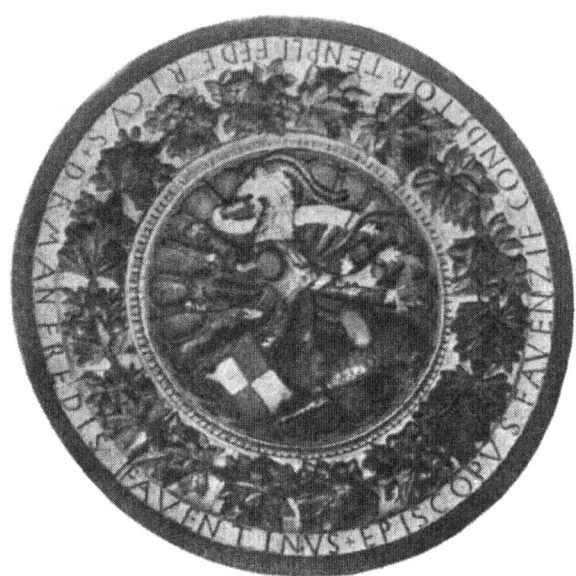

FIG. 36.—MANFREDI STEMMA.

tions are alternately dark and light in colour.　The same fruits are found in Luca's garlands.　Grapes, oranges, pine cones, apples are succeeded by grapes, citrons, pine cones, zucche, in the direction of the hands of a clock. The outermost band of the frame is inscribed:

FEDERICVS ✦ DE MANFREDIS ✦
FAVENTINVS ✦ EPISCOPVS ✦ FAVENZIE ✦ CONDITOR ✦
TENPLI

It is in the composition and modelling of the garland that one particularly recognizes the hand of Andrea della Robbia.

2. Medallion of the north transept.

The central portion of this medallion is of plaster, and presents in a complicated form the arms of Bishop Manfredi.　An eagle with a motto and a dove with a motto are added emblems.　The motto issuing from the goat's mouth reads:　WAH HIC MAC (sic).　The inscription S(IGILLVM) ✦ D(OMI)NI ✦ FEDERICI ✦ DEMANFREDIS ✦ EPISCOPI ✦ FAVENTINI ✦ is more delicate in lettering than the inscription on the outer band of the frame.　The frame is less carefully

modelled than the frame of the medallion in the vault over the high altar—
an indication that Andrea della Robbia already employed assistants. It is
also composed with less skill—every alternate bunch consists of pine cones
—and was stupidly set in position, two of the eight sections having ex-
changed places, so that the inscription is meaningless. The outer inscription is the same as in the central medallion, but punctuated with ✛ instead
of ✚.

3. Medallion of the south transept.

The central portion of this medallion, on which is painted the Manfredi
arms, is also of plaster. The supporter is still a camel seated beside a
flame, a sack on his back and a helmet with mantlings on his head. The
crest consists of a conventional floral pattern; the scroll is inscribed

WAN: ICH ✛ MAG ✚

The frame, of glazed terra-cotta, is composed of eight sections, each with
two bunches of fruit, alternating in colour from dark to light. The dark
coloured fruits are grapes and pine cones; the light ones, citrons, oranges,
apples, and zucche. The fruit seems to have been modelled by the sculptor
of the first medallion, but the inscription given over to an assistant who
used heavier lettering, reversed the direction of the inscription and changed
the spelling of FAVENZIE to FAVENTIE ✚ It records the foundation
of the church in the same words as in the first medallion.

Bibl. :

Argnani, 21; C., s.v. Manfredi; Guasti, *Caffagiolo*, 157; Malagola,
101-102, 464; M., *R. H.*, 33-35, Fig. 30; Messeri-Calzi, 506-512; Ton-
duzzi, 12, 508, 511; Strocchi, 3.

29 STEMMA OF FRANCESCO DI LORENZO DELLA STUFA.
1478. Volterra, Palazzo dei Priori. Photo., Alinari, 34619.

Set against a blue, fluted disk on a pointed, oval shield are the della Stufa
arms: Argent, two lions combattant or; in chief a Latin cross couped
gules (Fig. 37). The frame of plain architectural mouldings encloses a
garland of fruit composed of triplex bunches, in colour alternately dark
and light, well separated and bound by narrow ribbons.

Below a winged cherub displays a curved scroll inscribed:

FRANCISCVS ✛ LAVRENTII
STVFE ✛ PRESES ✛ ET ✛ LEGATV
S ✛ DIGNISSIMVS ✛ 1464 ✛ ET ✛ 1478

Francesco di Lorenzo della Stufa had been Prior of Florence in 1463

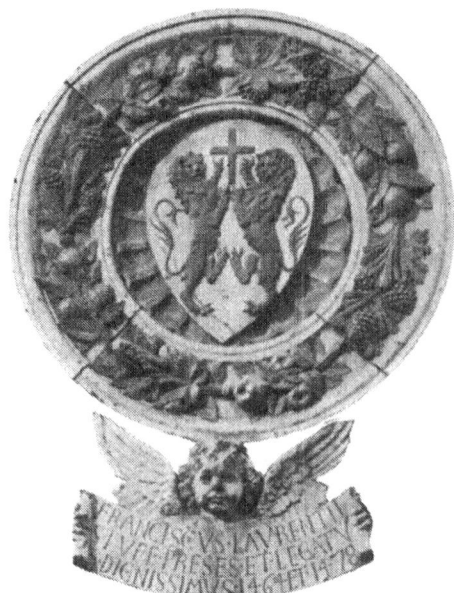

FIG. 37.—DELLA STUFA STEMMA.

and Gonfaloniere in 1482. His son Lorenzo became Vicario at Lari in 1524.

Bibl.:
C., s.v. Lotteringhi della Stufa; M., *L. D. R.*, 244-245; *R. H.*, 36, Fig. 32; P., 403-405; W., 176-177.

30 GOD THE FATHER BLESSING. Empoli. Galleria della Collegiata. Medallion. Diam., 1.28m. Photo., Alinari, No. 10124.

A representation of God the Father blessing, formerly in the Cappella di S. Lorenzo of the Collegiata above the altar adorned with Rossellino's S. Sebastiano (Fig. 38). It is to be attributed to Andrea della Robbia, though less beautiful than the representation of God the Father in the lunette of the Madonna della Cintola at La Verna. His eyes have dark blue brows and pupils, and yellow irises. He is surrounded by seven triple-winged cherubs. The frame is heavy and the bunches of fruit somewhat conventional, but not without decorative charm.

Bibl.:
Burckh., 434; Carocci, *Il Valdarno*, 75; C-M., 232 No. 169; Cr., 337; Giglioli, *Empoli*, 54.

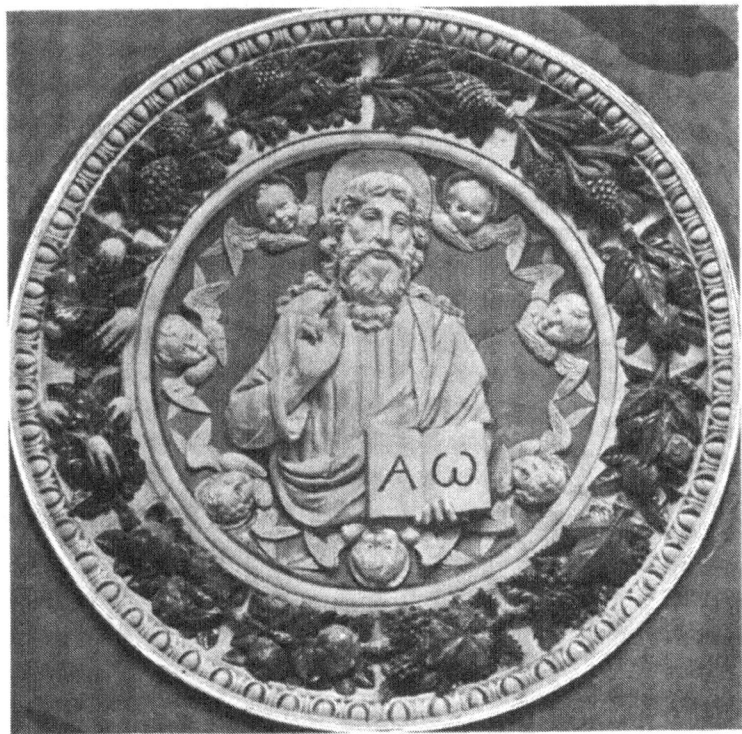

FIG. 38.—GOD FATHER BLESSING.

31 PAVEMENT TILES. Empoli. Museo della Collegiata. 2.40m. ✕ 1.53m.

Before the altar of the Cappella di S. Lorenzo in the Collegiata at Empoli was a Robbia pavement (Fig. 39), recently removed to the Museo. The central portion consists of hexagonal white tiles, decorated with complicated rosettes, blue, green, white and yellow, bordered with foliage of violet, green and blue. At either side is a border, 0.28m. wide, showing a net work of cubes, black, green and yellow. It did not compose well with the central pattern. In front a border, 0.23m. wide, shows a fringe and a charming pattern of opposing yellow palmettes united with blue and violet lilies. The tiles were set so that the fringe, which obviously belonged on the outer edge, is on the inner edge of the border. To the right of the altar was set a rectangular corner tile ornamented with a rosette. Evidently these tiles were adapted to, not originally designed for, this locality.

The altar of the chapel contains a statue of S. Sebastiano by Antonio Rossellino, who died in 1479; and on the wall is a coat of arms in Robbia

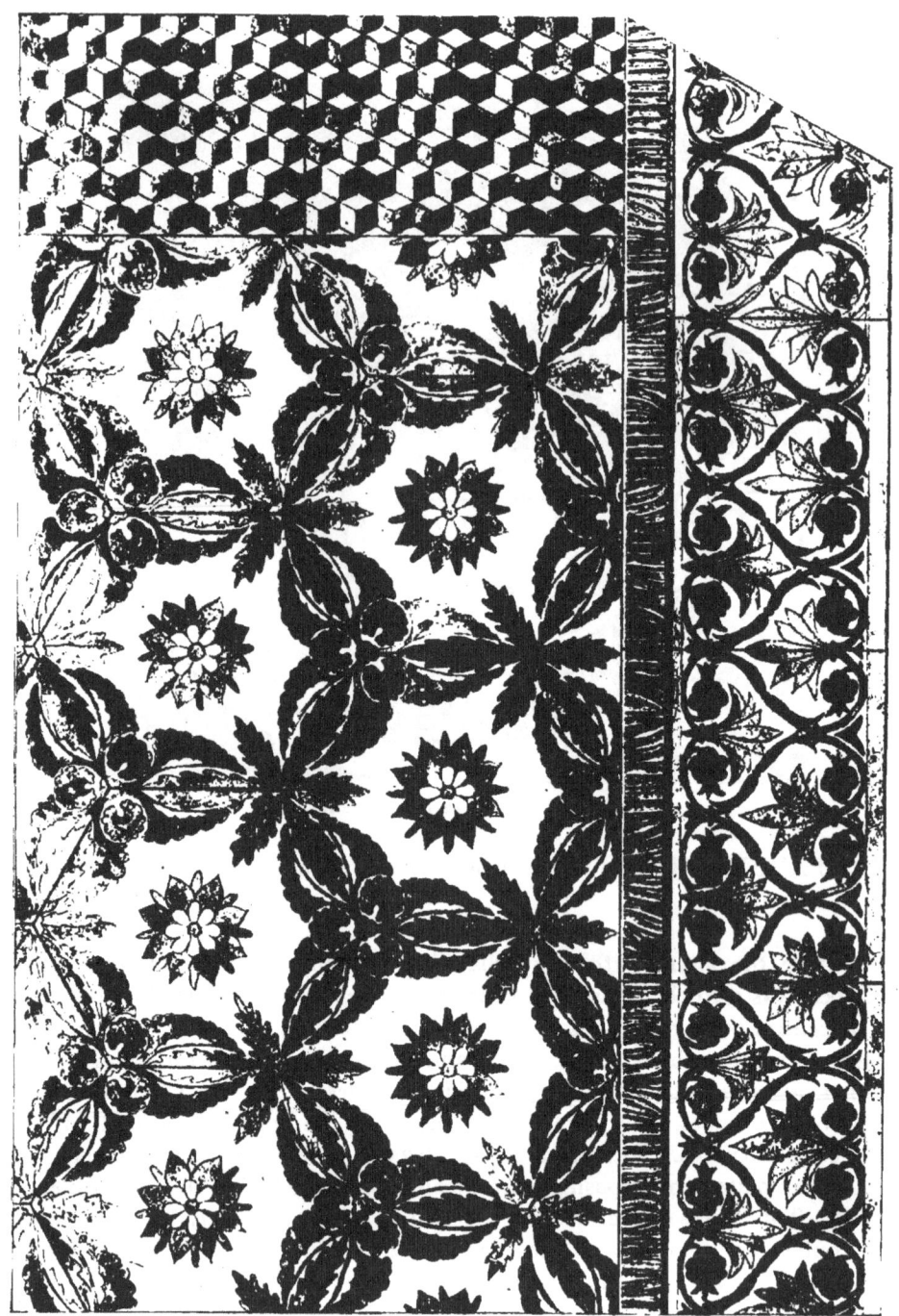

FIG. 39.—PAVEMENT TILES.

ware inscribed: ADIMARI, which may be dated approximately at 1475. The tiles were probably laid in this chapel at the same time as the medallion of God the Father. The pattern of the pavement as I have suggested elsewhere was probably designed by Luca della Robbia, but was reproduced several times in the atelier of his nephew.

Bibl.:
Cr., 337; M., *Br.* 1902, 55-56; *L. D. R.,* 91-92, Fig. 53.

32 SIMILAR TILES. S. Gimignano. Museo della Biblioteca. Photo., Private.

In the Museo della Biblioteca may be seen some tiles taken from the Cappella di S. Fina in the Duomo. This chapel was designed by Giuliano da Maiano in 1466, and enriched by Benedetto da Maiano with a tabernacle and altar in or about 1475. It is probable that the pavement was at that time laid like a rug in front of the altar. The tiles which remain show: (1) a corner tile, showing a rosette set within concentric circles and these in a square; (2) border tiles of opposing palmettes and a fringe, as at Empoli, and S. Fiora; and (3) central tiles, hexagonal in form bordered with blue, violet and green foliage and enclosing a large central rosette, as at Empoli.

Bibl.:
M., *Br.,* 1902, 55-56; *L. D. R.,* 91-92, Fig. 53.

33 SIMILAR TILES. S. Gimignano. S. Agostino, Cappella di S. Bartolo.

In the church of S. Agostino there may be seen some fine Robbia tiles, now in a poor state of preservation. They consist of hexagonal tiles, like those from S. Fina, decorated with varigated rosettes, but surrounded with elongated hexagons adorned with opposing bunches of fruit and flowers. The border tiles differ from those from S. Fina and are decorated with a series of palmettes, alternately blue and yellow, the blue ones being accompanied by cornucopias of fruit.

34 SIMILAR TILES. S. Fiora (Monte Amiata). Madonna della Neve.

Before the altar of Conte Guido Sforza in the church of the Madonna della Neve or della Piscina, are laid some tiles of hexagonal form exhibiting a polychromatic rosette in white ground surrounded by leaves of green, blue and violet; together with border tiles showing opposing palmettes and lilies, similar to those at Empoli, S. Gimignano, and Montevarchi.

Bibl.:
    M., *Br.*, 1902, 55; *L. D. R.*, 92.

34a SIMILAR TILES. Montevarchi. Collegiata di S. Lorenzo.

In the Cappella di Contte Guido Guerra with other remains of della Robbia monuments are some tiles of similar pattern to those at Empoli, S. Gimignano, and S. Fiora. Some are octagonal with central rosettes surrounded by foliage, others are border tiles with the fringe pattern.

Bibl.:
    M., *Br.*, 1902, 55-56.

35 ALTARPIECE OF THE ANNUNCIATION. Là Verna. Chiesa Maggiore, Cappella Niccolini. H., 2.10m.; W., 2.10m. Photo., Alinari, No. 9831. Cast, Cantagalli 484; Lelli 373, 386.

Although the mountain of La Verna was given in 1213 to S. Francesco by Conte Orlando Catani, Signor of Chiusi, the support of the monastery came chiefly from Florence—from the Arte della Lana, the Municipio, and several well known families.

The principal church, erected in 1348, suffered from fire in 1472. How destructive this fire may have been may be inferred from the fact that the general decoration of the church and the Robbia altarpieces may all be assigned to a period later than the fire. As we look toward the choir we see two baldachinos, not unlike those which shelter Luca's two tabernacles at Impruneta, forming private chapels. To the left is the Cappella Niccolini with the altarpiece of the Annunciation, to the right the Cappella Brizi with the altarpiece of the Adoration. The Cappella Brizi bears the date 1479. At this period Luca della Robbia was nearing his end, and Andrea, long since recognized as a master, was enjoying well earned success.

Both reliefs breathe the dignity and sobriety of Luca's compositions. The Annunciation altarpiece (Fig. 40) is composed in part as we might expect Luca to have designed it, with the Virgin to the left and the Angel to the right; various details are also reminiscent of Luca. But the Virgin is in type like Andrea's early Madonnas; S. Gabriele is the counterpart of the S. Michele from Faenza; the detached fleecy clouds recall those of the S. Egidio Madonna; and the introduction of the Dove, and of God the

Father in a glory of cherub heads, is thoroughly characteristic of Andrea.
The bench on which the Virgin is seated recalls those in several of Luca's
Madonnas, but is also found in Andrea's Annunciations in predella scenes
at Siena, Assisi, Aquila, Prato, Gradara Rocca, Foiano, the Misericordia at
Florence, in the Museum of Berlin, Città di Castello, and Florence.   At S.

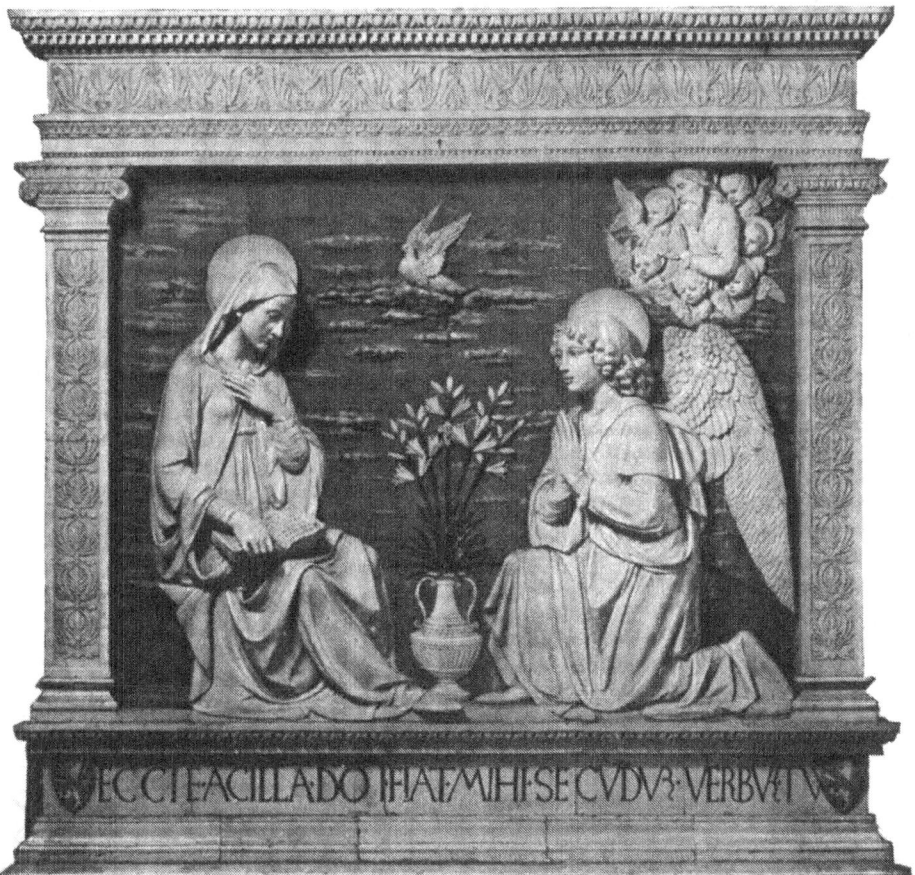

FIG. 40.—THE NICCOLINI ANNUNCIATION. LA VERNA.

Fiora a projection of the wall serves instead of a bench.   On the whole in
Andrea's earliest representations of the Annunciation the Madonna is
seated on a bench.   Later she is represented as kneeling or standing.   Here
she wears the mantle drawn over her head like a hood, with the characteristic triangular fold over the forehead.   It may be conceived as fastened
by the cord with buttons, and it falls in carefully arranged folds to her
feet.   Her tunic is supported below the breast with the usual linen girdle.
Her eyes have yellow irises, and violet brows, lashes and pupils.   The book

which lies open on her lap is inscribed *Ecce Virgo concipiet et pariet filium, et vocabitur nomen eius* the remainder of the quotation (Isaiah, VII, 14: S. Luke, I, 30) being covered, except for a few letters, by her right hand. The symbolic lilies are not presented by the angel, but are symmetrically arranged in a decorated amphora set on the ground. S. Gabriele, with thick, curly hair and fine wings, clad in tunic with shoulder capes, deacon's stole and flowing mantle, is on his knees, not waiting to deliver his message but having delivered it, to which the Virgin has replied in the words (S. Luke I, 38) inscribed below:

ECCIE ✦ A(N)CILLA ✦ DO(MIN)I ✦ FIAT ✦ MIHI ✦
SECV(N)DVM ✦ VERBVM ✦ TVV(M).

On either side of this inscription are the Niccolini arms: Azure, a lion rampant guardant argent, debruised of a bend gules.

The Niccolini family furnished many priors to Florence. We mention only Lorenzo di Lapo di Giovanni, Prior in 1446, 1453, 1465, 1468 and Gonfaloniere in 1465. His brother Otto was ambassador to Rome in 1453, 1455 and 1464. Agnolo di Otto di Lapo Niccolini, Prior in 1479, may be suggested as possibly the donor of this altarpiece. The frame, including the predella and cornice, constitutes a perfect square, an unusual form for altarpieces. The severely stylized palmette decoration of the pilasters suggest the influence of Mino da Fiesole rather than that of Luca della Robbia. This motive together with that of the cornice was repeated for the Coronation altarpiece at the Osservanza.

Bibl.:

Beni, 360; B., *Kf.*, 16; *Ital. Bildh. Ren.*, 81; *Denk.*, 83, 85, Taf. 251; *W. d. R.*, 8, Taf. 33; Burl., 119; C-M., 92, 256 No. 327; C., s.v. Niccolini; Cr. 162-163, 326; D.D., 33 Abb. 50; Fov., 89, 101; Lupattelli, 16; M., Scribner's 1893, 688, 697; *R. H.*, 30-31; Mencherini, 248-251; Michel IV, 123; Nagler, XIII, 226; P., 436; R., *D. R.*, 160; *Sc. Fl.*, 152; Reumont, *Kunstblatt* No. 206 (1831); S., 104-105, Abb. 107; Vas., II, 198; V., VI, 589, Fig. 395; W., 158-159.

36 HEAD OF THE ANNUNZIATA. London. Collection of Miss Florence Gilbert. H., 0.27m.; W., 0.17m.

This very beautiful fragment (Fig. 40a) was published for the first time by Miss Cruttwell, who characterized it as "by far the most important and beautiful work of Andrea in England." When I saw it in 1911 I hesitated to accept this attribution for the following reasons:

(1) The glaze covers the inside as well as the outside surface of the

head. This I had observed in two modern heads, but not in Robbia works
in the few instances where observation was possible.

(2) The glaze shows a crackle, more common in modern than in Robbia glazes.

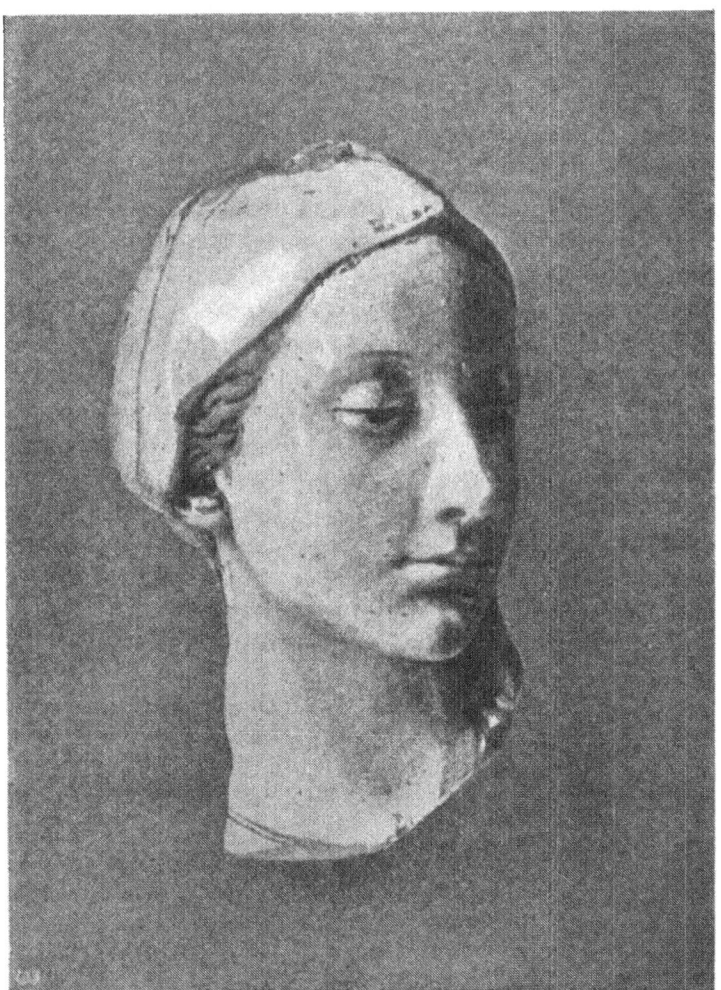

FIG. 40a.—HEAD OF THE ANNUNZIATA. LONDON.

(3) The mode of colouring the eyes is more summary than was customary with Andrea.

Notwithstanding these details, the general impression conveyed by this
head with its beautiful brows, delicate nose, sensitive mouth, and finely
modelled chin incline me to accept it as from the hand of Andrea himself.
Unfortunately nothing is known of its provenance. Possibly it came from

an Annunciation altarpiece, somewhat similar to that in the Niccolini chapel at La Verna.

Bibl.:
Cr., 176, 326; Mag. of Art, 1903, **414**; S., 123, Abb. **140**.

37 ALTARPIECE OF THE ADORATION. 1479. La Verna, Chiesa Maggiore, Cappella Brizi. H., 2.40m.; W., 1.80m. Photo., Alinari, No. 9830. Casts, Cantagalli, 484, 442-443, (detail), 341 (detail); Lelli, 381, 382, 428.

The chapel on the south side of the central aisle, corresponding to the Niccolini chapel on the north side, was founded by Jacopo Brizi of Pieve S. Stefano in 1479. The balustrade is inscribed *Istam Capellam fecit fieri Jacobus Britii de Pieve Santi Stephani* A.D. MCCCCLXXVIIII. The altarpiece (Fig. 41) is approximately of the same period, and presumably of a slightly later date than the Annunciation in the Niccolini chapel. The general form is not a square, but a rectangle of which the height exceeds the breadth. The predella is composed of simpler mouldings; the pilasters are slenderer; and the frieze consists of cherub heads. But the general spirit, the facial types, various details of drapery, the character of the clouds, the lettering of the inscription, show that the difference in date is insignificant. In the decoration of the pilasters Andrea makes use of somewhat slenderer floral forms rising similarly from a foundation group of leaves. The pilaster to the right is less skilfully executed and contains eight instead of nine palmettes. The capitals of the columns are of the Brunelleschian type used by Luca della Robbia in the tabernacle of the Holy Cross at Impruneta. It may be noted also that the central cherub of the frieze is posed en face, the others with heads more or less tilted toward the centre. The predella is inscribed

VERBVM CARO ✦ FATTV(M) ✦ EST ✦ DE VIRGINE ✦ M(ARI)A

The central relief is composed in semi-symbolic fashion. The Virgin is posed upon her knees upon a ledge which also contains the Child outstretched upon a rock-like mass of light green hay. There is no other indication that the scene is laid upon the earth. The sky, more realistically treated with gray and black clouds some of which are in relief, is surcharged with figures. There is a fine God the Father with outstretched hands surrounded by six cherub heads, the Holy Dove, and eight angels. Two of the latter hold a scroll inscribed: GLORIA IN EXCELS(IS) DEO. In this composition the Christ Child is given an isolated position and gazes out upon the world. He is the object of the adoration of almost every one represented in the composition. He and the Virgin are distinguished by a cream coloured glaze not so white as that of the heavenly creatures. 'This does not indicate, as Miss Cruttwell suggests, more than one designer, since God the Father, the angels, cherubs and Dove are as surely as the Virgin and Child characteristic products of Andrea's personal handiwork.

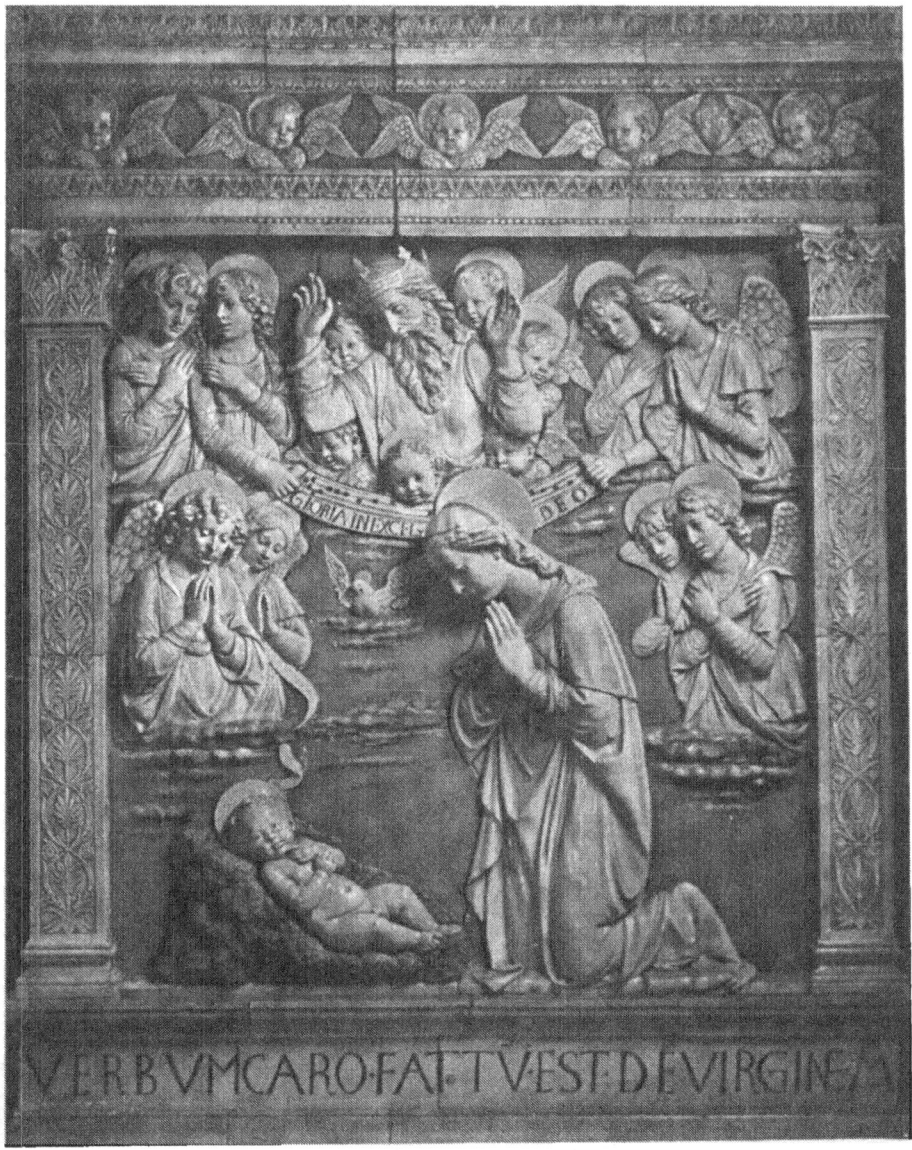

FIG. 41.—THE BRIZI ADORATION. LA VERNA.

The Adoration of the Child is derived from the more complex subject of the Nativity, which in Andrea's compositions no longer represented the birth itself, but, in stable or cave or in open air, the Child adored by his parents, the shepherds, the Magi, the heavenly hosts, and even by the ox and ass. Here the angels singing the Gloria are retained, but the other accessory figures are absent. In their place appears God the Father with his cherubs, and the Holy Dove.

Bibl.:

Beni, 357; B., *Kf.*, 16; *It. Bildh. Rcn.*, 81; *It. Pl.*, 93; *Denk.*, 83, Taf. 250; Brockhaus, 57; Burl., 73, 119; C-M., 256 No. 328; Cr., 148, 163-164, 326; M., *Scr. Mag.*, 1893, 697; *D. R. A.*, 64 Fig. 27; Mencherini, 245-248; Michel, IV, 123; R., *D. R.*, 156; *Sc. Fl.*, 149, 152; S., 103 Abb. 106; Vas., II, 179, 198; V., VI, 584 Fig. 301.

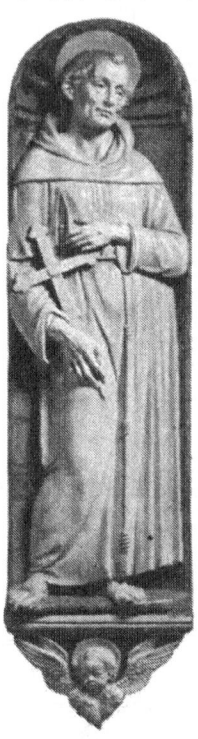

FIG. 42.—S. FRANCESCO.

38 S. FRANCESCO. La Verna. Chiesa Maggiore. H., 1.70m. Photo., Alinari, No. 9832.

This very expressive relief, formerly in the Brizi Chapel, represents S. Francesco (Fig. 42) standing in a blue niche which is capped with a shell with green ribs. S. Francesco in monastic robes holds a cross and points to his wounded side. His stigmata are raised knobs. His eyes have violet brows, lashes, and pupils. The irises are now hardly distinguishable from the pupils. The console is ornamented with a cherub head with three pairs of wings.

Bibl.:

Beni, 359; Burl., 119; C-M., 256 No. 329; Cr., 356; M., *Scribner's*, 1893, 697; Memorie della Verna. Ms. segnato Biblioteca Marucelliana, B. I, 19, c. 93; Mencherini, 254,-255, 257; R., *D. R.*, 176; *Sc. Fl.*, III, 162.

39 S. ANTONIO ABATE. La Verna. Chiesa Maggiore. H., 1.70m. with console. Photo., Alinari, No. 9833.

A companion piece to the S. Francesco, and formerly in the **Brizi** Chapel. S. Antonio, in monkish robes, carries a book and a staff (Fig. 43). He was popular with the poor, and with the Franciscans who exalted

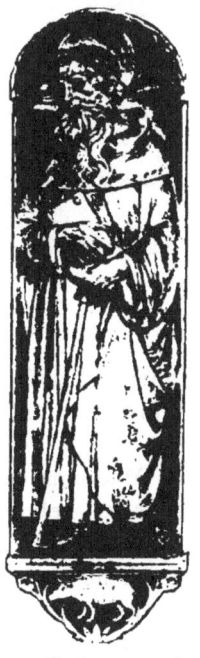

FIG. 43.—S. ANTONIO ABATE.

poverty as a virtue. His symbol, the pig, is represented on the console. Details of colour as in the preceding.

Bibl.:

Same as the preceding, and M., *R. H.*, 74.

40 MADONNA AND CHILD BETWEEN ANGELS. Florence.
Badia. Over entrance. Lunette. Photos., Alinari 2046-2046a;
Brogi 9913-

When in 1871 the Via del Proconsolo entrance to the Badia was recon-
structed in the style of Benedetto da Rovezzano, this beautiful lunette (Fig.
44) was embodied in it. It was in itself too small for the position, but the
Manufattura Ginori made for it a wide garland frame and the architects
fitted out the remaining space with a succession of plain and decorated
mouldings. The relief itself could not have been supplied by the Ginori

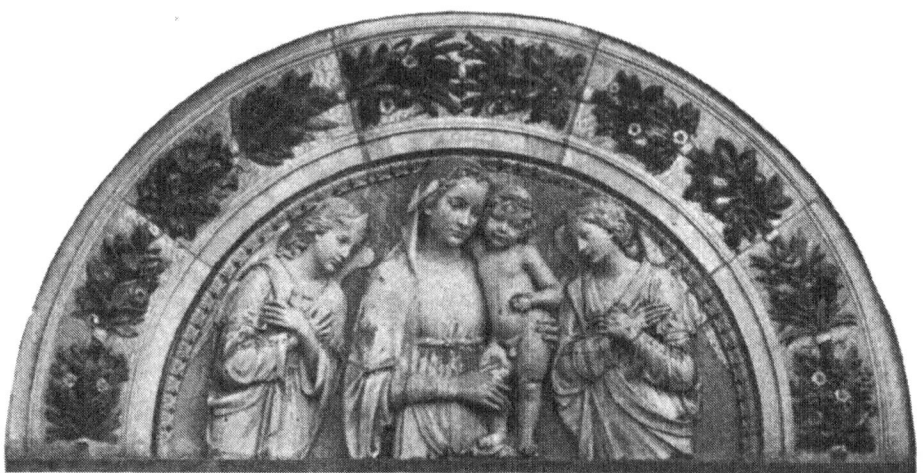

FIG. 44.—THE BADIA LUNETTE.

factory, as a close examination shows that it is covered with a hard Robbia
glaze whiter than that of the frame and without its iridescent quality, and
that its blue background is finer in colour and more uniform than that of
the frame.

The lunette is undoubtedly the Madonna over the "porta laterale verso
la strada publica" (via del Proconsolo) referred to by Puccinelli in 1664,
and further defined by Bocchi-Cinelli in 1677 as a very beautiful Madonna
with two adoring angels, "by Luca della Robbia." Richa in his Chiese
Fiorentine (1754) does not mention it. Possibly it had been removed, for
Barbet de Jouy in 1855 locates it within the Badia in the Cappella Salviati.
In 1878 Milanesi classed it as all that remained of the decorations made
for the chapel of Bernardo del Banco by Benedetto Buglioni (Vas. IV,
182). Subsequent writers, including Bode, Bacci, Burlamacchi, Cavalucci
and Molinier, Cruttwell, Perkins, Reymond, and Schubring follow Milanesi's attribution. On stylistic grounds however, we may say that it ex-

hibits none of the characters shown in Buglioni's works. The background is here a deep, beautiful blue, not the light, faded blue with which Buglioni was satisfied. The angels with their coronals, capes and graceful draperies, their gentle refined spirit may be paralleled in the heavenly hosts with which Andrea della Robbia surrounded his Madonna adoring the Child at La Verna. They have no parallel in the works of Benedetto Buglioni. The Madonna and Child show strongly the influence of Luca della Robbia, both in composition and details. The Child might be viewed as an emanation from Luca's stemma of the Silk Merchants on Or San Michele, and the Madonna as the prototype of the Madonna Lunga at Stia. Where in all of Benedetto Buglioni's work can we find even a remote parallel to this charming creation?

Documents:
1. "Sopra la Porta laterale verso la strada pubblica fu adatta
   l'effegie di Nostra Signora di terra robbia invetriata,
   vaga e bella per il disegno e maestria."
[P. D. Placido Puccinelli, *Istoria dell'Eroiche Attioni di Ugo il Grande.* Con la Cronica dell' Abbadia di Fiorenza. Milano, MDCLXIV. Cronica dell' Abbadia Fiorentina, c. 119.]

2. "E sopra la Porta di questa Ciesa in vn mezzo tondo vna
   bellissima Vergine col Bambino Giesù, e due Agnolini
   di terra vetriata di mano d(e)l Luca: Esprimono gli
   Angeli nel se(m)biante la devozione, e riverenza, che
   si deve all'eterno Verbo molto acconciamente."
   [Bocchi-Cinelli, 389.]

Bibl.:
Bacci, *Riv. d'Arte*, II(1904), 49-50; B-J., 89; Bocchi-Cinelli, 389; B., *Kf.*, 23; Burl., 107; C-M., 144, 205 No. 3; Cocchi, 113-114; Cr., 253, 341; Marcotti, 111; Perkins, *T. Sc.*, I, 201; *H. H.*, 145; R., *D. R.*, 223; *Sc. Fl.*, IV, 48; Richa, I, 198; S. 73, Abb. 69; Vas., II, 185 note 1, 192; IV, 182.

ANDREA DELLA ROBBIA

1480-1490

41 TWO ANGELS. Florence. Duomo. 1481-1482.

On the 15 of March 1481, and later in 1482, Andrea della Robbia through his son Marco (then 13-14 years of age, later became Fra Mattia) received payments from the Opera di S. Maria del Fiore for two angels made for the Cathedral. Their whereabouts is unknown.

Documents: [Copied by Mr. Rufus G. Mather.]

1. "+ MCCCC°LXXXI°

Andrea di marcho di Simone dellarobja de dare adj 15 dj marzo l. dodicj picciolj porrto marcho suo figliuolo per partte dj due agnolj fa per lopera paghonsi per poliza del provvedittore n° 45 - l 12 sol —

E adj 30 di marzo 1482 l. dodicj piccioli fattj buonj daprile a piero di ser lore(n)zo proveditore per partte dj 2 agnolj fattj per la chiesa per poliza dj detto piero proveditore n°60 l 12 sol —

2. "+MCCCCLXXXIJ 24 —"

Ricordo Spese dopera deono dare...

. . . .

E deono dare l. ve(n)tiquatro per loro a andrea di marcho dellarobia posto debj avere in questo c. 50 f - lib. 24 sol -"

[Arch. dell 'Opera di S. Maria del Fiore. Quaderno di Cassa 1481 n. I, c. 49t, 50, 76t; published in *L'Arte*, XXII(1919), 205.]

3. "+ MCCCCLXXXII

Andrea di marcho di simone della rob(b)ia de avere l ventj quatro per lluj da spese dopera posto debjno dare in questo c 77 l 24 s — de qualj affatto debitore al quaderno giornale p c. 97 al suo cōto(conto)."

[Idem, idem, c. 50.]

Bibl.:

R. G. Mather, *L'Arte*, XXII (1919), 205 (Doc.).

42 CORONATION OF THE VIRGIN. Siena. Osservanza. Rectangular altarpiece. H., 2.65m.; W., 2.30. Photo., Alinari, No. 9138;

Lombardi No. 2169, 2220, 1361-1364; Casts, Cantagalli, 290, 350 (detail), Lelli, 372, 375(detail).

The Osservanza at Siena contains several of Andrea's works and among them his masterpiece, the Coronation of the Virgin (Fig. 45). The lunette, with the monogram of Christ and the winged cherub heads, appears to have belonged to some other monument. The altarpiece itself, its frame and predella must be dated shortly after the Annunciation at La Verna. The frame is less square in form, with slightly elongated pilasters decorated with similar palmettes (ten instead of nine) and provided with similar capitals. The architrave shows the same mouldings, the frieze the same decoration, but the cornice richer ornamental forms. The predella is composed of three panels separated by flat pilasters. The two lateral ones exhibit an elaborate blue flowering plant containing the escutcheon of the Ugurgieri family: Or, three lions azure supporting a wheel gules. It may be noted that Magio Ugurgieri was one of the Nine in 1482, capitano in 1490, and four times Gonfaloniere. The central pilasters show delicately outlined vases containing bunches of single or double roses. The reliefs of the predella show: (1) an Annunciation with seated Virgin, not far removed from its La Verna prototype; (2) an Assumption, in which the Virgin, seated on clouds in the midst of a violet edged mandorla supported by four angels, has risen through clouds from a plain sarcophagus; and (3) a Presepio of the cave type, in which the Child rests on light green hay in a yellow crib, behind which are the large heads of the ox and ass, and at either side S. Giuseppe and the Madonna. Outside of the gray blue cave is a shepherd blinded by the sight of an angel whose scroll is inscribed not with the Annuntio Vobis, but GLORIA INESCIESIS (sic) DEO.

The principal relief exhibits the Coronation of the Virgin in the presence of five saints. The saints are posed upon a white projecting base, with neither clouds nor earth to indicate where they are standing. S. Girolamo, holding a stone, with breast exposed, gazes upward; S. Antonio of Padua, in Franciscan garb, holds a flame and book; S. Chiara is on her knees adoring; a young female saint (Rosa, Lucia) with martyr palm, stands behind; to the right is S. Francesco holding the cross. Their eyes have yellow irises and dark blue brows, lashes and pupils. That the Coronation scene takes place in heaven is indicated by the clouds in the blue sky over the entire background. God the Father with all seriousness places the crown on the head of the beautiful Virgin, whose robe retains much of its original gold ornament. They are surrounded by winged cherubs and between them flutters the Holy Dove. Eight angels, with trumpets and pipes arranged in pairs on either side, are evidently by the same hand that de-

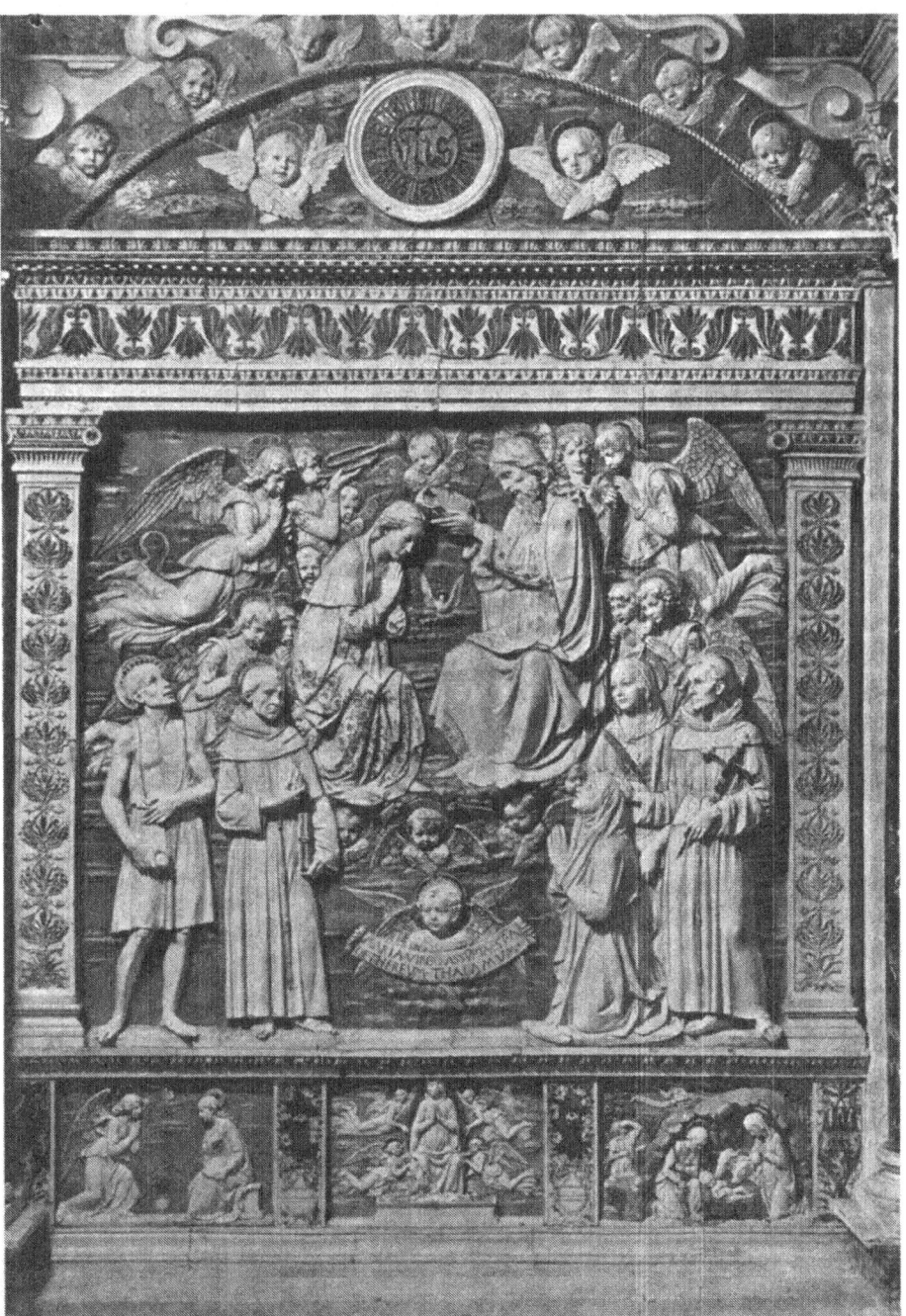

Fig. 45.—The Osservanza Coronation.

signed the Adoration altarpiece at La Verna. Below this group is a cherub holding a scroll inscribed:

MARIA ✦ VIRGO ✦ ASSV(M)PTA ✦ EST ✦ AD ETHEREUM ✦ THALAMVM ✦

In no other monument did Andrea della Robbia produce more beautiful forms.

Bibl.:

> B. J., 91; B., *Kf.*, 17, 25; *Denk.*, 84, Taf. 261; Brogi, *Inv.*, 229; Burl., 72-73, 117; C., s.v. Ugurgieri; Cr., 174-176, 326; Fov., 108; *D. D.*, 33, Abb. 52; M., *Scr. Mag.*, 1893, 697; *D. R. A.*, 68, 85; *R. H.*, 29-30; Michel, IV, 124; Perkins, *H. H.*, 142-143; *T. S.*, 197; R., *D. R.*, 168-170; *Sc. Fl.*, III, 158-159; *S.*, 105-106, Abb. 109; Vas., II, 194.

43 THE ANNUNCIATION. Siena. Osservanza. Two statues. H., 1.80m. Photos., Lombardi.

On either side of the high altar in the chapel of the Osservanza, set in plaster niches in the wall are two statues: (1) S. Gabriele; and (2) the

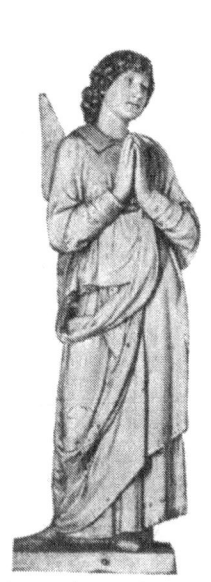

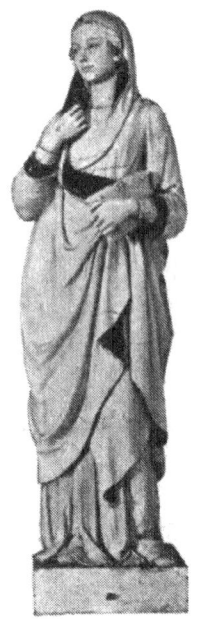

FIG. 46.—S. GABRIELE.   FIG. 47.—THE ANNUNZIATA.

Annunziata. S. Gabriele (Fig. 46), though of the same height as the Annunziata, is a stocky standing figure, with curly hair, wings without sculptured detail, and his white robe and mantle once covered with gilded ornament. The Annunziata (Fig. 47), in contrast, has extraordinarily long lower limbs, as if the sculptor were guided by some special impulse rather than by a fixed sense of proportion. Her hair was gilded and her eyes have violet brows, lashes, pupils, and yellow irises. She has a refined, beautiful face—a prototype rather than a copy of that of the Prato Cathedral Madonna. At some later period some one has painted in green over the white glaze the reverses of her mantle, without completing his work by giving her a blue mantle over a red tunic.

Bibl.:

B., *Kf.*, 25; *W. D. R.*, Taf. **43**; Brogi, 231; Burck., 435; C-M., 249 No. 274; Cr., 225-226, 330; Fov., 97, 103; S., 123, Abb. **138**.

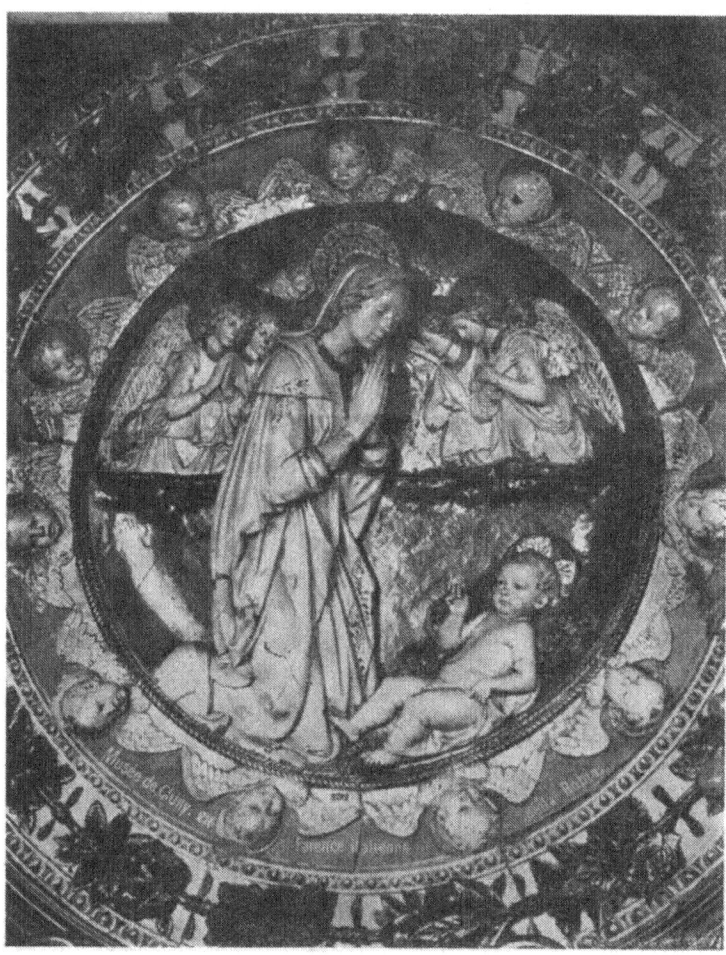

FIG. 48.—THE CLUNY ADORATION.

44 MADONNA ADORING THE CHILD. Paris. Musée de Cluny, No. 2792. Medallion. Diam., 1.85m. Photo., Mieusement or Leroy, No. 216.

This medallion (Fig. 48) resembles in general Luca's Adoration in the Foulc collection at Nimes, but has been transformed by Andrea. The four angels are arranged in pairs facing each other with little reference to the Child whom they are adoring; the Madonna resembles the Annunziata in the Osservanza at Siena; the clouds are in strong relief; the Child, playing with the drapery beneath him, blessing with his right hand, reclining on green hay, is less lifelike than the Child in the Foulc medallion. All the figures are given nimbuses.

The frame consists of an outer zone of polychromatic fruit arranged schematically on white ground, and of an inner zone decorated with eleven cherub heads. The innermost double cord or braid moulding occurs on other works by Andrea della Robbia.

Bibl.:

Burl., 84; C-M., 64 note 1, 272 No. 418; Cr., 351; M., *A. J. A.*, IX(1894), 25 note; *D. R. A.*, 67; R., *D. R.*, 160; *Sc. Fl.*, III, 151; Du Sommerard, *Cat.*, No. 2792.

45 MADONNA WITH SAINTS. Gradara Rocca. Cappella di Conte Morandi. Rectangular altarpiece. H., 2.13m.; W., 1.86m. Photos., Alinari, No. 14813; Moscioni, Nos. 4987-4990.

The Castello at the Rocca di Gradara, near Pesaro, was built in 1463. The framework of this altarpiece (Fig. 49), including the decoration of the frieze, the pilasters, and predella link it with Andrea's early works at La Verna (1479). The Madonna is a prototype of the Madonna of 1489 in the Museo dell'Opera del Duomo, Florence. The predella, with its painted pilasters, is to be classed with the predella of Andrea's altarpieces at Assisi and Siena. The three scenes of the predella are: (1) S. Francesco receiving the stigmata; (2) the Annunciation; (3) S. Maria Egiziaca. In the first a winged cherub is substituted for the glorified Christ. The modelling of all three scenes is inferior to that of the central relief. The large relief represents S. Lodovico, whose cloak was gilded with fleurs-de-lys; S. Caterina of Alexandria, crowned, and standing with folded hands by her wheel; the Madonna, seated on a violet bench, holding on her lap the nude, standing Child with his left thumb in his mouth; S. Maria Maddalena with the box of ointment; and S. Girolamo, holding a stone against

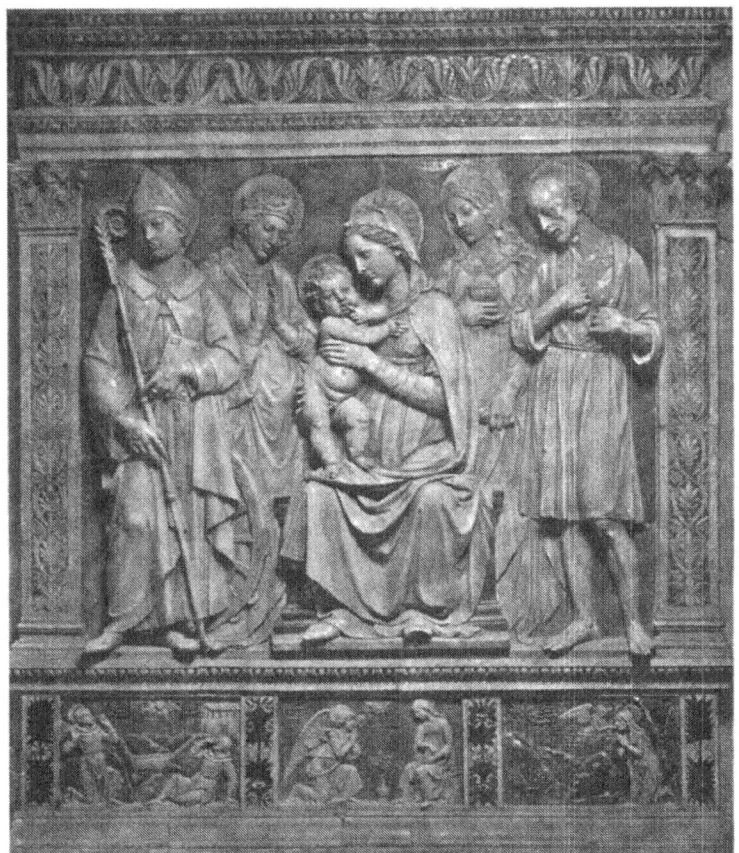

FIG. 49.—THE GRADARA ROCCA ALTARPIECE.

his bared heart. Their eyes have blue brows and lashes, copper coloured irises and dark pupils.

Bibl. :

Anselmi, *A. S. A.*, VIII(1895), **444**-446; *I. A. e. I.*, I(1893-4), **78**-79; B., *Kf.*, 16, 26; Burl., 114; C-M., 106, 235 No. 188; Cr., 178, 326; Giglioli, 54; Michel, IV, 124; R., *D. R.*, 164-**165**; *Sc. Fl.*, III, 155-156; S., 103 Abb. **104**.

46 MADONNA AND CHILD WITH SAINTS. Prato. S. Lodovico, also known as Oratorio della Madonna del Buon Consiglio. Rectangular altarpiece. W., 1.38m. Photos., Alinari, Nos. 10079-10082; Brogi, No. 12769. Casts, Lelli, 439-440.

The altarpiece (Fig. 50) is a replica of the one at Gradara Rocca, showing the Madonna and Child between SS. Lodovico, Caterina, Maria Maddalena, and Girolamo, with the predella scenes of S. Francesco receiving the stigmata, The Annunciation, and S. Maria Egiziaca. Slight

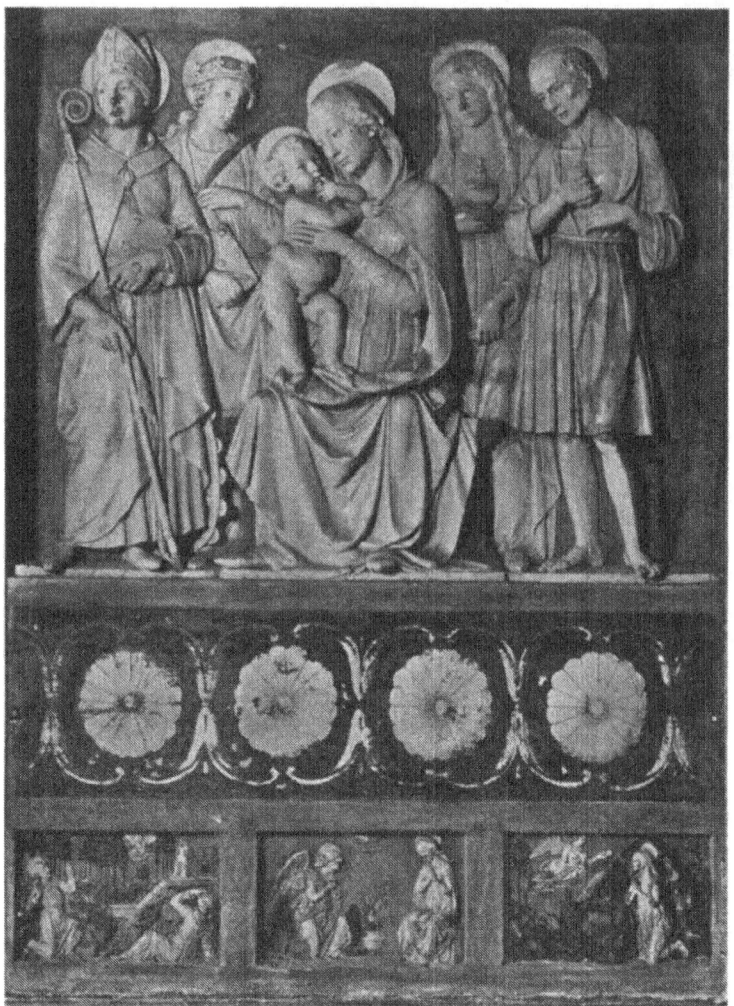

FIG. 50.—THE PRATO ALTARPIECE.

variations may be noted in the poses of the figures—also in some details, e.g., S. Caterina, who at Gradara Rocca stood with folded hands, here holds a green martyr's crown and a book.

The charming frame of the Gradara altarpiece, if repeated here, has been destroyed. The insignificant framing is of late date.

Bibl.:

Anselmi, *A. S. A.*, VIII(1895), 446; *I. A. e. I.*, I(1893-1894), 79; B., *Kf.*, 17, 24; Corradini, 44, 45; C-M., 106, 245 No. 250; Cr., 223. 330; Giglioli, 52-55; R., *D. R.*, 165, 166; *Sc. Fl.*, III, 156.

47 GOD THE FATHER AND ANGELS. 1484. Montepulciano. Museo Civico. Rectangular altarpiece. H., 2.92m.; W., 2.50m. Photo., Alinari, No. 9176.

This altarpiece (Fig. 51) was made for the Franciscan church of the monastery at Fonte Castello in 1484. In 1785 the monks were transferred to S. Agnese and in 1787 their church was suppressed. Their beautiful altarpiece was placed in the Misericordia, where it remained until in 1905 it found a resting place in the Museo Civico. The predella was designed as a ciborium for the Sacred Host. Above this is the altarpiece, with a central niche in which is a painting of the Dead Christ. About it is a narrow frame of cherubs; overhead a medallion, God the Father, the Holy Dove, cherubs, and adoring angels. God the Father, in a circular glory bordered with cherubs, raises both hands in well restrained grief over the death of his Son. This is perhaps Andrea's most majestic representation of the Father. Twelve angels with folded hands or arms crossed on breast are symmetrically distributed on either side. The outer frame of the altarpiece consists of an entablature, the frieze of which is an enriched variant of the palmette friezes at La Verna, the Osservanza, and elsewhere—supported on two slender pilasters ornamented with an arabesque based on Luca's pilaster decoration at Impruneta and used frequently by Andrea and his followers.

The predella is charming in its simplicity—the two outer pilasters are decorated with a network of cubes, a pattern used several times by Luca, and the central pilaster (one of which has been defaced) by a mosaic pattern of rosettes and quatrefoils. Both patterns are found in other works of Andrea at La Verna, Arezzo, and elsewhere. These pilasters separate the central ciborio with its opening framed with a frieze of cherub heads, from two panels figuring the Nativity and the Adoration of the Magi. These are charming compositions. The Nativity or Adoration of the Child by his parents, and the ox and ass, in an open landscape with one or two trees was repeated in predella reliefs at Aquila, Arezzo (Camposanto, Cathedral) Berlin Museum, Florence (Misericordia), Foiano (S. Domenico, S. Francesco), but nowhere in such perfection as here. The Adoration of the Magi was represented by Andrea in an interesting predella composition at Assisi. Here it is reduced to the Madonna, Child, and the three Magi. Almost a repetition of this composition may be seen at Aquila, but the predella reliefs of the same subject at Florence (Misericordia) and

London (Victoria and Albert Museum) are inferior. Marcel Reymond appears to stand alone in a proper appreciation of this beautiful altarpiece.

Document: [Published by Carocci, *Ill. Fior.*, 1906, 158.]
"8 Dec. 1484.

Item ex consilio eiusdem vinculum et obtentum fuit per lupinos albos undecim, rubeo nullo in contrarium existente, quod operarii gloriosae Ver-

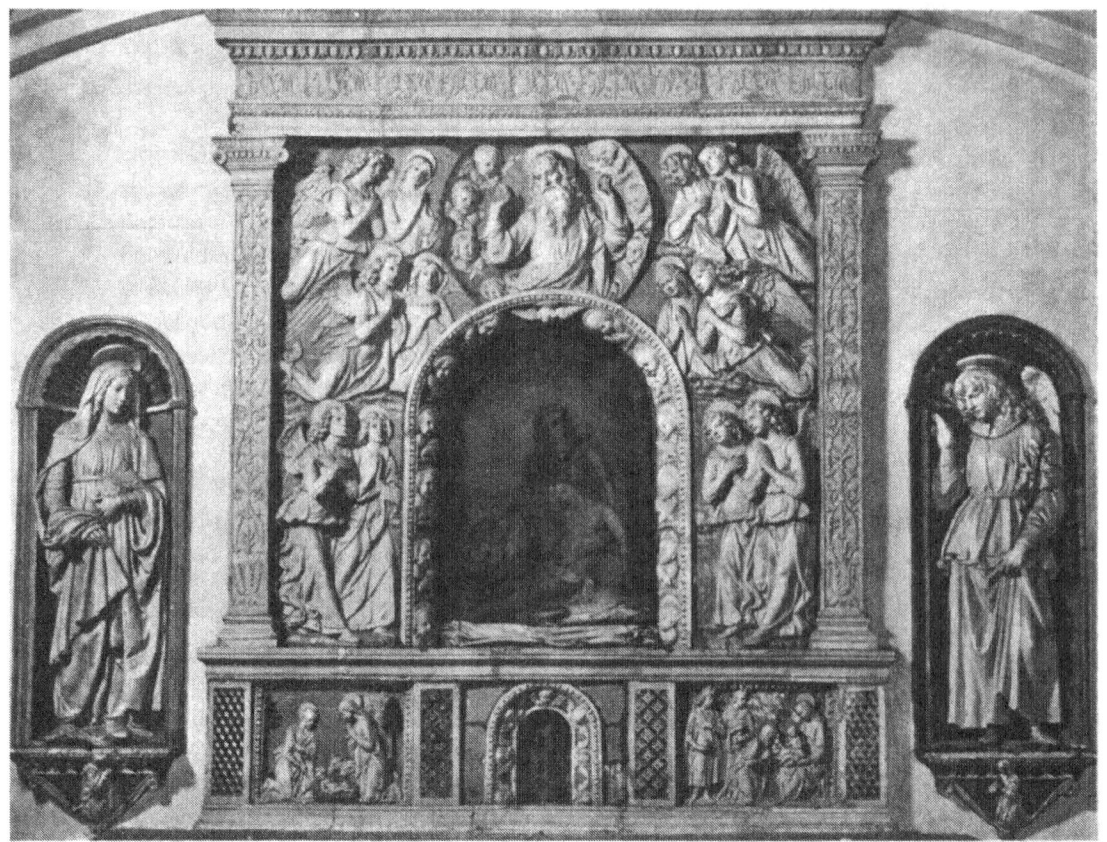

FIGS. 51-53.—THE MONTEPULCIANO ALTARPIECE AND ANNUNCIATION.

ginis Mariae de Fonte Castello possint et eis licitum sit extraere impune de comitatu Montis politiani staria centum grani pro solvendo tabulas per eas factas a Magistro Andrea Marci de Rubio de Florentia."

[Deliberazioni del Comune (of Montepulciano), 8 Dec. 1484.]

Bibl.:
Brogi, 306; Burl., 69, 115; Carocci, *Ill. Fior.*, 1906, 157(Doc.); C-M., 239 No. 210; R., *D. R.*, 173-174; *Sc. F.*, III, 160-161; Repetti, s.v. Montepulciano; S., 143, Abb. 157.

48 THE ANNUNCIATION. 1484. Montepulciano. Oratorio della Misericordia. Statues. H., 1.60m. (with console). Photo., Alinari, 9176.

In blue niches capped with violet conchs stand on either side of the altarpiece the white figures of S. Gabriele and the Annunziata. Their positions are reversed when compared with the Annunciation group in the Osservanza and their proportions more normal, and yet they should be attributed to Andrea himself at the time when the adjoining altarpiece was made. (1) The Annunziata (Fig. 52) reflects a face which we may see perhaps for the first time in the S. Rosa (?) of the Osservanza altarpiece. It recurs again in many works by Andrea and his followers. Below her is a console with a frieze of laurel leaves and containing a kneeling figure of the donor. (2) S. Gabriele (Fig. 53), holds a branch of lilies in his left and blesses with his right hand. Below him is a console with kneeling figure of the donor's wife.

Bibl. :
Same as preceding.

49 S. PIETRO MARTIRE. 1484. Florence. S. Maria Novella (formerly).

In a XVII century Ms. a record is preserved of a terra-cotta statue of S. Pietro Martire so injured as to be replaced by a new one in the XVII century. Although no mention is made of the Robbias one thinks naturally of such statues as the S. Pietro Martire at Arezzo, the S. Domenico at S. Croce etc.

Document: [Copied by Mr. Rufus G. Mather.]
" Sa Ma Novella
Sopra la colonna di S. Felicità eravi li statua di S. Pietro Martire di terra cotta consumate dal tempo, parte cade, e parte fu levata per parvi la nuova. Dentro un braccio di detta statua vi fu un vaso della stessa terra coperto con lastra di rame e dentro il quale eravi una lamina dipiombo con la segnente inscrizione
Amerigus, olim Tribaldi Guernieri de Rubeis et Tribaldus eius filius, et alii de Rubeis hanc figuram S. Petri Martiris apponi cura(ve)runt Anno Salutij MCCCCLXXXIV"
[Arch. di Stato, Sched. Manoscritti, No. 176, busta 15, carte del Sec. XVIII.]

50 MADONNA WITH NUDE STANDING CHILD HOLDING DRAPERY, TWO CHERUBS. Nimes. Musée de Peinture et Sculpture. Eduard Foulc Collection. Medallion. Photo., Private.

Of this composition (Fig. 54) there are replicas at London, Prague, Florence, New York, Baltimore, Messina, Paris and Sèvres, but none finer than the Foulc Madonna. I am inclined to think that the composition was evolved from a seated Madonna, though all indications of a chair and of the Madonna's knees have disappeared. The two cherub heads are not like

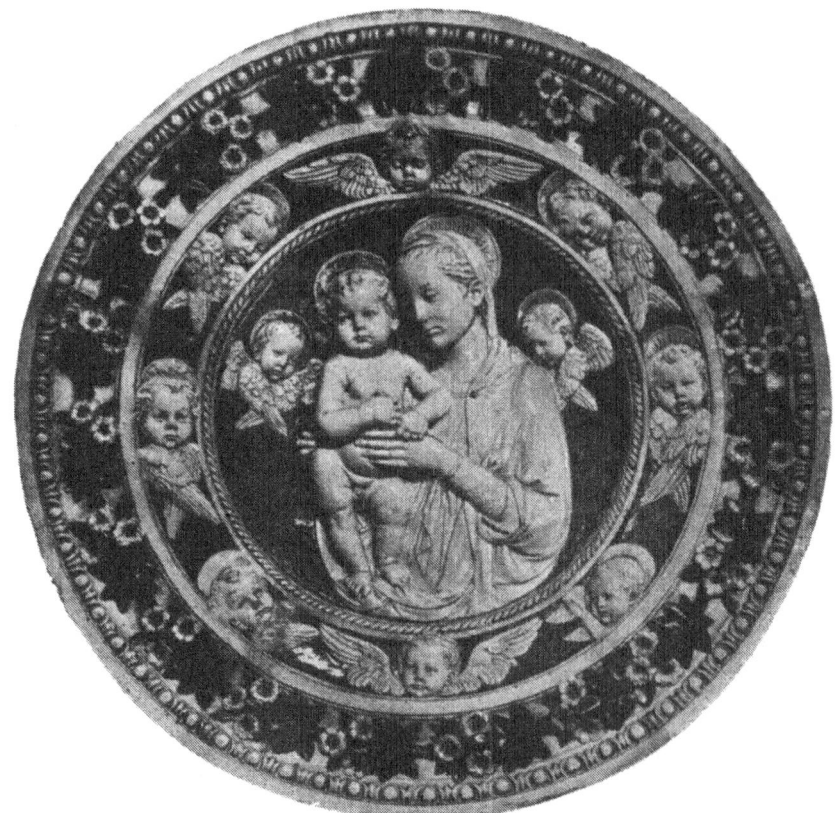

FIG. 54.—THE FOULC MADONNA.

a glory or a nimbus, but are space-filling decoration. Usually, however, clouds are indicated beneath them. This type of Madonna, possibly modelled from life, is full of grace and charm. The Child also is very lifelike. With her two hands the Mother steadies her Child whose standing might otherwise seem insecure. The Child is seen almost en face, as if Andrea realized that the Child would thus be rendered more emphatic.

The frame with its twisted cord, egg and dart, bands of cherub heads and of roses link this frame with that at S. Simone. Single and double roses, triangularly arranged, succeed each other with almost perfect regularity. Had there been eighteen instead of nineteen bunches the regularity

would have been complete. The cherubs at the top and base of the frame
have outspread wings. The other cherubs have folded wings.

Bibl.:

B., *Denk.*, Taf. **26** ; Frizzoni, *Rass. d'Arte*, IX(1909), 30; M.,
D. R. A., 45; V., 588, Fig. 394.

NOTE. Bode, Frizzoni, and Venturi all erroneously publish this Madonna
as in the Museo Nazionale.

51 SAME SUBJECT. London. Victoria and Albert Museum, No.
5633-'59. Medallion. Diam., 0.53m. Photo., Private.

This relief (Fig. 55), formerly in the Soulages collection, was obtained
by the Museum in 1859. It is a fine example of the Madonna of the Foulc

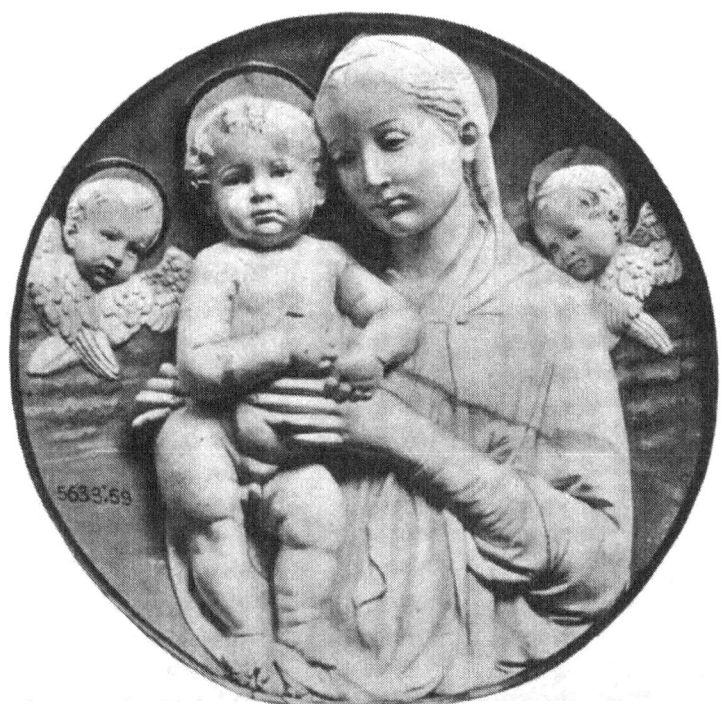

FIG. 55.—MADONNA OF THE FOULC TYPE.

type, probably slightly earlier, as here the sky is full of clouds painted in
Andrea's manner. The facial types, modelling, the colouring of the eyes
also betray Andrea's authorship. It is not easy to see in this medallion,
with Miss Cruttwell, an "imitation of Verrocchio."

Bibl.:

Burl., 120; C-M., 267 No. 382; Cr., 346; M., *D. R. A.*, 45; Robinson,
66 No. 5633.

52 SAME SUBJECT. Florence, Palazzo Vieri-Canigiani. Medallion.
Diam., 0.53m.

In this replica of the Foulc Madonna the head of the Madonna and the
forehead of the Child are somewhat damaged. It shows, however, Andrea's
workmanship, even to the colouring of the eyes.

Bibl.:
Burl., 59; Cr., 342; M., *D. R. A.*, 45.

53 FRAME, CHERUB HEADS AND ROSE GARLAND. Florence.
S. Simone. H., with console 1.65m.; W., 1m. Photo., Brogi, No.
9705.

In the church of S. Simone, Florence, there is a charming tabernacle
(Fig. 56), the central relief of which was apparently removed some years
ago. When I saw it in 1894 it contained a standing polychromatic Madonna of the Robbia school, set on a low pedestal inscribed: SACELLV(m)
C(orpus) C(hristi).

Now it contains a Gothic shrine inscribed: CORPVS XPI, intended to
serve as a ciborio, but used to shelter a bust of S. Orsola. At the base of
the shrine are the arms of the Risaliti and of the Baldovinetti families. I
cannot believe with Miss Cruttwell that the Robbia tabernacle was originally designed as a frame for this earlier shrine. More probably, it was
designed to frame one of Andrea's now frameless Madonnas, like that in
S. Egidio; or the one in the Belmont Collection at Newport, R. I.; or one
in the Museum at Palermo. There is documentary evidence that in the
year 1651, it framed a door of carved walnut. But this carved door must
have been removed by 1754 when Richa speaks of it as "un tabernacolo di
Maria."

The mouldings of the frame are those which we find in Luca's later
works and the floral wreath a conventionalized variation of his rose garland. These rise from vases not unlike those of the frame of the Madonna
of the Architects, but the garland is even more Andrea-like in its rhythmic
alteration of single and double petalled roses arranged in regular triangular pattern, like the wreath on the Salviati stemma of 1484 at S. Giovanni
in Valdarno (Fig. 158). The cherub heads and the inscription are thoroughly characteristic of Andrea's handiwork of the period 1480-1490.

The inscription PELL ANIMA ✦ DI GIERI ✦ RISALITI ✦ EDI
IACOPO ✦ SVO FILGLVOLO ✦ E DE DISCIENDENTI ✦ DI
DETTO ✦ IACOPO ✦ 1363 ✦ implies that this is a votive offering for
the souls of Gieri Risaliti, of his son Jacopo and the descendants of Jacopo.

The date 1363 is known to be the date that Gieri made his will and, from its occurrence here, probably also the date of his death.

The console is attractively designed. A cherub head with outspread wings recalling those of the S. Michele from Faenza supports a laurel wreath on which are combined the arms of the Risaliti family: Azure, two

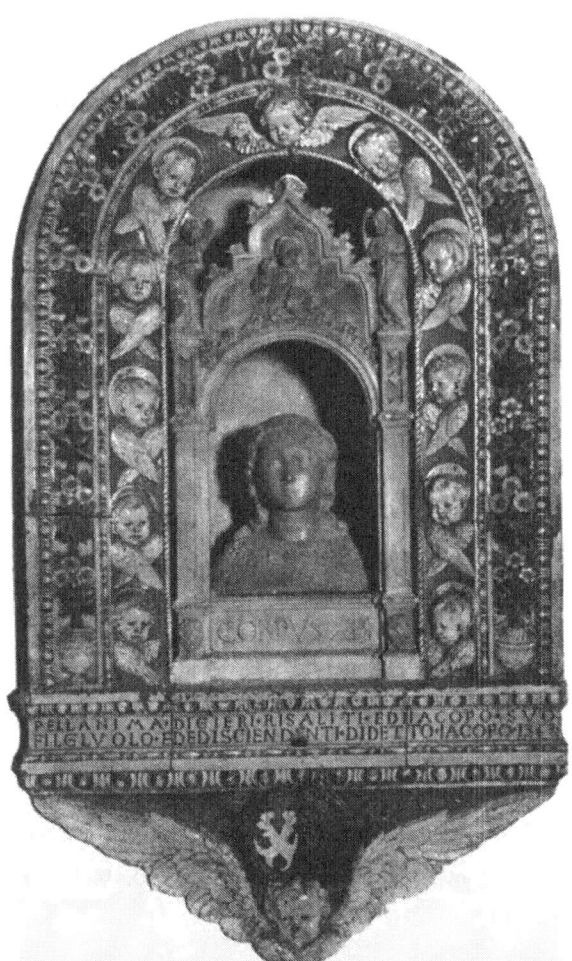

FIG. 56.—THE S. SIMONE TABERNACLE.

lions' paws erased per saltire, argent, with those of the Baldovinetti family: Gules, a lion rampant, or. The union of these families occurred when Jacopo Risaliti in 1384 married Bartolommea Baldovinetti. This date is of course much too early for a Robbia tabernacle, and the inscription implies that this tabernacle was not erected by Jacopo but by his descendants.

On Sept. 4, 1449 Ubertino di Gherardo Risaliti, the uncle of Jacopo, made a will providing for services to be held in perpetuity before the altar of the Virgin of the Annunciation, in the chapel of the Risaliti family. The Risaliti chapel passed into the hands of the Romena family, and the church became thoroughly renovated.

Documents:

1. "HOC OPUS ..... AN. DOMINI M.... DIE IV IVLII
Questa memoria era nella Tavola della Cappella dell'Annunziatione fondata dalla famiglia de Risaliti, la quale fu tirata a terra l'anno 1625 e era dove di presente si vede nel Santuario la Statua di S. Simone, e nella Custodia o Ciborio dell'Altar Maggiore gl' infrascritti caratteri, trovati colla detta Custodia in luogo seccoso, e acciò non si perdesse tanta memoria di Noi, mentre f... romo al governo di questa chiesa, l'adattassimo sopra la porta al didentro della chiesa, acciò servisse d'ornamento e custodia d... testa delle compagne di S. Orsola.
Pelli Anima di Gieri Risalti e di Jacopo suo figliuolo e discendenti   or
    detto Jacopo Mccclxiii"
[Memorie che sono nella chiesa di SS. Apostoli Simone e Giuda Padronato dell' Abbadia Fiorentina.   Milan, 1664.]

2. "1449, Sept. 4. Item in perpetuo qualibet anno die 8 Decembris cuiuslibet anni dare et tradere Haeredis debeant Presbitero sue Rectori Ecclesiae S. Simonis de Flor. libram unam, et solidos 10 et libram unam cerae cum hoc quod dictus Presbiter, se Rector, qui pro tempore fuerit in dicta Ecclesia, debeat in perpetuam quolibet anno in dicta die facere unum sacrum sub commemoratione conceptionis Beatissimae Virginis ad Altare dicti Testatoris institutum sub nomine Annuntiatae."
[Quoted by Richa, *Chiese Fiorentine* I, 249-250 from the papers of the Signori della Rena, No. 78.]

3. "1651, Marzo, 26. Sopra la porta verso il lavatorio uno tabernacolo di terracotta de Risaliti ed suo sportello di noce intagliato."
[Inventory of S. Simone, Convento 79, No. 350, fol. 232.]

Bibl.:
Ammirato, fol. 78-79; Ancisa, CC fol. 485; EE. fol. 602; II, fol. 385; Archivio di Stato, Carte de Epocci, Famiglia Risaliti; Carte Gargani, Fam. Risaliti; B. J., 46 note, 89; Burl., 108; C-M., 212 No. 46; C., s.v. Baldovinetti, Risaliti; Cr. 172 note, 342; Richa, I, 249 (Doc.); Rosselli, Sepoltuario, I, fol. 144-145; W., 126, 169.

54 MADONNA WITH NUDE CHILD SEATED ON A CUSHION. DOVE, FIVE CHERUBS. Palermo. Museo Nazionale. Round headed relief. H., 0.87m.; W., 0.56m. Photos., Alinari, No. 19588; Brogi, No. 13974.

Alinari's photographs of this relief shows remains of gilding on the haloes, as well as on the Madonna's girdle and sleeves and on the tassels of the cushion. When Brogi's photograph was taken the gilding of the haloes had been removed, together with the superficial paint or accumulated dirt which concealed from view Andrea's characteristic clouds. The lower right hand corner has been injured and repaired, so that the chair on which the Madonna is seated is indistinctly indicated.

In this composition (Fig. 57) the Holy Dove remains, but God the Father is omitted. The five cherub heads do not surround the Madonna and

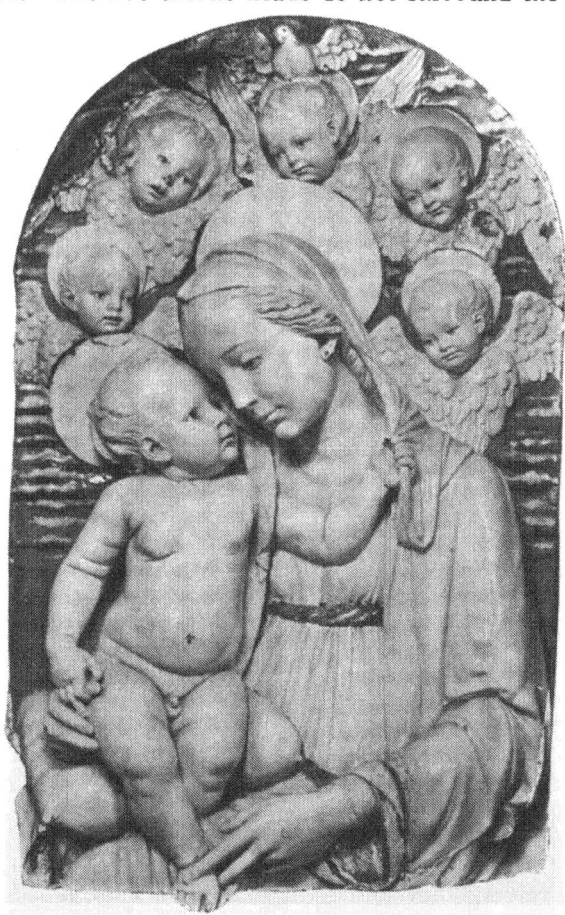

FIG. 57.—THE PALERMO MADONNA.

Child as a glory, but are arranged above their heads like a nimbus. These heads are disproportionately large. In other reproductions of this Madonna in the Museo Nazionale, Florence, in the Cathedral and at S. Maria delle Grazie at Arezzo, the Kunst Gewerbe Museum at Hamburg, and in the Vanderbilt Collection, New York, the Dove is omitted and cherub heads reduced in number. The Madonna of the Cushion is found in one of Luca's altarpieces at Pescia, but in a variety of forms it occurs in the works of Andrea and his followers. The Palermo example is perhaps the earliest. In type the Madonna is not unlike the Madonnas previously described. Her eyes show violet brows, lashes and pupils, and hazel or copper coloured irises.

Bibl.:
Burl., 69, 115; Cr., 158; M., *D. R. A.*, 54; La Grassa-Patti, *L'Arte*, VI(1903), 44-45.

55 MADONNA DELLA CINTOLA. c. 1486. La Verna. Chiesa di S. Maria degli Angeli. H., 3.88m.; W., 2.36m. Photo., Alinari, Nos. 9821-9823.

The earliest church established at La Verna by S. Francesco was that now known as the Chiesa di S. Maria degli Angeli (1216-1218). In 1486 the Capitolo Provinciale held at Bosco di Mugello granted to Domenico Bartoli and his brothers Leonardo and Lorenzo permission to restore and adorn this church according to their good pleasure provided they did not alter its form. Its chief altarpiece is the Madonna della Cintola (Fig. 58) by Andrea della Robbia. The subject was not unpopular at the close of the XV and in the early years of the XVI century. Altarpieces with this subject from Andrea's atelier may be seen at Foiano, Frankfort, Florence, S. Fiora, London, and a lunette at the Accademia, Florence, but this would seem to be the only example entirely by Andrea's hand.

The composition may have been in part suggested by Nanni di Banco's relief over the northern portal of the cathedral of Florence, but Andrea's possesses superior charm. The Madonna, represented as somewhat older than in Presepio, Adoration, and Coronation scenes, has been transported to the skies. Four angels, with most delicately feathered wings and light, fluttering draperies uphold the mandorla, which, detached from the background, is bordered by ten cherub heads. She is clearly seen to be seated upon clouds. Below the mandorla is a decorative, space-filling cherub head. The four saints, S. Gregorio in Bishop's garb, the Dove at his ear, S. Tommaso receiving the cintola, S. Francesco holding a cross, and S. Bonaventura, the seraphic Doctor whose mantle is covered with cherub

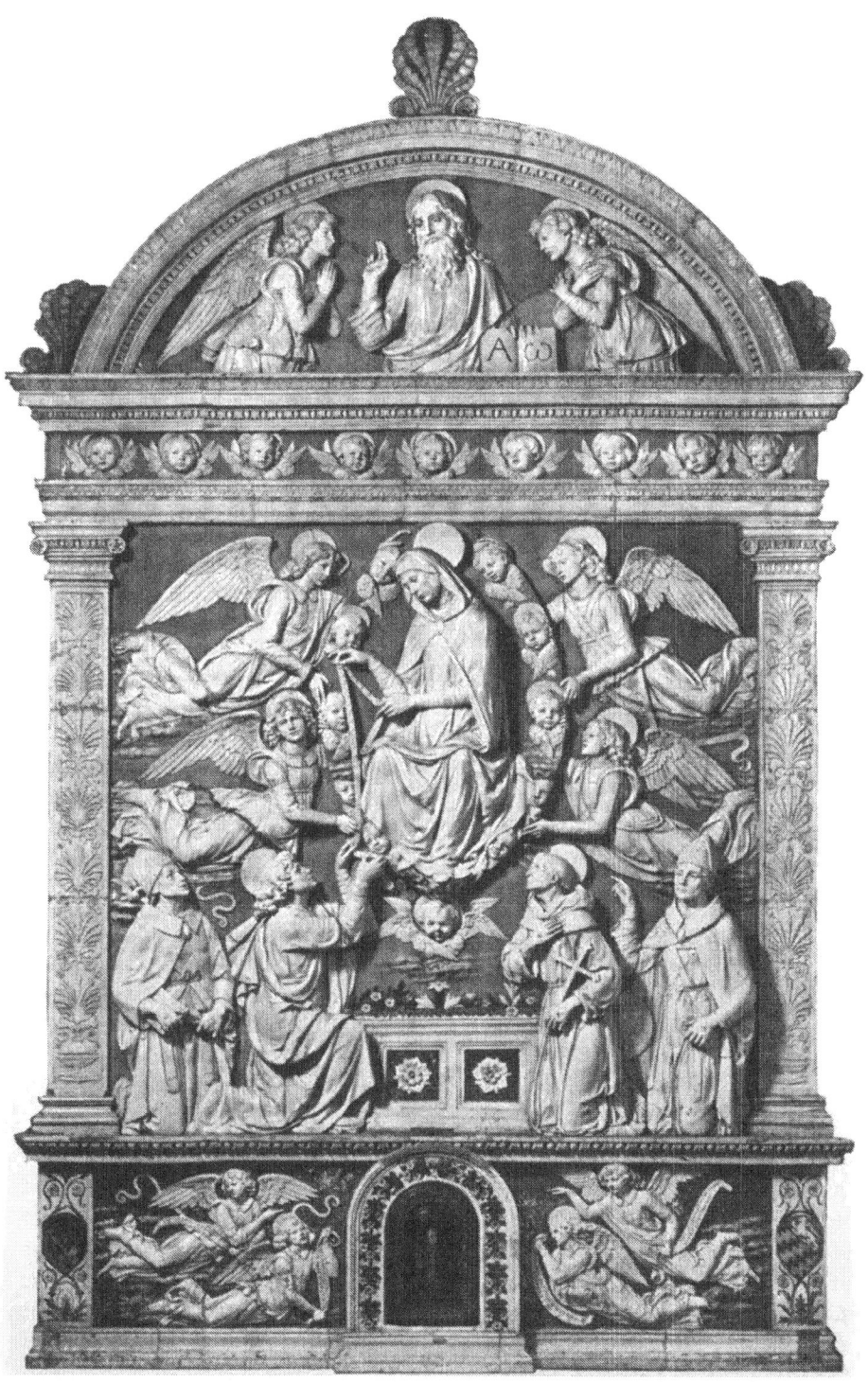

FIG. 58.—THE LA VERNA MADONNA DELLA CINTOLA.

heads, are all upon their knees, apparently upon the earth, for between them is the sarcophagus ornamented with red and green porphyry panels and covered with roses and lilies. Their eyes, as in Andrea's early works, have yellow irises, and violet brows, lashes and pupils.

The frame has many points of interest. Its general proportions tend to

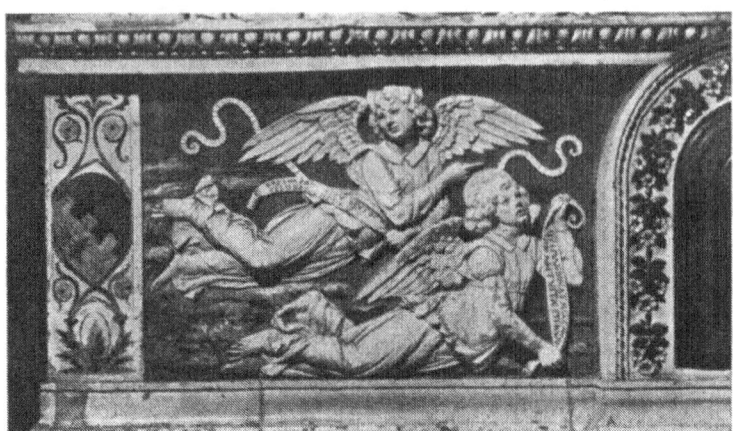

FIG. 58a.—DETAIL OF PREDELLA.

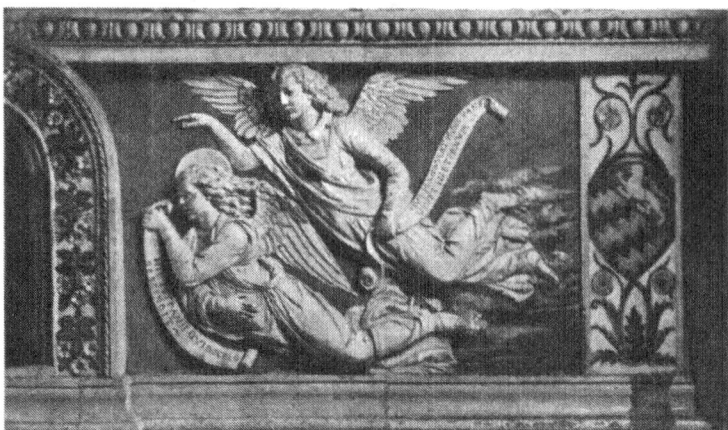

FIG. 58b.—DETAIL OF PREDELLA.

greater height. This is attained by superadding a lunette to the somewhat slenderer rectangle. Its acroteria of fluted palmettes occur here for the first but by no means the last time. Its decoration consists of a beautiful figure of God the Father blessing between two adoring angels. A very similar God the Father may be seen in the altarpiece of 1484 at Montepulciano. In the cherub frieze we note that the five central heads form a balanced group but that the two heads at either end are posed without regard to the next.

The slender pilasters have capitals not unlike those of the Annunciation altarpiece at La Verna and of the Coronation altarpiece at the Osservanza but the palmette decoration is more elaborate and springs not from a base of leaves but from vases which have no handles. Henceforth vases occur frequently in pilaster decoration.

The predella is charming, evidently inspired by Luca's work at Impruneta. At either end are flat pilasters with floral scroll work enclosing coats of arms. To the left are the arms of Domenico Bartoli: Per bend embattled gules and or, accompanied by two stars of eight rays each counterchanged. To the right are the Rucellai arms: per bend gules, a lion passant argent; in base, barry indented azure and or. As Domenico Bartoli married Maddalena di Paolo Rucellai in 1448, we are satisfied that this altarpiece was their gift to the church. The sportello of the ciborio is framed by pendent bouquets of six petalled, white roses with green leaves arranged in Andrea's favorite method. On either side, as at Impruneta, are angels bearing scrolls. Figs. 58a, 58b.) These are inscribed:

(1) EGO SVM PANIS VIVUS QUI: DE CELO DESCENDI·
(2) QVI MANDVCAT MEA(M) CARNEN· ABET VITA(M) ETERNA(M)·
(3) HIC EST PANIS· QVI DE CELO DESCENDIT·
(4) QVI MANDVCAT HVNC PANE(M) VIVET IN ETERNVM·

The inscriptions, differing in version and spelling, seem to have been written by two different hands.

Bibl.:

Ancisa, G. G.; Beni, 257-358; B., *Kf.*, 16; *Denk.*, 84 Taf. **258**; Burl., 119; C-M., 92, 257 No. 335; Cr., 166-167, **169**, 326; M., *Scr. Mag.*, 1893, **691**, 697; *R. H.*, **69**-71; Mencherini, 65, **72**; R., *D. R.*, 161-**162**; *Sc. Fl.*, III, **154**; S., 106-107, Abb. **110-112**; Vas., II, 198.

55a HEAD OF AN ANGEL. Boston. Museum of Fine Arts. Loaned by Mrs. T. O. Richardson. H., 0.35m. Photo., Baldwin Coolidge, 8900.

Fragment of an angel, possibly a mandorla supporter from an altarpiece representing the Assumption of the Virgin (Fig. 59).

Bibl.:
M., *D. R. A.*, 85-86, fig. **34**.

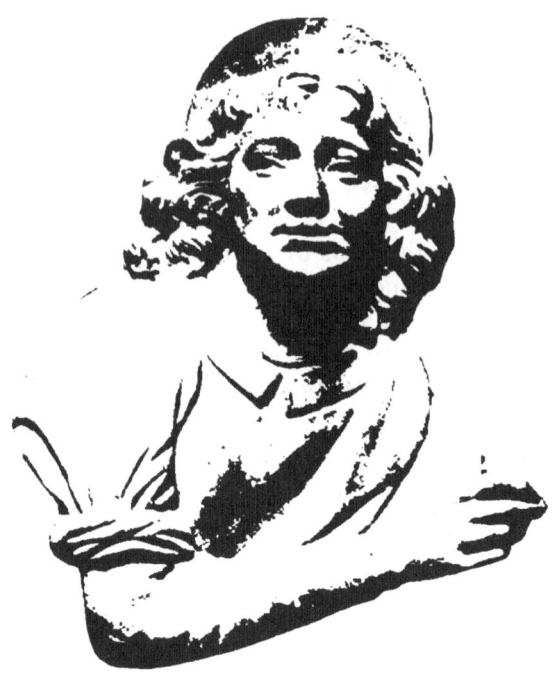

FIG. 59.—HEAD OF AN ANGEL.

56 NATIVITY, GLORIA AND SHEPHERDS. Borgo S. Sepolcro.
S. Chiara. Altarpiece. H., 3.60m.; W., 2.40m. Photo., Alinari,
10376.

This (Fig. 60) is not strictly a Nativity. Here is no Virgin stretched
upon a couch or mattress, no midwives, no child being washed. Such representations do not occur in Robbia iconography. It is rather an Adoration
of the Child by his father and mother, shortly after the Nativity, and before their removal from the stable, when the angels are bursting forth into
their Gloria in Excelsis and proclaiming the glad tidings first of all to the
shepherds. In spite of polychromatic details this is essentially a sculpturesque monument of white figures against a blue sky. It belongs to a
period when Botticelli, Leonardo, and others were also engaged in complex representations of similar themes.

The stable or shed type of Nativity does not occur often in Robbia works.
We find at Militello a copy of this relief, in which the entire composition
is reversed, and in the Victoria and Albert Museum a medallion of the
Adoration of the Shepherds and a rectangular altarpiece of the Adoration
of the Magi in all of which the shed occurs, but none is attributable to
Andrea's own hand. Here the Child reclines in a manger or cradle of
green hay held in by yellow cords. He is playing with his scanty garments,

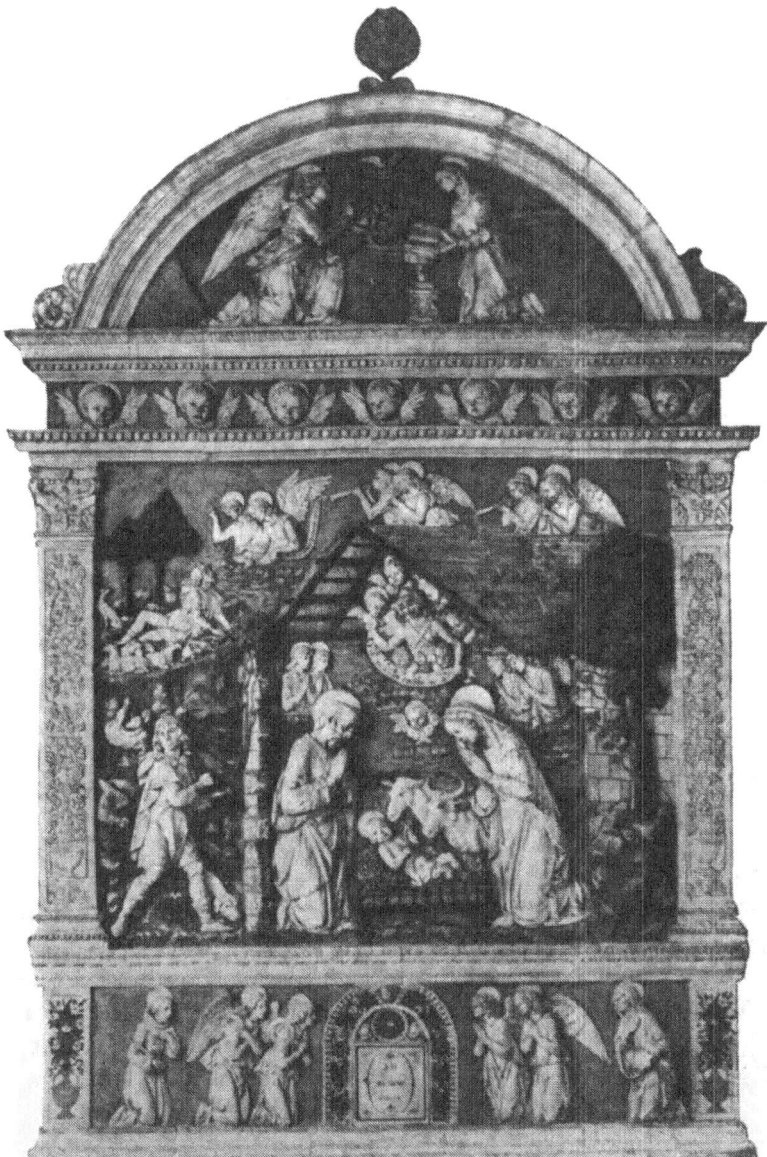

FIG. 60.—Nativity Altarpiece. Borgo S. Sepolcro.

like the Child in the Adoration relief in Genoa. His adoring parents are manifestly of an earlier type than those in the Nativity altarpieces at Bibbiena and Città di Castello. The ox and ass are here naïvely eating hay. The shed is like a ruin with partially standing walls against which stands a tree and over which clamber vines. Through the broken walls are seen not only the Holy Family but adoring angels with folded hands; an archangel surrounded by cherub heads displays a scroll inscribed *Gloria in Excelsis Deo*. Outside the shed the news is being proclaimed to the world by trumpeting angels. In front of them are two angels one of whom bears a scroll inscribed *Annuntio vobis gaudium magnum*. The shepherd, resting near his sheep, eagerly receiving the news,—even his dog turns his head toward the angels—and below is seen another striding, with sheep over his shoulder and dog at his feet, toward the spot to which he has been directed.

The frame has been improperly adjusted. A comparison with the Militello altarpiece or with the Cintola altarpiece at La Verna will show that architrave and predella cornice have changed places, thus interfering with general proportions of the monument. The pilasters have ornamented bases, shafts with floral arabesques rising from vases and capitals showing crochets and pendent palmettes. The frieze of seven cherub heads is similar to that of the altarpiece in the Metropolitan Museum. The lunette recalls that of the Innocenti Hospital, but is simpler and perhaps earlier in type. A serrated palmette and rosette with semi-palmettes serve as acroteria.

The predella has lateral pilaster strips on which are painted blue vases as at the Osservanza, containing bunches of white roses and green leaves. In the central panel is a sportello or ciborio for the sacred wafer and chalice framed by a frieze of roses in triplex composition, as in the Cintola altarpiece at La Verna. To the left and right are kneeling figures of S. Francasco and S. Chiara and four angels charmingly designed.

Bibl. :
Brockhaus, 59; C-M., 229 No. 150; Cr., 186, 223, 327; Michel, IV, 124; R., *D. R.*, 182-185; *Sc. Fl.*, III, 166.

57 STEMMA OF THE ARTE DELLA LANA. 1487. Florence. Opera del Duomo. (1) Sala della Deputazione. (2) Vault of Hall. Diam., 0.95m. Photo., Alinari, 17098. Cast, Lelli, 1156.

The Arte della Lana took a leading part in the building of the Cathedral and of the Palazzo for the Operai. The old Palazzo in 1390 was decorated with stone medallions emblazoned with the stemma of the Arte della Lana. In 1432 the residence of the Operai was transferred to the rear of the Cathedral. Here are two Robbia stemmi of the Arte della Lana (Fig. 60a). On a field azure is the Agnus Dei, nimbed, argent, carrying a banner inscribed with a Croce del Popolo, gules. In chief is a label of five points enclosing four lilies of the Commune, gules. The garland consists of triplex bunches of fruit separated by fluted (yellow) ribbons. Two examples of this stemma still exist in the Opera del Duomo. The one in the vault of the hall appears to be the "chompasso della volta della stanza dell'Opera" ordered from Andrea della Robbia in 1486 and paid for in 1486 and 1487.

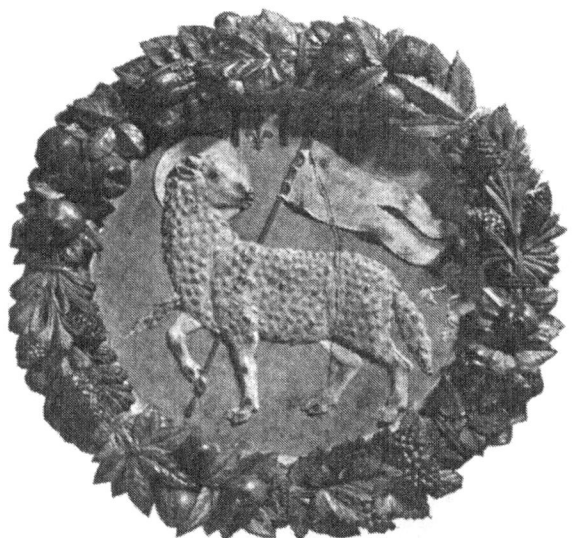

FIG. 60a.—STEMMA OF THE ARTE DELLA LANA.

Documents: [Copied by Mr. Rufus G. Mather.]

1.   "+ MCCCCLXXXXVJ
Andrea di marcho della Robbia de dare adj iij di marzo l dodicj s x picciol. porto giovannj suo fig-luolo contantj per parte dun chonpaso dato allopera per la volta sopra e minjstrj per poliza del proveditore dj no 63-
          l 12 s 10 dj —
1487 E di dare adi xxvij di marzo 1487 l dodicj sx piccioli porto e detto chontanti per Resto del chonpasso delle volta della stanza dellopera per poliza del provedi-tore —   l 12 s 10 dj —"

3.   "+ MCCCCLXXXVIJ
Spese dopera di Santa maria del fiore deono dare

2.   "+MCCCCLXXXVJ
Andrea di marcho della Robbia chontro scritto de avere adi xxx di giungnjo l ventj cinque piccoli per luj da spese dopera posto debbjno dare in questo c. 69-   l 25 s —"

— — — — —
— — — — —
— — — — —

E deono dare adi xxx di giungnjo
l ventj cinque piccioli per loro a
Andrea di marcho della robbia
posto debbj avere in questo c 42
chonpassi fattj allopera per poliza
del proveditore di n° 281

125 s —"

[Archiv. dell'Opera di S. Maria del Fiore, Quaderno di Cassa di Tomaso di nicholo giovan Kamerario per 6 mesi comiciati adi primo di giennaio MCCCCLXXXVIJ c. 41ᵗ, 42, 69.]

Bibl.:

M., *R. H.*, 57 Fig. 57, 58(Doc.); *R. G. M.*, *L'Arte*, XXI(1918), 205(Doc.); Poggi, *Cat.*, 7-12, 23; Staley, 164, 168.

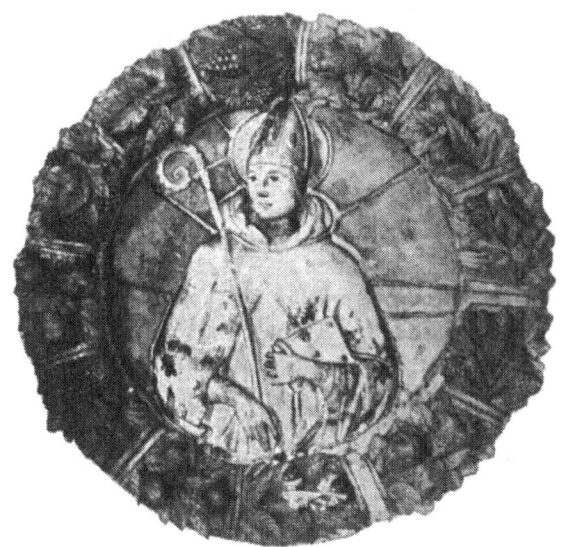

FIG. 61.—S. LODOVICO.

58 (1). S. LODOVICO DA TOLOSA.   (2). S. BONAVENTURA. Siena. Osservanza (in the ceiling). Medallions. Photos., Private.

Set into the vault of the nave of the church are two medallions respresenting S. Lodovico Episcopo and S. Bonaventura.

1. S. Lodovico (Fig. 61) is posed somewhat as in the altarpieces at

Prato and Gradara Rocca, but has the greater charm of naiveté. He wears the nimbus, episcopal mitre, and gloves, and carries a crozier and book. His mantle is decorated with large fleurs-de-lys. The heavy frame of fruit and foliage, almost devoid of flowers, is composed in triplex bunches separated by double or triple unfluted bands straight across.

2. S. Bonaventura (Fig. 62), also arrayed in episcopal attire, carries a

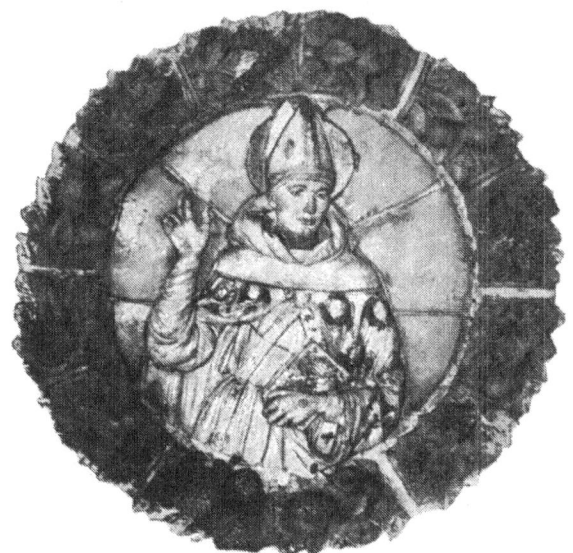

FIG. 62.—S. BONAVENTURA.

book and is blessing. His mantle is painted with cherub heads. He is here younger than in the medallion on the porch of the hospital of S. Paolo. The frame is similar in style to that of its companion piece, but with reversed movement.

Bibl.:
Brogi, 230; S., *Pl. Siena's.* 205.

59 MADONNA DELLE GRAZIE. Arezzo. S. Maria in Grado. Round-headed altarpiece. H., 2.60m.; W., 2.33m. Photo., Alinari, 9722.

Vasari mentions this altarpiece as being by Andrea's own hand and calls it "una tavola bellissima con molte figure." It represents the Madonna della Misericordia, del Soccorso, or delle Grazie (Fig. 63). Beneath her cloak are sheltered the people of Arezzo, nuns and ladies to the left, ecclesiastics and civilians to the right. Amongst the latter in full face is a portrait head possibly of the elder Luca della Robbia. In type and composition this Madonna seems to be not far removed from the Madonna in the lunette of the Cathedral at Prato. The Child is almost a replica of the Child in the Prato lunette. The Madonna's eyes have blue brows and lids,

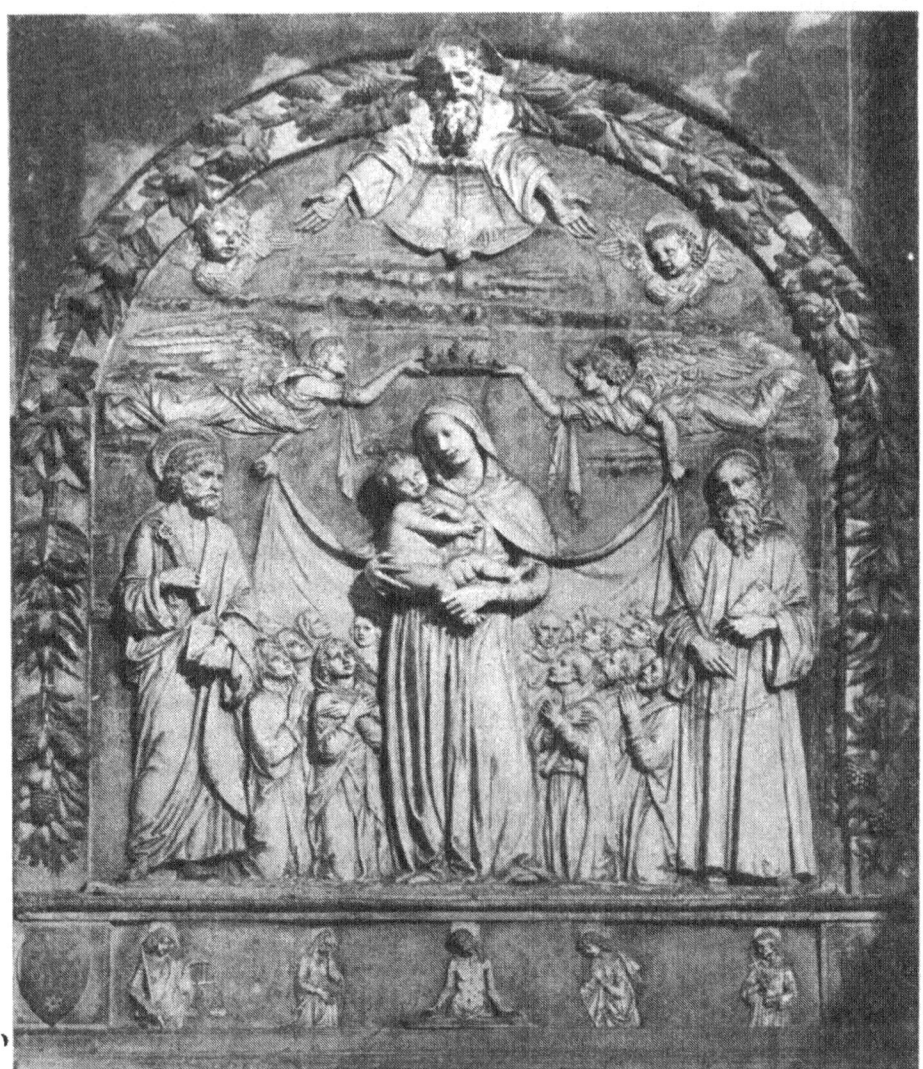

FIG. 63.—MADONNA DELLA GRAZIE.

dark copper coloured pupils and golden irises. To the left stands S. Pietro with book and key, and to the right S. Benedetto with aspergill and book. Both types were inspired by Luca's Apostles in the Pazzi chapel. Overhead are two charming angels who draw back the Madonna's mantle and hold above her a lilied, golden crown. Still higher are the outspread hands of God the Father, the Holy Dove and two cherubs. The finely modelled head of the Father, with its unusual triangular nimbus, appears to have been designed for the position it occupies, although Miss Cruttwell declares it to be a modern stucco addition. From either side hang garlands of fruit arranged in conventional triplex bunches, separated so as to reveal the background, their stems bound by narrow ribbons. The predella shows half figures of S. Michele, the Mater Dolorosa, Christ in sepulchre, S. Giovanni, and S. Francesco. At either end is an oval shield displaying the Carbonati arms: Gules, two mounts of six tops vert; in base a rose or. According to Sac. Anastasio Baini, the founder of the chapel and donor of the altarpiece was probably Sig. Valerio Tommasi Carbonati, member of a noble family of Arezzo.

Bibl.:

B. G., sub Feb. 7; B. J., 76; B., *A. S. A.*, II(1889), 3; *Denk.*, 87; Burckh., 434; Burl., 112; C-M., 84, 90-92, 224 No. 115; Cr., 182, 325; Fov., 108; M., *R. H.*, 75, Fig. 76; Pasqui, *Invent. d. Mon. di Toscana ed Opera d'arte della Provincia d'Arezzo-schede per S. Maria in Gradi di Arezzo* (Manuscript). R., *D. R.*, 197-199; *Sc. Fl.*, III, 172-174; Vas., II, 179.

60 S. AGOSTINO(?). Borgo S. Sepolcro. Duomo. Statue. H., 2m. Photo., Alinari, No. 10373.

S. Agostino(?) or S. Antonino (Fig. 64), in episcopal garb, is an early and fine example of polychromatic enamelling by Andrea della Robbia. His face, left unglazed, was painted in flesh colour, his mitre adorned with green, violet, yellow, and blue jewels. His cloak, of a rich blue, with green collar and lining, has a broad border with an arabesque derived from Luca's work at Impruneta and used by Andrea at La Verna, Assisi, Empoli and elsewhere. It has also a fringe of green, yellow and blue. He holds a violet book studded with yellow. The console adorned with cherub heads and olive leaves is evidently Andrea's design.

There were nine Florentine Capitani and Commissarii at Borgo between 1480 and 1490 whose stemmi in Robbia ware decorate the Palazzo Tribunale. One of these, possibly Lorenzo di Giovanni Bartoli, may have been the donor of the statue.

Bibl.:

Cr., 335; Graziani, 150 note 1, 152; Repetti, s.v. Sansepolcro.

61 S. BENEDETTO. Borgo S. Sepolcro. Duomo. Statue. H., 2m. Photo., Alinari, No. 10372.

S. Benedetto (Fig. 65), patriarch of the order of the Camaldolesi, clad in white, carries the aspergill and a green book with yellow fittings. His

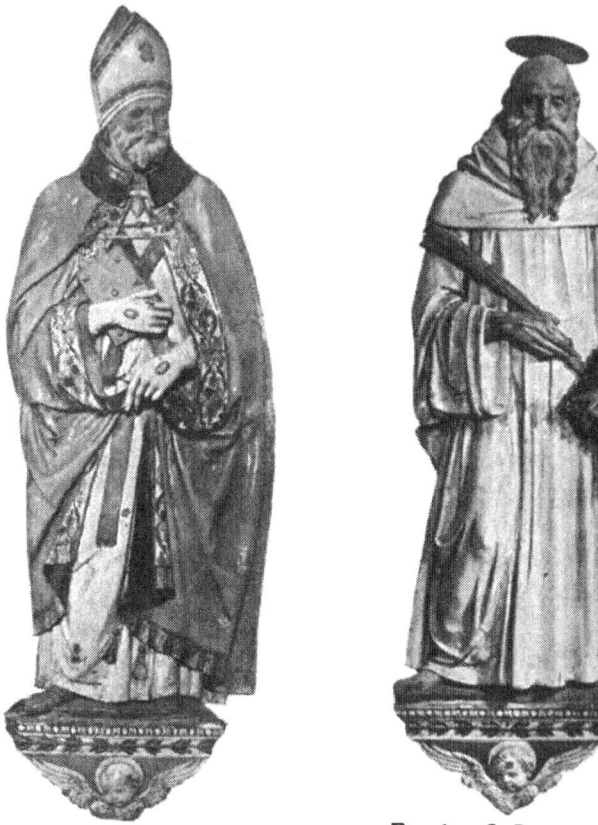

FIG. 64.—S. AGOSTINO (?)   FIG. 65.—S. BENEDETTO.

face and hands are unglazed. The console with cherub head and olive leaves resembles that of the companion statue in the same Cathedral.

It may be recalled that the cathedral at Borgo S. Sepolcro was founded as a Camaldolese abbey.

Bibl.:
Cr., 335: Graziani, 150 note 1, 151.

62 MADONNA AND CHILD BETWEEN SS. STEFANO AND LORENZO. 1489. Prato. Duomo, over entrance portal. Lunette.

H., 1.63m.; W., 2.63m.   Photos., Alinari, No. 10005; Brogi, No. 12707.

The lunette over the entrance portal of the Cathedral of Prato (Fig. 66) is not only a documented, dated work by Andrea della Robbia but a fine example of his handiwork.

The pointed form of the lunette was determined by the architect, Giovanni Pisano, in the XIV century.   Into the foliations of the arch, Andrea could not resist placing a series of cherub heads.   They are set against a

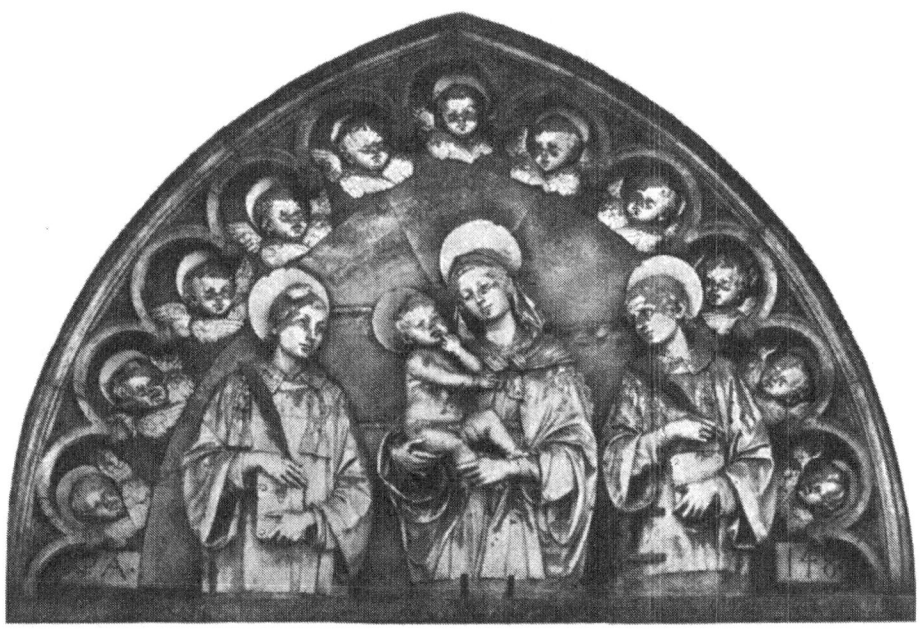

FIG. 66.—THE PRATO CATHEDRAL LUNETTE.

dark blue background.   According to the contract there should be cherub heads below as well as on the sides and above the lunette.   There is no lower, limiting moulding, hence in some cases the clipping of the lower wings of the cherubs is unpleasing.   Andrea has however, treated the heads sympathetically and with facile variety.   Note the absence of monotony in the treatment of the hair, the eyes, the mouths, and how even the pose of the heads does not follow schematically the lines of the arch.   At the base is inscribed OP(ER)A ✠ 1489.

The background of the central relief is of a lighter blue and the clouds, used to conceal the joints, are vaguely indicated.   The Madonna is delicate and beautiful.   Her veil doubly folded shows very slight kinks above the forehead and is loosely tied into a knot on her breast.   Beneath it four long

tresses of hair fall upon her left shoulder. Her mantle, once ornamented
with gold, hangs in somewhat complicated folds over both arms, but elsewhere is simpler. The smoothly modelled Child places the middle finger
of his left hand in his mouth. S. Stefano, with a stone on his head, and
S. Lorenzo, standing by his gridiron, are similarly clad in deacon's robes
and carry green palms. Their eyeballs are flattened, and have dark pupils
and copper coloured irises. Eyebrows and lashes are violet. The collars
of both deacon saints are decorated with palmettes.

Documents: [Revised by Mr. Rufus G. Mather.]

1.   "die 3 novembre 1489

partito dellalogazione della nostra donna sopra alla porta della pieve

Prefati operaij Cappelle cingulis Virginis marie de prato
congregati in eorum audientia inter eos misso et fermato
per 4 fabas nigras nulla alba in contradio locaverunt Andrea
marci simonis della robia populi S. laurentii de florentia in-
frascriptam rem vulgariter videlicet una meza nostra donna
col figliuolo in bracio con dua santi dalato nel quadro cioè
'narchuo della porta maggiore della pieve di prato cioè
quella che va inverso al veschovado in questo modo cioè una
meza nostra donna col figliuolo in bracio dalato dirito di
terra chotta e a esser nel champo azzuro e dalato ritto a
esser Santo stefano e dalato mancho S lorenzo e medesimi
santi anno avere uno campo azurro buono e di sotto dallato
e di sopra che gira intorno a esser uno archulo di serafini e
quali figure anno a esser bianche invetriate e tutte le sopra-
dette chose dove bixognasse anno a esser adorne doro fine
e ne chanti da parte debbe fare nelluno chanto el segno dellopera e nellaltro canto el mileximo tutte le dette chose
adorne in buona forma E se paresse a detti operai fare
cholorire detti santi e figure detto andrea sia tenuto a fargli
la quale opera debba avere fatta e posta in prato nella detta
opera a tutte le sue spese di gabella e vettura per tutto el
mese di marzo proximo avvenire e debbe stare qui continov-
amente a metterla sopra detta porta e detti operai sieno
tenuti a fare fare e ponti e dare un maestro di cazuola e
galcina bixognando adogni spesa di detta opera e detti
operai in nome di detta opera promettono dare e pagare a
soprascritto andrea per suo pagamento fiorini venticinque
larghi doro in oro cioè f xxv larghi doro in oro finita detta
opera e detto tondo e fiure dorate debbono corrispondere
secondo alluogho dove anno a esser sopra detta porta

partito che
lorenzo cam°
(camerario)
paghi f 5
larghi a
Andrea di marcho

Item prefati operaij servatis servandis deliberano quod Lorenzo coci camerario de dare solvere soprascripto andrea pro parte solute f quinque larghi dauro in auro e in...... soprascripto lorenzo ...... soprascripta Indictione flore (nos) quinque largos in presentia nostra soprascripti operaij"

[Archivio del Patrimonio Ecclesiastico, Prato. Opera della Cappella del Sagro Cingolo, Libro delle Deliberazioni-segnato C., Vol. I, c. 29.]

2.   "1496, 9 maggio.

Antonio di geri muratore e domenicho di puccio debono avere infino a dì...daprile per quattro opere... mesono a rompere e murare sopra alla porta dove si mise la vergine maria l. tre s. quattro e a rimurare e aiutare la vergine maria"

[*Op. cit.*, c. 276.]

Bibl. :

B. J., 72; B., *Kf.*, 16, 24; *Denk.*, 85, Taf. **266**; Burl., 116; Corradini, 10, 15; C-M., 104, 245 No. 246; Cr., **179**, 326; Desc. d. Catt. d. Prato, 27; Fov., 107; M., *Scribner's*, 1893, 686; Papini, *L'Arte*, 1912, 38-39 (Doc.); R., *D. R.*, **168**; *Sc. Fl.*, III, **157**; Vas., II, **199**; V., VI, 584.

63 S. LORENZO. Brancoli. S. Lorenzo. Photo., Alinari, No. 8387.

In the church at S. Lorenzo at Brancoli is a statue in high relief of S. Lorenzo (Fig. 67) set in a niche. He wears diaconal robes, carries a green palm and a book. A black gridiron is at his side. It may be dated soon after the S. Lorenzo of the Prato Cathedral lunette (1489) and before that at the Quercia, Viterbo (1507-1508).

The gilded borders of the robe follow Andrea's patterns.

Bibl. :

Burl., 116; C-M., 242 No. 228; Cr., 335; R., *D. R.*, 258; *Sc. Fl.*, III. IV, 64; Ross and Erichsen, 320.

64 THE NATIVITY. 1489. Florence. Palazzo dell'Arte de'Giudici e Notai, Via Proconsolo (formerly). Lunette. Over new door.

This relief is no longer in place and its whereabouts is unknown. The composition we may believe did not vary greatly from that of the Nativity altarpiece at S. Chiara, Borgo S. Sepolcro. The document noted by Milanesi, was published for the first time by Mr. Rufus G. Mather.

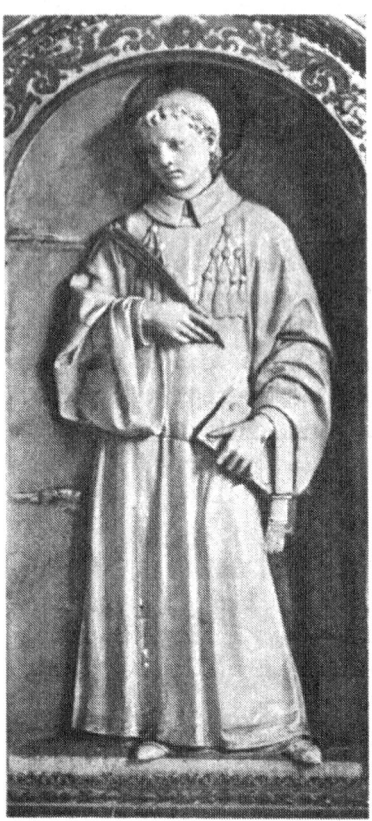

Fig. 67.—S. Lorenzo.

Document: [Copied by Mr. Rufus G. Mather.]
"Die XXVI novembris 1489.

1.   prefati d(omi)n(u)s Proco(n)sul et co(n)sules una
simul cu(m) co(n)siliarijs del xij dicte artis.
In sufficie(n)tibus numeribus collegiabiter co(n)gregati
etc. servatis servandis et obte(n)to partito
secundum ordinem.   Deliberaveru(n)t et Stantiaveru(n)t
Quod came(rarius) dicte artis de pecunia
sui cameratus det et solvat ut i(nfra) vz(videlicet) . . .

. . . .

Andrea della Robbia pro quoda(m) cholmo nativitatis d(omi)nj Yhu Xpi pro colloca(n)dum super
dicta(m) Janua(m) nova(m) dicte artis de terra chocta
i(n)vetriata etc. florenos quinque larghos aurj i(n)
auro vz(videlicet) i(n) totu(m) l. trigi(n)ta duas.-   f - l 32 - sol - dj -"

[Archiv. di Stato, Arte de'Giudici e Notai, Libro d'Atti e di entrata, 2 Sept.-29 dicembre 1489, segnato Arti I, cod. 258, c. 44.]

2. "Exitus Die 28 nove(m)bris 1489.

Andree della Robbia pro quoda(m) cholmo
nativitatis Yhu Xpi sito super dictam Janua(m)
l. trigintaduas vigorj stantiamenti in isto a
c. 44 -   l. 32. sol. - dj—"

[Archiv. idem, Cod. idem, c. 46.]

Bibl.:

> R. G. M., *L'Arte,* XXI(1918), 205(Doc.); Milanesi, *Miscell.* 44
> III p, c. 74.

65 CRUCIFIXION. La Verna, Cappella delle Stimate. H., 6m.; W.,
4.20m. Photo., Alinari, No. 9835.

In the Cappella delle Stimate founded in 1263 by Count Simone da Battifolle the large altarpiece representing the Crucifixion was presented by some member of the Alessandri family, whose coat of arms—Azure, a bicapited lamb trippant, argent—appears twice upon the predella. It is not improbable that the donor of this altarpiece was Maso di Niccolaio d'Ugo di Bartolo Alessandri, Gonfaloniere at Florence in 1466 and 1488. His father Niccolaio was elected in 1432 by the Arte della Lana as one of the first of the Conservatori del Sacro Monte (La Verna). The altarpiece (Fig. 68) is one of the masterpieces of Andrea della Robbia.

The central composition represents the Crucifixion not as an historical event, but as a religious drama. As the old Nativity had been transformed into an Adoration of the Child, so the Crucifixion became a Lamentation over Christ crucified. Much of the old symbolism remains. Above the cross on a green pine tree, is the pelican, plucking her heart to feed her young with her blood. Immediately below is a scroll inscribed I(esus) N(azarenus) R(ex) I(udaeorum), on either side of which the sun and moon are transformed into melodramatic masks (possibly later insertions). The Christ—with his mustard yellow hair, livid body, and the blue nails that fasten his hands and feet to the cross on which the graining of the wood is carefully imitated—is more realistic than was customary with Andrea della Robbia. But had not Luca before him in the stemma of the Physicians at Or San Michele made a similar realistic colour experiment? The four couples of angels who in sorrowful adoration surround the cross are the most expressive of Andrea's angels—finer than those of the Cintola altarpiece at La Verna or of the Tabernacle in the Misericordia at Montepulciano. The clouds which are displayed over the entire background ·

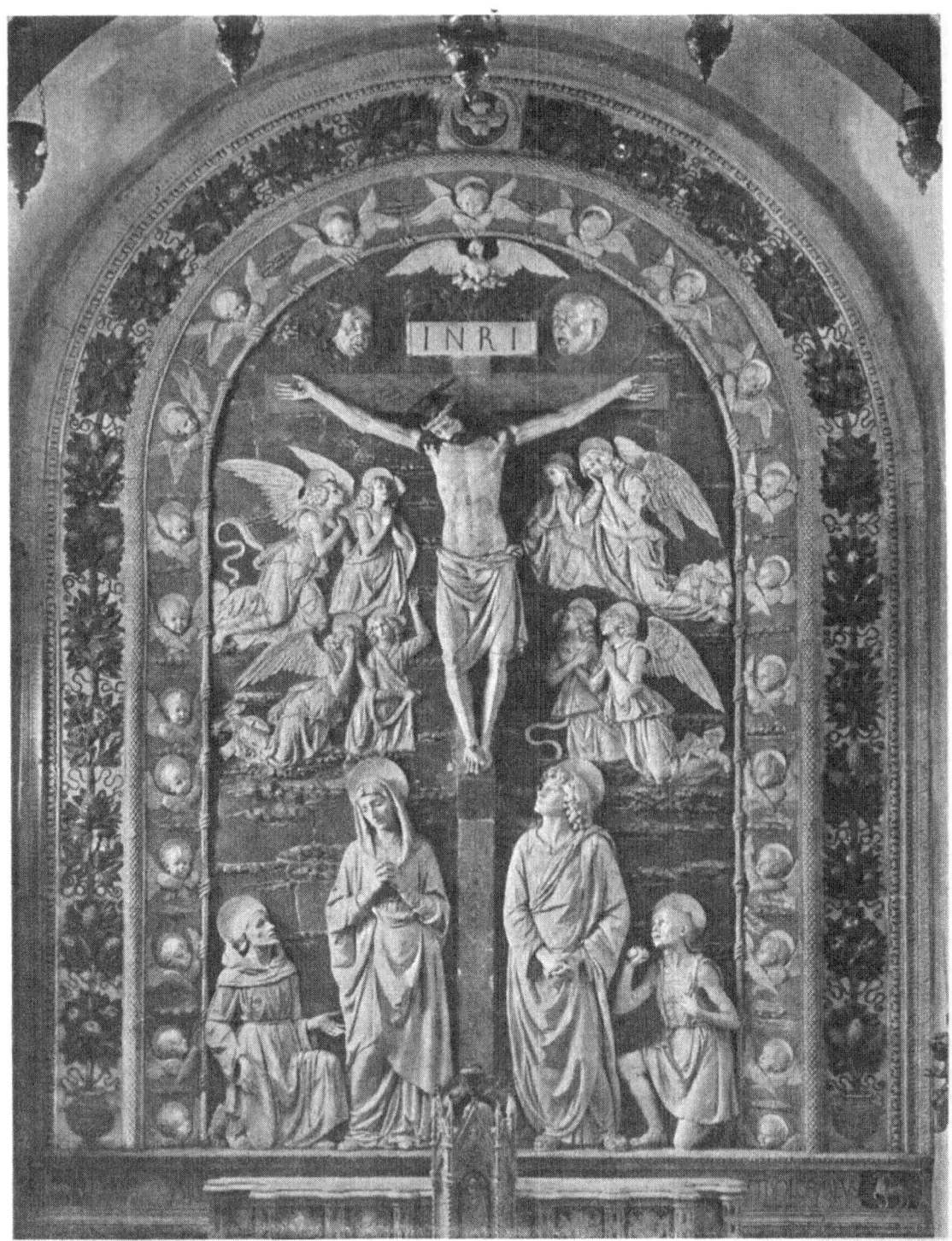

Fig. 68.—The La Verna Crucifixion.

are sharp and clear as in some of Andrea's earlier works. At the foot of the cross S. Francesco and S. Girolamo are subordinated to the Madonna and S. Giovanni. All are sorrowful, but the restrained quiet of S. Giovanni is most remarkable. As an artistic creation it is superior by far to Luca's S. Giovanni in the Crucifixion scene at Impruneta. It may be noted that the eyes of the four standing figures have yellow irises, blue brows and lashes and dark pupils.

On the predella is inscribed from the Lamentations of Jeremiah, I, 12:

O VOS OMNES QVI TRA(N)SITIS P(ER) VIAM ATTE(N)DITE ET VIDETE SI EST DOLOR SICVT DOLOR MEVS

The frame is the finest example of the double frames which occur not infrequently in Andrea's works. The outer frieze consists of a succession of bunches of fruit (no flowers) tied together by light polychromatic, sinuous ribbons and rising from light blue amphorae. At the apex of the arch enclosed in a circle is the Holy Dove emitting flames of fire. Between a rounded billet and a knotted cord moulding is a fine series of cherub heads, twenty-three in all, each with three pairs of wings. In general, the cherubs look inward toward the central picture. On the curved portion of the frieze they are set perpendicularly to its direction, on the vertical portions they are parallel to it. Clouds are set between each head.

Bibl.:

Beni, 361-362; B., *Kf.*, 16; *Denk.*, 84, Taf. **259**; *W. D. R.*, Taf. **38**; Burl., 119; C-M., 92, 257 No. 333; C., s.v. Alessandri; Cr., **168**-**170**, 327; Fov., 108; Gerspach, *Rass. d'Arte*, VI(1906), 15; M., *D. R. A.*, 119; *R. H.*, 72-73; Mencherini, 69-70, **204**-**208**; P., **455**-**457**; R., *D. R.*, **174**-**176**; *Sc. Fl.*, III, **155**, 161; S., 108 Abb. **113**; V., VI, 591; W., 125.

66 WALL TILES. La Verna. Cappella delle Stimate. Photo., Private.

Below the altarpiece of the Crucifixion, the entire wall is decorated with Robbia tiles (Fig. 69). This imitation of three rugs with charming borders and fringes which enclose a series of squares of incongruous patterns crudely framed, was evidently not originally designed for this locality. I am inclined to believe that the border was designed by Luca della Robbia for the pavement of the study of Piero de'Medici and was used by Andrea at Empoli, at S. Gimignano, and at S. Fiora. The pattern in the inner squares: (1) nail or diamond heads; (2) quatrefoils enclosing rosettes; and (3) cubes—used by Andrea at Arezzo, Montepulciano (1484) and

elsewhere—were employed also by Giovanni and other designers in the
Robbia school.

Bibl.
    M., *L. D. R.*, 91-92, Fig. **53**; *R. H.*, 72, 73, Fig. **73**.

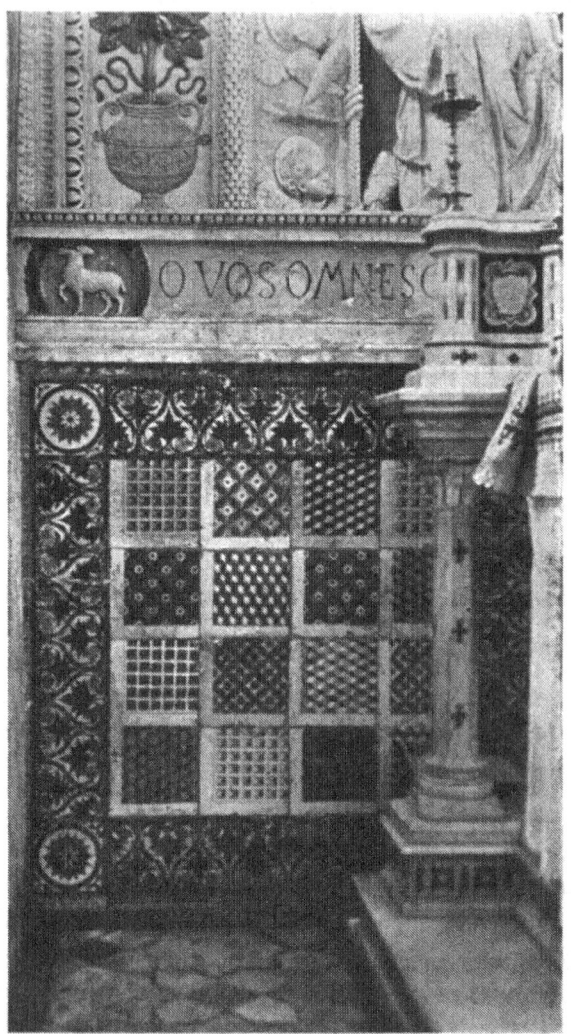

FIG. 69.—WALL TILES. LA VERNA.

67 THE TRINITY AND SAINTS. Arezzo. Duomo. Cappella della
Madonna. Altarpiece. H., 3.70m.; W., 2.60m. Photo., Alinari,
No. 9702.

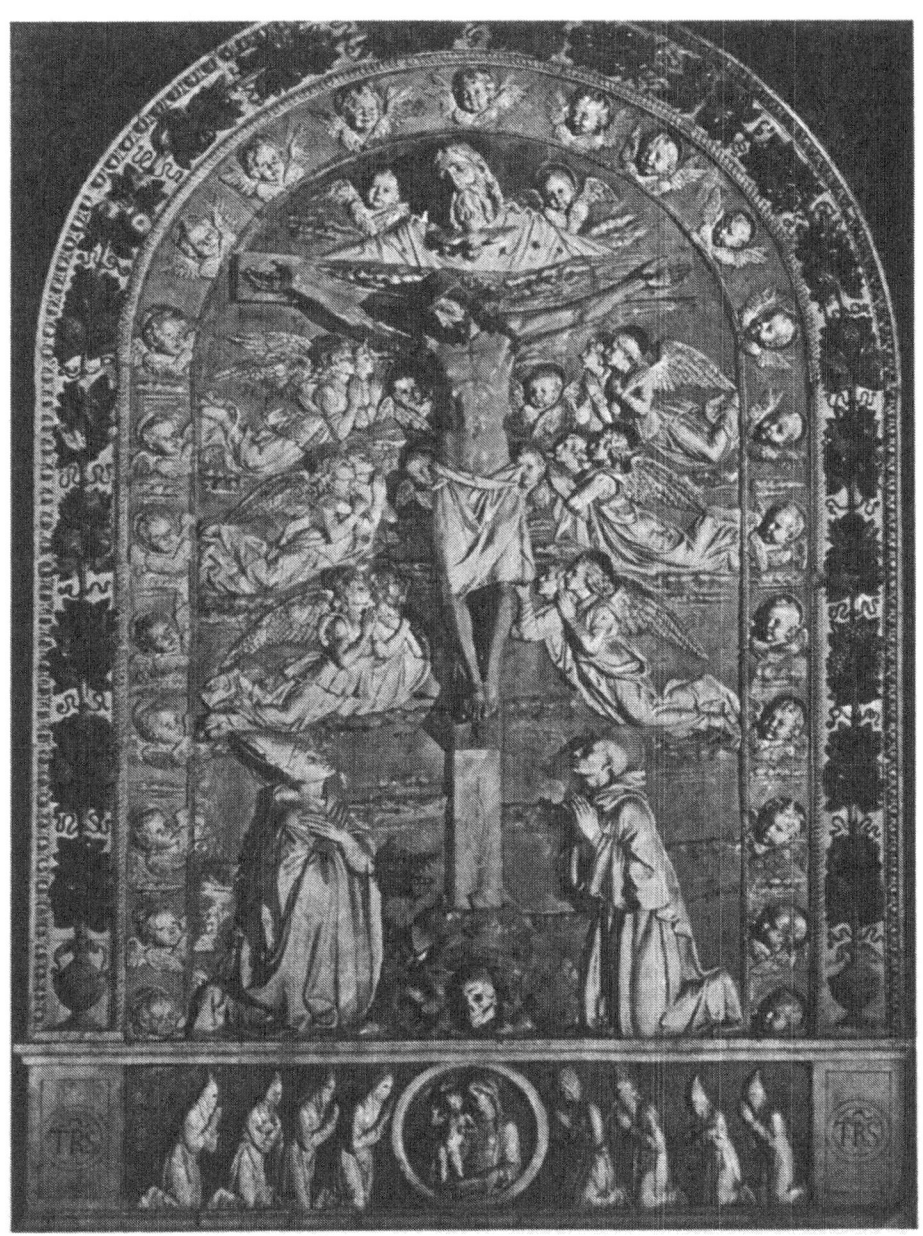

Fig. 70.—The Trinity Altarpiece. Arezzo.

Vasari, in his account of Andrea della Robbia, says "also in the Compagnia della Trinità, by the high altar there is by his hand an altarpiece in which God is represented upholding in his arms Christ crucified, surrounded by many angels, and below on their knees S. Donato and S. Bernard." This monument (Fig. 70) was transferred in 1811 to the Cappella della Madonna of the Cathedral of Arezzo. On the predella is at either end the monogram TR(INITA)S, and in the centre the brothers of the compagnia kneeling before an image of the Madonna. This Madonna, seated, holding a nude standing Child blessing, occurs in an altarpiece in the Campo Santo, Arezzo; in rectangular reliefs in the Endicott collection, Boston, and the Liechtenstein Collection, Vienna; in a round-headed relief formerly in the Bardini collection (No. 512 in sale catalogue of 1902); and in tondi in the Berlin Museum (No. 107), and at Valenzano. An inferior copy is in the Museo Buonarotti, Florence.

The Crucifixion is less realistic, more doctrinal than the Crucifixion at La Verna, where Saints and Angels are overcome with sorrow. Here the divine nature in its Trinitarian aspect is emphasized. Father, Son and Holy Ghost form a visible unit. The six pairs of angels, the six cherubs, the kneeling S. Donato and S. Bernardino are not overwhelmed with grief, but are filled with wondering adoration. The Christ has yellow hair, a green crown and livid greenish flesh. The cross imitates the colour and graining of wood, and its upper portion is enveloped in clouds. Below it is wedged into the ground which is indicated as Calvary by its symbol, a skull. S. Donato's dragon is green with dark spots.

Of the outer frame the bunches of fruit are more monotonous and their ribbons less complicated, than in the Crucifixion at La Verna. The architectural mouldings and the cherub frieze are also slightly inferior in the Arezzo altarpiece.

Bibl.:

B. J., 74-75; B., *Kf.*, 16; *Denk.*, 84, Taf. **260**; C-M., **77**, 84-85, 223 No. 110; Cr., 170, 325; D. D., 33, Abb. **51**; Fov., **108**; M., *D. R. A.*. 36; Michel, IV, 124; Nagler, XIII, 226; Pasqui, 140-141; Perkins, H. H., 144; R., *D. R.*, **177**; *Sc. Fl.*, III, 162, **163**; S., 108, Abb. **114**; Vas., II, 179; V., VI, 590 Fig. **397**; Vita, 53, Fig. **76**.

68 MADONNA AND CHILD BETWEEN SAINTS. Florence. Accademia dei Belle Arti. Vestibule. Lunette. H., 1.30m.; W., 2.60m. Photos., Alinari, 3656; Brogi, 3542.

The polychromatic lunette (Fig. 71) now in the entrance vestibule of the Accademia is said to have come from the convent of S. Orsola, a Benedictine establishment which in 1435 came under Franciscan rule and was merged with the sisterhood of S. Agata. It is difficult in the absence of distinctive attributes, to determine whether the sainted martyr to the right is to be called S. Orsola or S. Agata.

I am inclined to attribute this lunette to Andrea della Robbia at the time when he made polychromatic works, like the altarpiece in the Cathedral of Arezzo and the medallions on the loggia of S. Paolo. In type the S. Fran-

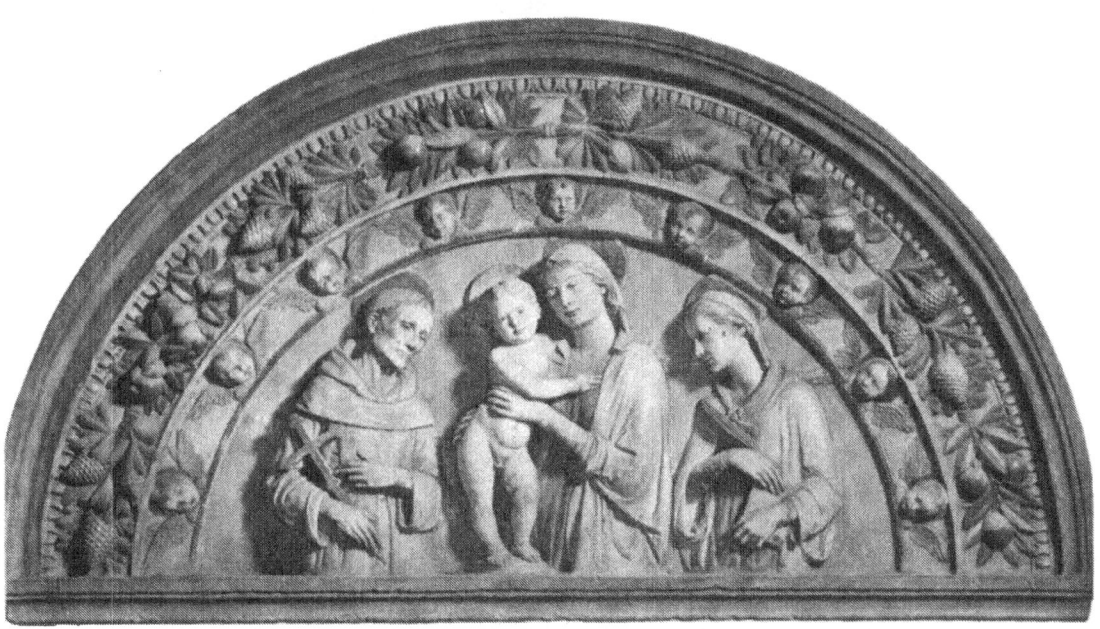

FIG. 71.—LUNETTE OF THE MADONNA AND SAINTS.

cesco is not far removed from the S. Francesco in a niche at La Verna. The S. Orsola in violet tunic with white mantle is most charming. The composition of the Madonna and Child occurs later over the Pistoia Cathedral portal, but with lessened grace. She is clad here in violet, and her blue mantle has a yellow lining. The attempt to give flesh colour to the cheeks and to portray ruby lips may not altogether be endorsed by the aesthetic standards of today, but Luca della Robbia, in the Madonna on Or San Michele, and Andrea, on the loggia of S. Paolo, conformed as here to the demands of the day.

The frame consists of an inner frieze of cherub heads, with blue wings and variously coloured hair, and an outer frieze of triplex bunches of fruit. alternately light and dark, and rigidly bound.

Bibl.:

B., *Kf.*, 16, 24; C-M., 222 No. 101; Cr., 320; R., *D. R.*, 204; *Sc. Fl.*, III, 175; Richa, VII, 42ff.; Vas., II, 192.

69 THE ANNUNCIATION. Berlin. Kaiser-Friedrich Museum, No. 100 (I, 149). H., 0.395m.; W., 0.49. Photo., Berlin Museum.

This very charming relief (Fig. 72), formerly a predella piece, was acquired by the museum in 1888. The background is a light blue, the sloping base upon which the angel kneels imitates green porphyry, and the bench on which the Virgin is seated red porphyry. The figures themselves

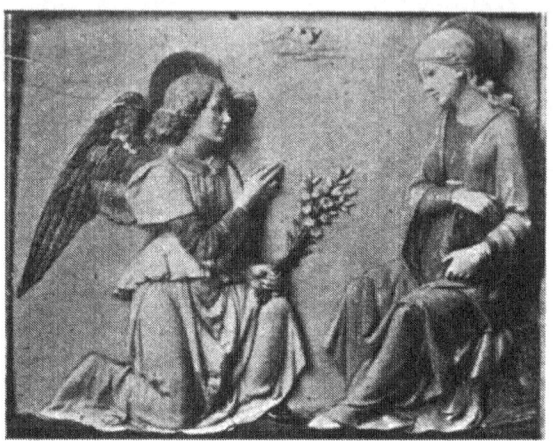

FIG. 72.—POLYCHROMATIC ANNUNCIATION. BERLIN.

are coloured. S. Gabriele wears a violet tunic beneath white robes ornamented with blue. His hair is light yellow, his wings streaked with yellow, white, violet and blue. The Virgin also has yellow hair and wears a violet tunic over which is a blue mantle lined with yellow. The book she carries is green. The composition and the types recall the Annunciation in the predella of the altarpiece at Assisi. Even the lilies have the same rose like forms.

Bibl.:
B., *It. Pl.,* 93; Cr., 333; Schottmüller, 43 No. **100.**

70 S. GREGORIO AND S. AGOSTINO. Berlin. Kaiser-Friedrich-Museum, No. 104 (I, 4999)-105 (I, 5000). Medallions. Diam., with frame, 0.76m. Photo., Bardini; Berlin Museum.

These medallions belong to a series representing the four Fathers of the church, of which two are in the Berlin Museum and a third in Vienna. Formerly in the hands of Bardini of Florence, of J. Bohler of Munich, and in the collection of J. Simon of Berlin, they were purchased by the Museum in 1904.

1. S. Gregorio (Fig. 73), wearing the papal triple tiara, is seated on clouds, inspired by the Holy Dove. He holds a book in his right hand. His pallium is adorned with crosses. The polychromatic fruit frame is

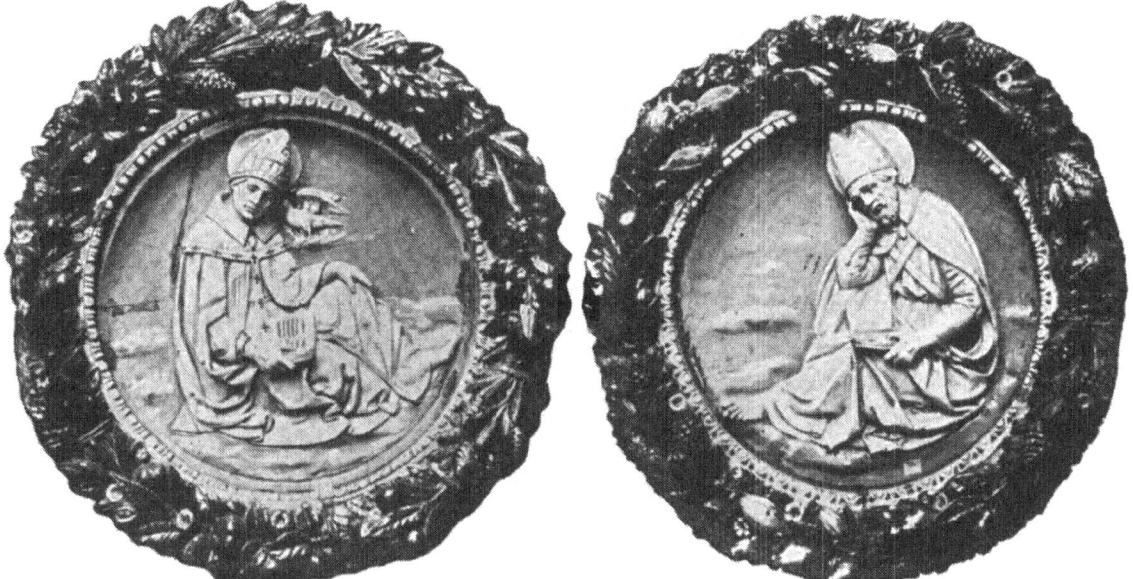

FIG. 73.—S. GREGORIO. FIG. 74.—S. AGOSTINO.

somewhat irregularly composed: six regular bunches of fruit alternately dark and light in colour, being balanced by two long and one short bunch.

2. S. Agostino (Fig. 74), bearded, wearing a Bishop's mitre, holding a book in his left hand, is seated on clouds, pensively anxious. He recalls Luca's S. Agostino at Impruneta. The frame is more regularly composed of nine equal triplex bunches of fruit, separated by plain ribbons straight across. The egg and dart moulding was evidently executed by assistants.

Bibl.:

Cr., 334; Schottmüller, 45 Nos. 104, 105; J. Simon Coll., *Cat.*, Nos. 27, 28; Tschudi, 83, Taf. 60.

71 S. AMBROGIO. Vienna. Collection of Prince Liechtenstein. Medallion. Diam with frame, 0.76m. Photo., Liechtenstein Gallery.

This medallion (Fig. 75) was formerly in the hands of Bardini of Florence and formed part of a series representing the Four Fathers of the Church. Two of the series are in the Berlin Museum.

This must represent either S. Ambrogio or S. Agostino. On Luca's bronze doors these two Fathers were indistinguishable. In these medallions both wear mitres, but one is bearded and wears the piviale, the other

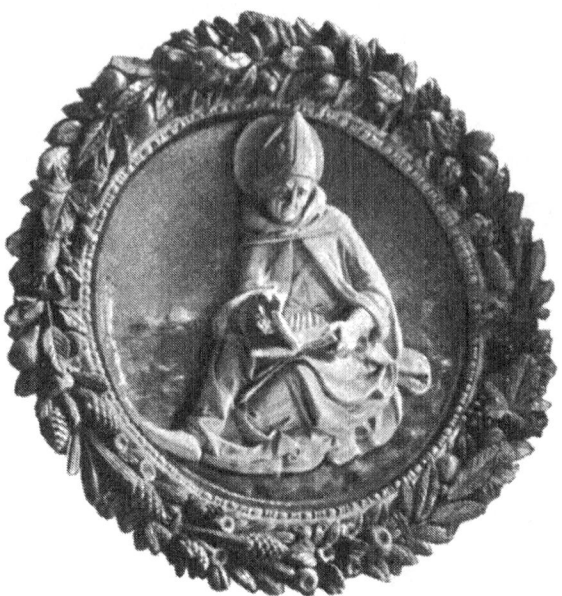

FIG. 75.—S. AMBROGIO.

beardless and is clad in monastic garb. Probably the latter is S. Ambrogio, who is represented as a beardless monk in a Robbia altarpiece at Empoli.

The frame is in six sections separated by ribbons straight across, each section consisting of two triplex bunches of fruit and flowers. The motion here is the reverse of that in the Berlin medallions.

ANDREA DELLA ROBBIA

1490-1500

72 STEMMA OF LORENZO AND FRANCESCO DAVANZATI.
1490. Pistoia, Campanile. Photo., Private.

Unframed, in a kite-shaped shield, are the Davanzati arms: Azure, a
lion rampant or (Fig. 76). Below, a tabella ansata is inscribed:

LORENZO ✦ DI PIERO ✦
DAVANZATI ✦ P(ODEST)A ✦ 1486 ✦
E FRANCESCO ✦ SVO ✦ FI
GLIOLO ✦ P(ODEST)A ✦ 1490 ✦

Lorenzo in Piero Davanzati had been Prior in Florence in 1461 and 1485,
and his son Francesco in 1488.

Bibl.:

C., s.v. Davanzati; M., *R. H.*, 76-77; Fig. 77; P., 267-269; W., 137.

73 WOODEN CRUCIFIX. 1491. Florence. Duomo (formerly).

The archives of the Opera del Duomo show that on January 24, 1491
(O. S. 1490) Andrea della Robbia was commissioned to make a wooden
Crucifix with moveable limbs, and that he completed it on the 29th of
April of the same year. On Good Friday, this miraculous image was to
be displayed to the people. Its present whereabouts is unknown, but a
similar one is said to be preserved in the Museo Civico at Treviso.

Documents: [Revised by Mr. Rufus G. Mather.]

1. "Mcccclxxxx°
Dcā die xx quarta Januarij

pro crucifixo
conficiendo

Item quod fiat quidam crucifixus ligneus ita congregnatus
ut membra moveri videantur et serviat pro illum ostendendo
popolo in venere Scō quolibet anno a quicumque foret ex-
peditus in quo ad plus expendantur f sex largos pro valore—
f 6 largos pro valore"

[Archiv. di S. Maria del Fiore, Deliberazioni dal 1486 al
1491, c. 78ᵗ.]

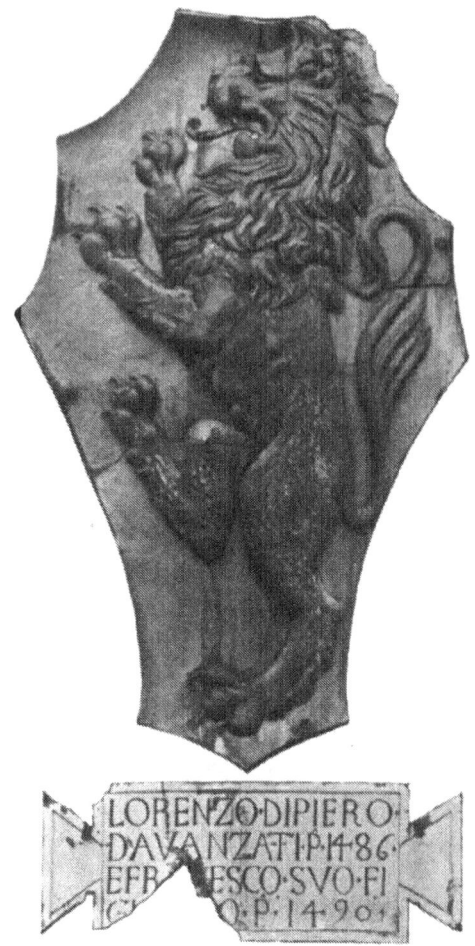

FIG. 76.—DAVANZATI STEMMA.

2.   "Mcccclxxxxj

Die xxiii° Aprilis Item quod solvantur Andree Marci dalla
in hoc a c. 78 Robbia f quinque largos pro valore pro un crucifixo per
eum constructum pro ebdomeda S°(sancta) vigore Deliber-
ationis in hoc a c 78 Sub Diem xxiij° Januarij Mcccclxxxxj*
p.(per) p.(pagina) n° 128-f 5"   per la valuta crocifixo
[Idem, c. 106'.]

3.   "MCCCClxxxxj

pro crucifixo
pretium   Item Dcā Die (xxviiij° Aprilis) appretiaverunt cruci-
fixum constructum per Andream della Robbia vz extima-

* error in text, should be Mcccclxxxx°

tionis, et valoris f quinque largos pro valore, et ita solvatur
dicto Andree etc.—"

[Idem, c. 107.]

Bibl. :

Cr., 199, 308 (Doc.), Fabriczy, *R. f. K.*, XXIX
(1906), 284-285 (Doc.); *J. k. p. K.*, XXX(1909),
Beiheft, 31 No. 94.

74 FOUR EVANGELISTS. 1491. Prato. S. Maria delle Carceri.
Vault. Medallions. Photos., Alinari, 10068-10071; Brogi, 12758-
12761.

In S. Giobbe, Venice, and in the Pazzi Chapel, Florence, vaulted ceilings
had been decorated with glazed terra-cotta Evangelists. The former were
half figures emerging from clouds, the latter full figures seated on clouds,
highly polychromatic, in the midst of a golden radiance.

1. S. Matteo (Fig. 77). On a flat blue disk on which are scattered
clouds in relief S. Matteo is seated, legs crossed and sole of right foot
exhibited, as in the Pazzi Chapel medallion. He holds an open Gospel,
and dips his pen into an ink pot held before him by an angel who also displays to him the inspired book. From the center of the relief radiate shafts
of golden light with trident extremities. The treatment of the hair is more
plastic and folds of garments more complicated than customary. Nimbuses,
collar and borders of mantle decorated with gold.

2. S. Marco (Fig. 78). He is seated on clouds, looking to the right
holding pen and book, and reading from the Gospel held by the emblematic
lion. Lines only, with no attempt at lettering, are seen in the books. His
nimbus, and borders of his garment are gilded. This is a finely modelled,
thoughtful figure of S. Marco, but the lion is less successful.

3. S. Luca (Fig. 79). He is seated on clouds, looking to the right,
writing in a book, while the symbolic ox holds before him a Gospel. The
clouds are in relief against the blue sky; about him is a golden radiance.
His mantle is decorated with gilded borders.

4. S. Giovanni (Fig. 80). He is seated on clouds, looking to left, writing in a book. The nimbed eagle holds an ink pot before him. The nimbuses are gilded and about him is a golden radiance. The borders of his
mantle are decorated with gold.

The documents show that Andrea della Robbia had completed these
Evangelists in the summer of 1491. Document No. 5 indicates that
Andrea's brothers were also concerned with this order. One of them,
Simone, was a member of the Arte dei Maestri di Pietra e Legname.

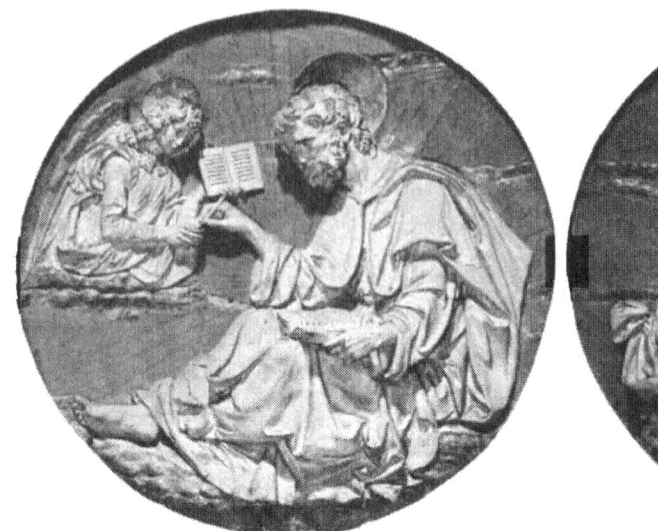

FIG. 77.—S. MATTEO.

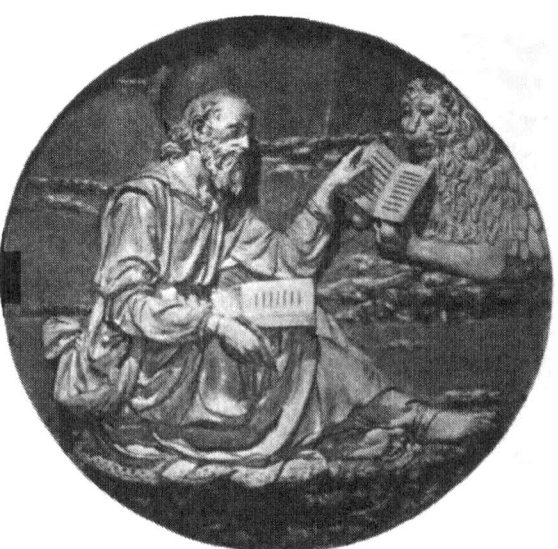

FIG. 78.—S. MARCO.

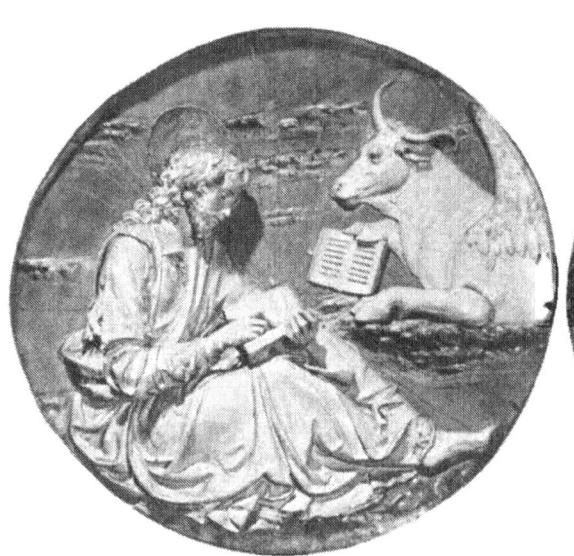

FIG. 79.—S. LUCA.

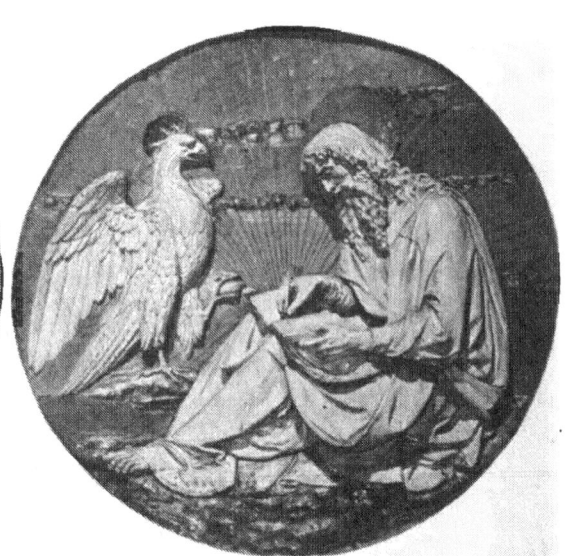

FIG. 80.—S. GIOVANNI.

Documents: [Copied by Mr. Rufus G. Mather.]

1.

a Messer brano di lionardo spedalincho konto della muraglia
dare adi 12 di magio 1 sessanta cinque ebe per noi da
messer girolamo spedalincho della misericordia di prato per
stanzamento degli operaj di questa opera   l 65 s —
          alibro 98

a Andrea di marcho dalla robia da firenze dare adi
13 di magio 1 sessanta cinque per me da messer brano
spedalincho e konto di questa opera et per mia poliza   l 65 s —
         alibro 108"

[Archivio di Patrim., Prato. Opera di S. Maria delle Carceri, Giornale
della Muraglia, segnato F. VII, 32, c. 17ᵗ.]

2.

'+1491 adi 22 di giugno

a Andrea di marcho dalla robbia da firenze de dare
adi 22 di giugno 1 tredicj per noi da messer brano
spedalincho e konto della muraglia di questa chasa e
per mia poliza   l 13 s —
         alibro 108

a Messer brano di lionardo spedalincho e konto di muraglia
di questa chasa avere detto di 1 13 pacho per noi a
andrea di marcho dalla robia e per mia poliza —   l 13 s —
         alibro 98

a Jacopo di stefano di guasparj vetturale de davere
adi 22 di giugno 1 4 s 4 sono per vettura di some 4 libbre-
da firenze con e quatro vangelisti per lopera   l 4 s 4
e de avere detto di per chabella pacho Indochana 1 tre dj 4
et per paglia per le some s quatro In tutto e per la prestanza
delle ceste   l 3 s 4 - 4
         alibro 110"   7.8.4

[Idem, c. 19.]

3.

"+1491

a Jacopo di stefano di guasparj vetturale de dare adi
primo di luglio 1 sette s otto dj quatro et per noi da
messer brano di lionardo spedalincho per konto della
muraglia di questa chasa e per mia poliza —   l 7 s 8 . 4
         alibro 110"

[Idem, c. 20.]

4.

"+1491 adi 13 dochosto
Andrea di marcho dalla robbia da firenze de avere per Insino
a questo di 20 dochosto f trentadua doro Inoro sono per quatro
vangelisti si ebbero daluj pelopera dachordo chonesso luj sono
l cento novantacinque   l 195 s –
questa partita la fo morire qui perche sono f 32 doro
quegli chesse fatto el marchato chonesso luj chome si vede
In questo karta 26
Andrea di marcho dalla robbia a dare adi 20 dochosto
f. dodici doro Inoro sono l settantaotto e per me da
messer brano e per mia poliza e qualj sono per ogni suo
resto di quatro vangelistj avutj da luj   l 78 s —
          alibro 108"
     [Idem, c. 25.]

5.

"+1491 adi 20 dochosto
Andrea di Marcho dalla robbia e fratellj da firenze
deono avere per Insino a questo di 20 dochosto f. trentadua
doro Inoro larghi sono l dugentotto e qualj danarj sono pella
monta de 4 vangelistj si sono autj dalloro per lopera e qualj
a fatto pregio andrea prop(r)io chon mia operaj e di chonsentimento
delluno e dellatro o fatta da prima scrittura
perche dissono esser dachordo In tutto —   l 208 s –
          alibro 108"
     [Idem, c. 26'.]

6.

"+1491 adi 26 dottobre
Andrea di Marcho dalla robia de dare adi detto l trentanove
sono per parte del fregio che luj fa Intorno alla chiesa di terra
cotta e qualj porto bart° di simone di bart° a firenze   l 39 s —
          alibro 108"
     [Idem, c. 32.]

7.

'1491 adi 3 di novenbre
Andrea di Marcho dalla robia a dare adi 8 di novenbre
l venti sei e per noi ebe da messer brano di lionardo spedalincho
della misericordia (?) e per mia poliza   l 26 s —
          alibro 108"
     [Idem, c. 32'.]

8.

"Adi 26 di Marzo 1492

M° Andrea di marcho dellarobia de dare adi ult° di marzo

f. dieci larghi doro ebbe da brano per mia poliza   165 - s —

        posto alibro b 121   a brano s 4

[Idem, c. 39.]

9.

"Adi 14 daprile 1492

M° Andrea di marcho dellarobia de dare adi 14 daprile(?) [badly written] f. tredici larghi doro inoro ebe dalospedale della misericordia per poliza deglioperaj per parte del fregio f x l 2 f tre larghi in oro per mordente e oro

        posto alibro b 121"   184 s 10

[Idem, c. 41.]

Bibl. :

B. J., 61; B., *Kf.*, 16, 24; *Denk.*, 85, Taf. **267**; Burl., 69, 116; C-M., 104-106, 246 No. 253; Cr., 184-**186**, 326; *Verrocchio*, 165; D. D., 32; Giglioli, *a Prato,* 55-58 (Doc.); Guasti, *Caffagiolo,* 157-158; M., *R. H.*, 90; Passerini, 231; R., *D. R.*, 186-**187**; *Sc. Fl.*, III, 167; S., 119, Abb. **130**; Vas., II, 181 note.

75 CANDELABRA AND GARLANDS, ARMS OF PRATO. 1492. Prato. S. Maria delle Carceri. Frieze. H., 0.80m. Photos., Alinari, 10063; Brogi, 12756.

The documents show that Andrea della Robbia was paid for this frieze

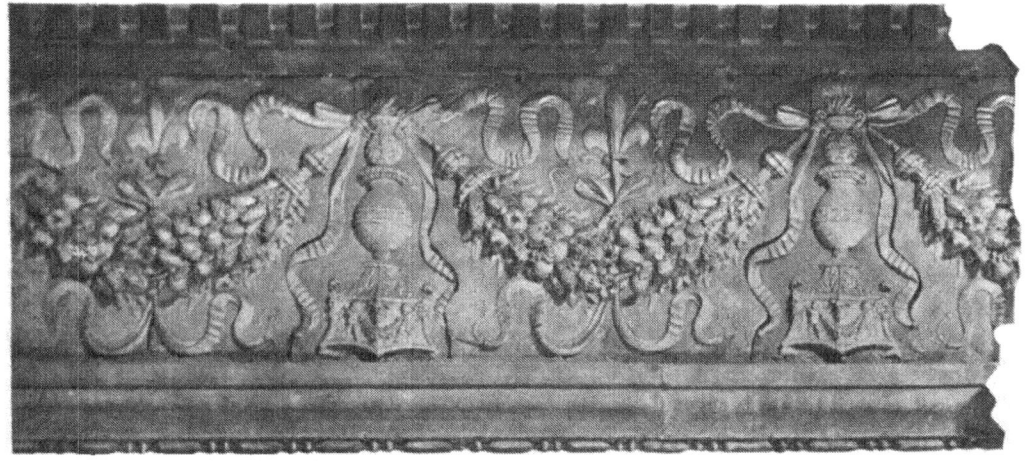

Fig. 81.—Candelabra and Garland Frieze.

(Fig. 81) in 1491-1492. Whether the designing of it was entirely in his hands or controlled by the architect Giuliano di San Gallo is more difficult to determine. A somewhat similar frieze decorates the church of S. Rocco in Rome. Candelabra more or less like these had been used by Antonio Rossellino, Benedetto da Maiano and others; and hanging garlands were common enough in Tuscan sculptures. On the other hand this very design is found again in Robbia ware at Brancoli and all the elements of it, garlands of fruit, fluted ribbons, candelabra, abound in the work of Andrea della Robbia. At intervals, above the pilasters, are wreaths of fruit, com-

FIG. 82.—PRATO STEMMA.

posed in accordance with Andrea's methods, containing shields of floriated Tuscan form, with the arms of Prato: Azure semé of fleurs-de-lys or (Fig. 82).

Documents: [See Documents 6-9 of the preceding.]

Bibl.:
Same as the preceding.

76 THE FOUR EVANGELISTS. Naples. Monteoliveto. Cappella S. Anna dei Lombardi. Medallions. c. 80m. diam. Photo., Private.

Set in frames consisting of a simple but well modelled egg and dart moulding are medallions of the four Evangelists, white on blue.

1. S. Matteo (Fig. 83) holds a pen in right hand, ink stand in left. To the left, an angel appears holding an open book.

2. S. Marco holds a pen in right hand, a book in left. To the right is a winged lion holding an inkstand.

3. S. Luca holds a pen in right hand, a book in left. To the right is a winged ox holding nothing.

4. S. Giovanni turns over the pages of a book. To the right is an eagle, no inkstand. The blue background somewhat spotty.

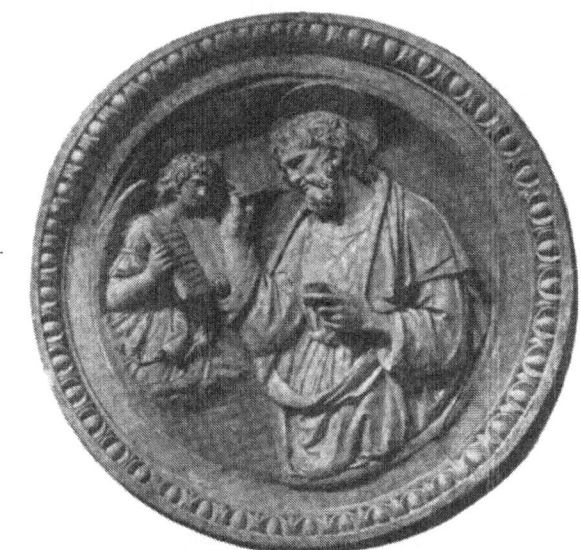

FIG. 83.—S. MATTEO, NAPLES.

77 ANNUNCIATION. Florence. Ospedale di S. Maria degli Innocenti. Cappella. Lunette. H., 1.54m.; W., 2.85m. Photos., Alinari, 3180; Brogi, 4696. Casts, Cantagalli, 340 (detail); Lelli, 406.

From the Cappella de'Pugliesi, where it once stood above an altarpiece by Piero di Cosimo, this lunette (Fig. 84) was removed to the position it now occupies above the door leading from the courtyard to the chapel of the Hospital.

It may be classed with the Evangelists of S. Maria delle Carceri in point of style, in view of the highly plastic treatment of hair and the crumpled drapery. The angel, kneeling, pointing, bearing the symbolic lilies recalls the S. Michele at Braunschweig. The covert or upper bank of feathers are treated in almost identical fashion in both reliefs. However, the Innocenti archangel is more mannered and his eyes with their yellow irises more in accord with Andrea's later usage. The vase with its full body and snake handles, recurs in the works of Andrea's followers. The base of the prie-dieu is ornamented with cherub head and garland against a brown background and the support for the book is ornamented with griffin legs. The book contains not mere lines as in the vault at Prato, but letters and abbreviations which suggest, if they do not indicate the words of the salutation, *Ave, gratia plena. . . Ne timeas, Maria. . . Ecce, concipies* etc. (Luke, I, 28-33).

As in the Prato Cathedral lunette the Madonna's head is of a rounded type and locks of hair fall from behind her kerchief. The ground upon

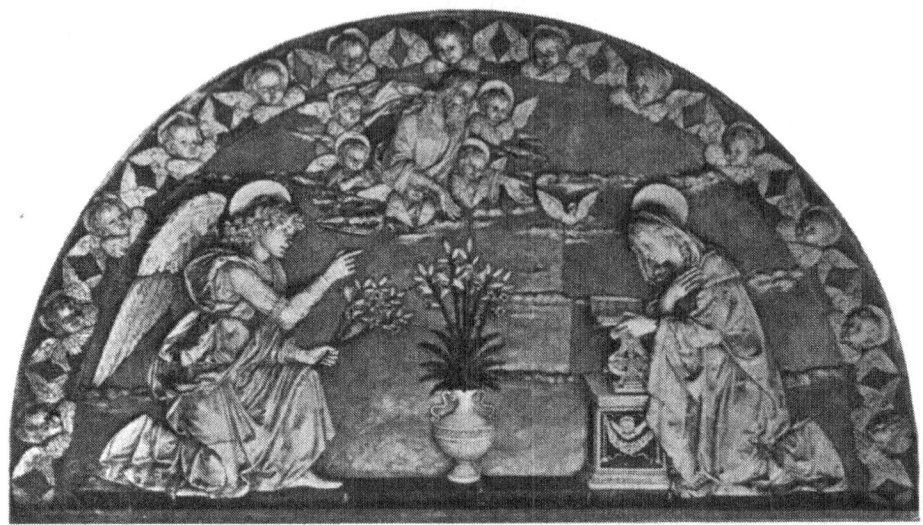

FIG. 84.—THE INNOCENTI ANNUNCIATION.

which the figures are kneeling is of a sea-green colour. Above is the blue sky, clouds in relief, God the Father in a glory of cherubs, and the Holy Dove.

An Annunciation of this type, in which both figures are kneeling, occurs again in the lunette of the altarpiece at S. Chiara, Borgo San Sepolcro, and in various works by Andrea's followers.

Document: [Copied by Mr. Rufus G. Mather.]

"Spedale degli Innocenti, La Chiesa.

All' entrare a man ritta in cappella ornata di colonne....... et addirimpetto una simile cappella del Pugliese dipinse la vergine con molti santi atorno Pier di Cosimo arrichita di teste di cherubini di terra invetriata di Luca della Robbia con la Verg.' annunziata"

[Ferdinando del Migliore, *Chiese Fiorentine*, Tomo I, Cod. carta Sec. XVII Segnato Magliab. II, I No. 316.]

Bibl.:

B. J., 64; B., *Kf.*, 16, 24; *Denk.*, 85-86, Taf. **265**; *W. D. R.*, 8, Taf. **42**; Bruni, I, 11; Burl., 55-56, 108; Car., *Ill. Fior.*, 1912, 33; C-M.,

93, 100-102, 209 No. 20; Cr., **186**, 326; Fov., **100**; Nagler, XIII, 226;
R., *D. R.*, 184-186; *Sc. Fl.*, III, 166-167; Richa, VIII, 129; S., 113,
Abb. **128**; Vas., II, 180, Note 2; *Z. f. b. K.*, XX(1885), 20.

78 STEMMA OF GIOVANNI DI GALEZZO TROTTI. 1492. Florence, Museo Nazionale, Cortile. Photo., Alinari, 2985.

Within a wreath of ten bunches of fruit of triplex composition, separated
by plain transverse ribbons, and with motion like that of the hands of a
clock, is set a flat blue plate on which is a tournament shield (Fig. 85)

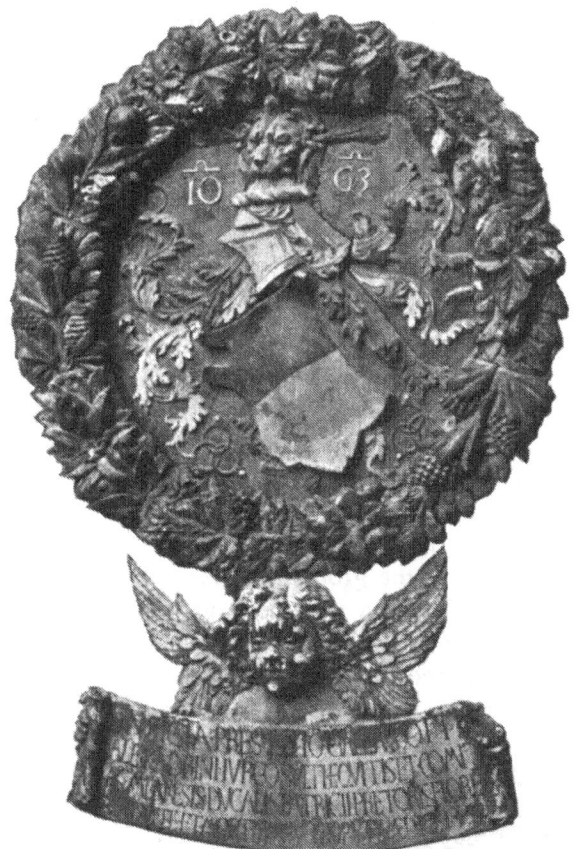

FIG. 85.—THE TROTTI STEMMA.

displaying the Trotti arms: Per fess or and azure.   Above this is a helmet
with foliated mantlings vert and argent drawn through a chaplet and held
in a lion's mouth.   Groups of Medici rings appear in the field above and
below.   In chief is the name IO(HANNES) G(ALEATVS)

Below, a winged cherub with wing locks unfolds a tablet inscribed:
INSIG(N)IA ✦ PREST(ANTISSIMI) · D(OMINI) · IO(HANNI) ·
      GALEATI · TROTTI ·
ALEXA(N)DRINI · IVR(IS)CO(N)SVLTI · EQVITIS · ET · CO-
      MIT(IS) ·
AC M(EDIO)LANE(N)SIS · DVCALIS · PARICII · PRETORIS ·
      FLORENTINI ·
ANNO VITE · ET · MORTIS · MAG(NIFICI) · LAVRE(N)TII ·
      MEDICE(I) · 43.

Gian Galeazzo Trotto, named from Gian Galeazzo Visconti, was a de-
scendant of Emanuele Trotti, one of the founders of Alexandria in Pied-
mont. The method of dating is interesting. Lorenzo de' Medici was born
in 1449; hence the forty-third year of his life, the year also of his death,
would fall in 1492.

Bibl.:
C., s.v. Trotti; Cr., 340; M., *R. H.*, 93-94, Fig. 94.

79 MADONNA AND CHILD AND SAINTS. Florence. S. Croce,
Cappella Medici. Altarpiece. H., 2.20m.; W., 2.10m. Photo.,
Alinari, 2165; Brogi, 3620. Casts, Cantagalli 462(detail), 492(de-
tail), 294(detail); Lelli, 378, 363-365(details).

The Madonna, in full length is seated on clouds from which emerge
cherub heads. She holds to right the partially draped Child who carries a
bird and is blessing (Fig. 86). Above are two charming angels, who are
setting a jeweled crown upon the Madonna's head. To the left and right
are six saints standing on the ground, in size smaller than the Madonna.
They are S. Antonio of Padua with book and flame, a female saint (S.
Elisabetta? Rosa? Dorotea?) with roses, S. Giovanni in hair cloth, pointing to the sacred Child and holding a cross and a scroll inscribed ECCE
AGNVS DEI, S. Lorenzo with green martyr's palm and gridiron, S. Lodovico, and S. Francesco with book and cross. The eyes have Andrea's
characteristic blue brows and lashes, dark, copper coloured pupils and yel-
lowish irises.

The frame shows signs of injury and of having been at some time
stupidly erected. We might have expected for so beautiful a relief a frame
comparable to those of the altarpieces at La Verna, instead of which we
find pilasters of a type common in Andrea's atelier at a somewhat later
period. The architrave of the entablature is set as a base moulding of the
predella, and the plain predella moulding put in its place. Fortunately,
however the frieze of seven cherub heads and the cornice remain intact.

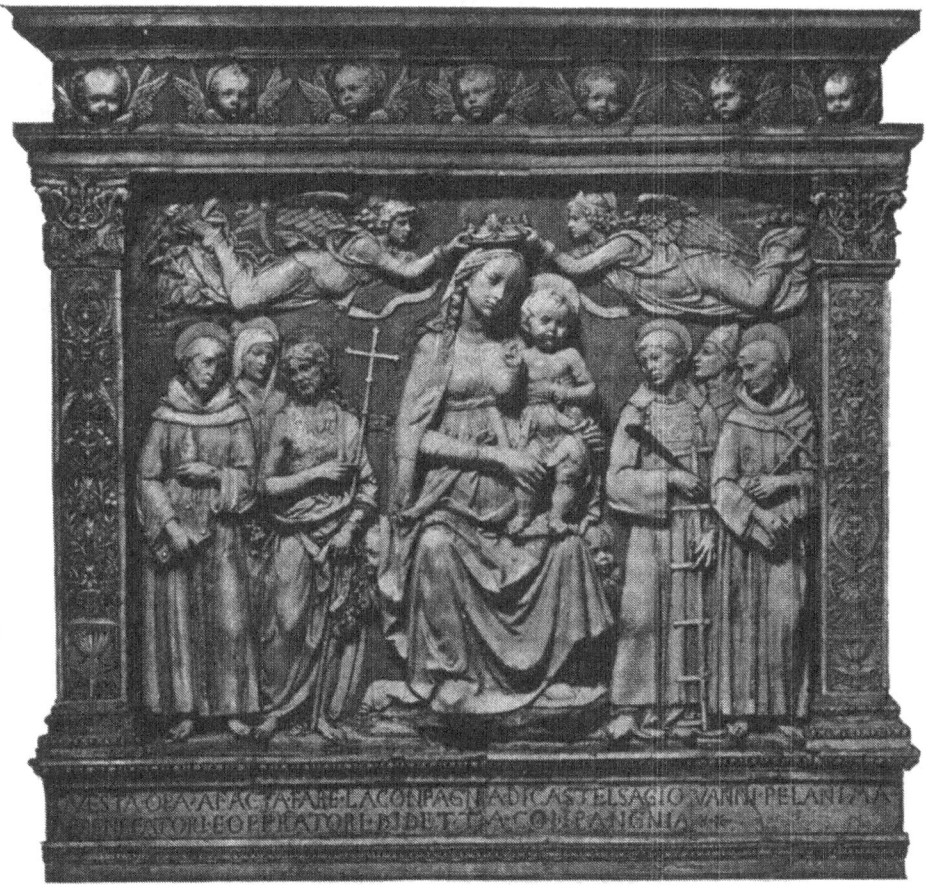

FIG. 86.—MADONNA AND SAINTS. S. CROCE.

The predella is inscribed: QVESTA ✦ OP(ER)A ✦ A FACTA ✦ FARE ✦ LA CONPAGNIA ✦ DI CASTEL SA(N) GIOVANNI ✦ PE(R) L'ANIMA ✦ DE(I) BENEFATORI ✦ E OPERATORI ✦ DI DETTA ✦ CONPANGNIA

Bibl.:
B. J., 66-67; B., *Kf.*, 23; Denk., 87; Burl., 57-58, 107; C-M., 206 No. 7; Cr., 173-174; 325; Fov., 108; R., *D. R.*, 171-172; *Sc. Fl.*, III, 160; S., 103, Abb. 105; Vas., III, 218.

80 CHERUB FRIEZE. 1494. Florence. S. Frediano, Cappella della Compagnia di S. Frediano.

In the church of S. Frediano, the Cappella della Compagnia di S. Frediano, founded c. 1490, was decorated with a frieze of cherub heads with other objects (cherubini e chosi). We recall in this connection the un-glazed cherub frieze of cherub heads and paschal lambs in the interior of the Pazzi Chapel, and the glazed frieze of cherub heads, lambs and Sacred Names on the exterior of the Cappella Maggiore di S. Chiara, now in the Victoria and Albert Museum. The S. Frediano frieze was glazed. Payments for the frieze began in 1494 and 1495; and were continued, or repeated, in the autumn of 1502. The individual members of the Robbia family appear to be indistinctly known to the Operai, for their indebtedness is recorded first to "Luca della Robbia," who died in 1482, and later to his successor, here recorded as Andrea di Lucha (sic) della Robbia. The Luca della Robbia first mentioned may, however, have been Luca di Andrea.

The payment for the frieze appear to have been in units of 11 lire and to have totalled 44 lire, from which we gather that the chapel was square in form and that the frieze was continued on all four sides. It was probably vaulted, for in 1518-1520 we find a Robbia lunette placed "sotto l'arco della cappella."

Documents · [Copied by Mr. Rufus G. Mather.]

1.   " + MCCCCLXXXXIIJ +
Operaj della chapella deono avere adi 21 daprile
1494 l 182 s 19 per tantti paghati a chabriello
scharpellino al ponte a santa trinita In 8 partite
come apare alibro deglioperaj tenuto per stefano
bonssj in questo a c 116   l 182 s 19 d–
E deono avere a detto libro a c 117 l 33 paghate
allucha della Robia per un fregio per detta chapella   l 33 s — d–
E deono avere a detto libro a c 81 l 1 s 12   sono
per detto libro si chonpero dant° chartolaio   l 1 s 12 d–
                                        217.11"

[Archivio di Stato. Compagnia di San Frediano, Libro Debitori e Creditori anni 1467 al 1522, segnato n° 112, c. Lxxxvij.]

2.
"E deon dare adi 24 daprile 1495 fi 5 Inoro
larghi et per lloro a franc° da bruscanese e
sono per dare andrea della robia per un
freg(i)o ci fa per detta chapella come apare
alibro deglioperaj a c 81 suddettj operaj abino
avere a detto libro a c 50 e dettj danarj
porto franc° da bruscanese detto diliscienza (di licenza) di
stefano bonssj proveditore di dettj operaj
a uscita a c 79"   L 33 —   d–

[Idem, idem.]

3.   "+ Mdj
Chapela murata di nuovo nela
chiesa di sanfriano ad dirinpetto
di quela muro lorenzo fornaio de
dare adi 27 daprile 1502 etc.........17

- - - - - -

- - - - - -

E de dare l 33 a lucha delarobia per
parte de cherubinj per detta chapella
in questo a c 87 nel chonto de opera
autj da lucha delarobia dare (in)
questo a c 113 davere in soma di l 44   l 33 s –
E de dare 1- s vij per 3 fasti (fregii) di
cherubinj e chosj da lucha delarobia
per la Chiesa di san friano pachatj
bartolomeo dant° vaiaio k° (kamerario)
c 8 a sua uscita   1– s 7
E de dare l undicj picciolj per tantj
fatti buonj andrea di lucha (sic) della
Robbja posto avere in questo a c 113
in soma di l 44 sono per resto dettj
charubinj autj dalloro per detta capella   l 11 s –"

    [Idem, c. 112.]

"c 113

4.   "+ Mdj
Andrea di lucha delarobia de dare
l 7 autj da bartolomeo dant° vaiaio
k° a c 8 portaglieli salvestro di
ser Ichopo adi 31 di marzo 1502
per parte de cherubinj di tera chota
per la nuova capela a uscita   l 7 s–
E de dare l 33 autj piu tempo fa
chome apare in questo a c 87 a
chonto di nostra chapela
delopera posto chapela (in) questo
a c 113 debitori per parte del
freg(i)o de cherubinj   l 33 s–
E de dare adi 15 di settèbre 1502
l iiij picciol. sono per e serafinj per la
chapela di sanfriano e peresto
di tutti e detti serafinj e fregio
di detta chapela soprascrita   .

"+ Mdj
Andrea di lucha delarobia de avere
l quaranta quattro picciolj sono per
ttuttj i fregi di cherubinj di tera chottj
Invetrjatj autj dalluj per fornire la
chapella di san friano dela nostra
conp(agnia) nella chiesa di sanfriano
                              [fatta
per gli uomjnj di detta chonp(agnia)
                              [posta
in detta chiesa di Rimpetto alla
chapella di salorenzo in detta chiesa
posto detta chapella dare in questo
a c 112 in 2 partite una di l 33 e
una di l 11   l 44 s–"

di agnolo berragli nostro
fratello   l 4 s– d–
          l 44 o o"
[Idem, c. 113.]
Bibl.:
B., *D. R.,* 150; *Sc. Fl.,* III, 147; Richa, IX, 177; Vas., II, 180-181 note.

81 S. ANTONIO BETWEEN TWO ANGELS. Prato. S. Antonio Abate. Lunette. H., 0.97m.; W., 1.90m. Photo., Alinari, 10077.

S. Antonio, with finely modelled head and hands, carries a book and a crutch (Fig. 87). He is robed in monastic (Camaldolesce) cowl and gown. The border of the latter was ornamented with a series of *tau* crosses, or

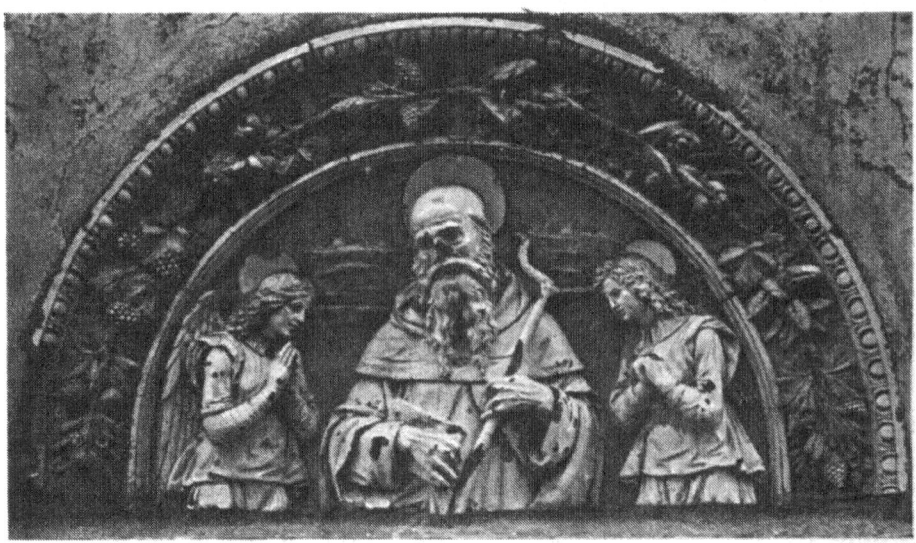

FIG. 87.—S. ANTONIO BETWEEN TWO ANGELS.

T's, emblem of the order of the Ospitalieri.—The adoring angels approximate those at S. Maria della Quercia, Viterbo. In execution it is finer than the lunette of S. Zanobi in the Opera del Duomo.

The frame, with its bunches of fruit and flowers bound into pendent garlands by narrow crossing ribbons, is fashioned according to Andrea's methods.

Bibl.:
Burl., 116; C-M., 245 No. 247; Corradini, 50; Cr., 227, 330.

82 (1). GARLAND. (2). LUNETTE OF S. ANTONINO. Prato
(near). Via del Ferro.

Not found. Recorded by Miss Cruttwell. Possibly confused with the
lunette of S. Antonio Abate, which in Alinari's catalogue is designated as
S. Antonio del Ferro.

Bibl. :
  Cr., 352.

83, 84 HISTORICAL RELIEF, A PIETÀ, S. GIOVANNI BAT-
TISTA, S. SEBASTIANO, AND OTHER DECORATIONS.
Montevarchi. Collegiata di S. Lorenzo, Cappella della Fraternità.
Photos., Alinari, 10387-10394.

The Collegiata at Montevarchi cherishes as a sacred relic a drop of the
Virgin's milk supposed to have fallen from the lips of the Child and to have
been miraculously crystallized during the Flight into Egypt. This was

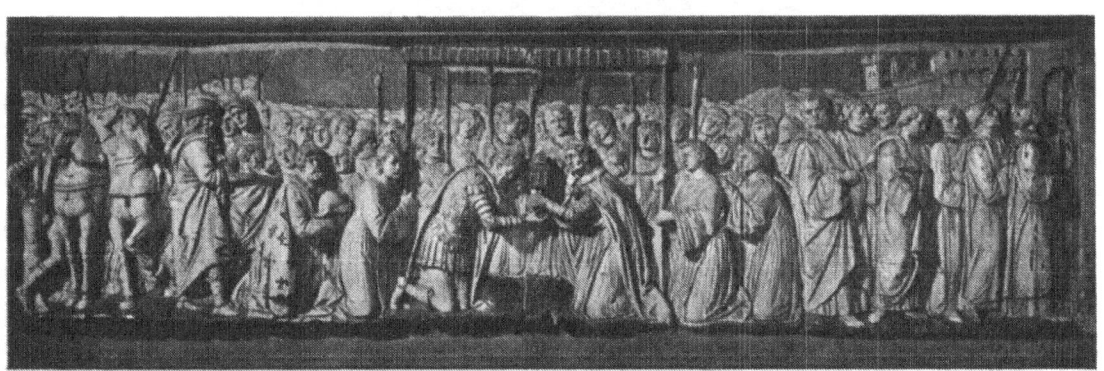

FIG. 88.—HISTORICAL RELIEF. MONTEVARCHI.

presented by Conte Guido Guerra who received it from Charles of Anjou,
to whose brother Louis it was presented by the Emperor of Constantinople.
This presentation was commemorated by a relief on the façade of the
church and by a chapel in the interior.

1. The Historical Relief. (Alinari, 10387-10389).

Formerly on the exterior of the church was a balcony, from which the
sacred relic was displayed. This balcony was decorated on the front by a
relief on which is depicted Conte Guido, in armour on his knees present-
ing the relic to the Ecclesiastical representatives of the church (Fig. 88).
Behind him may be recognized from his mantle decorated with fleurs-de-

lys, Charles of Anjou, accompanied by a host of attendants. On the other side is an ecclesiastic, also on his knees, attended by clerics and civilians. White figures, yellow details, standing on greenish gray ground.

2. The Stemmi (Alinari, 10390).

The sides of the balcony were decorated with coats of arms (Fig. 89) of the Guerra family, on oval shields upheld by winged putti: Gules, a points enclosing three lilies or. These reliefs are now inside the church in

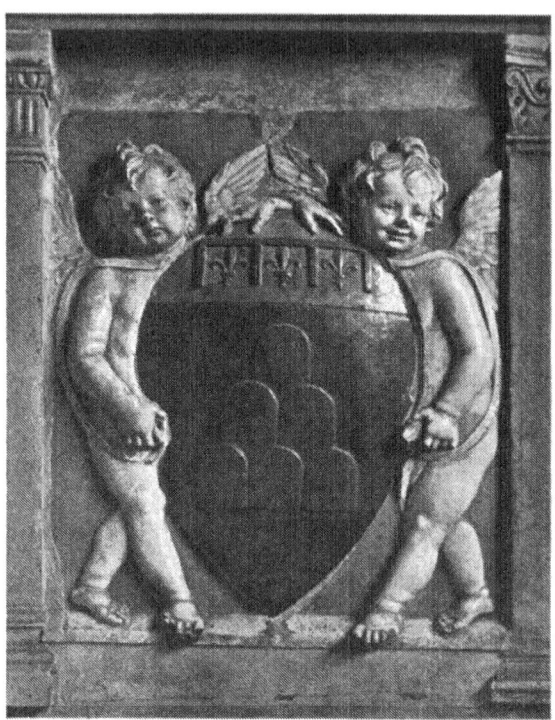

FIG. 89.—THE GUERRA STEMMA.

a chapel devoted to the preservation of the relic and known as the Cappella della Fraternità.

Von Rumohr states that the entire façade of the church not long before his day was decorated with glazed terra-cotta. This is probably an overstatement.

3. The Chapel Pavement.

Some hexagonal tiles from the pavement still remain. They show the pattern which Andrea used for pavements at Empoli, S. Gimignano, and S. Fiora, and which Giovanni also used as backgrounds for reliefs. Border tiles with fringe also survive.

4. The Ceiling.

Twelve of the coffered ceiling panels remain, showing square panels with white rosettes on blue ground, framed by rectangular panels decorated with triplex bunches of fruit, white on blue, and at the angles square panels, in each a ball, white on blue, not unlike the coffering of the vault at Pistoia.

5. The Wall-frieze (Alinari, 10394).

At the top of the wall ran a frieze of cherub heads, of which thirty-four still remain (Fig. 90). White on blue.

The Altarpiece.

Cavallucci and Molinier declare that the altarpiece once consisted of a central niche containing a Madonna suckling the Child, flanked by two

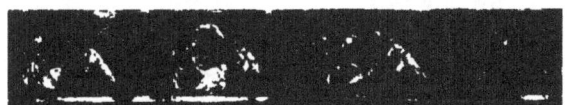

FIG. 90.—CHERUBS.

niches containing figures of S. Giovanni Battista and S. Sebastiano. The central niche, if it ever existed, has now disappeared, but there still remain a lunette with a Pietà, the two niches with Saints, and a long panel of angels adoring the secred relic. The dimensions and the frames do not readily admit of associating these reliefs into a single altarpiece.

6. The Lunette with the Pietà (Alinari, 10398). H., 0.74m.; W., 1.36m.

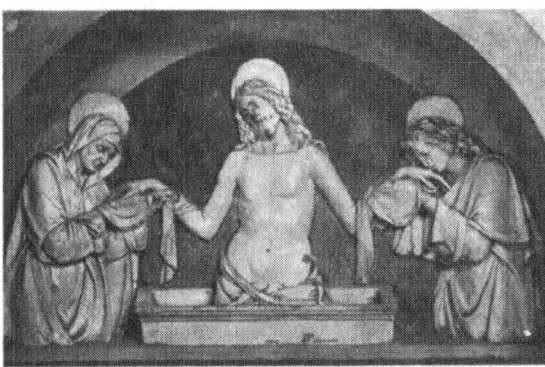

FIG. 91.—PIETÀ.

This relief represents Christ with eyes closed rising from the tomb, upheld by his Mother and the Beloved Disciple (Fig. 91). They perform an act of religious devotion rather than of physical assistance. This relief is more beautiful than the marble Pietà at Arezzo, more expressive of religious feeling than the Christ in the Piazza di S. Spirito, Florence. It deserves to be more widely recognized as one of Andrea's masterpieces.

7. S. Giovanni Battista (Alinari, 10392). H., 1.80m.; W., 0.84m.

Wearing hair·cloth and mantle, S. Giovanni Battista points with his index finger and carries a cross and a scroll inscribed ECCE AGNVS DEI TOLLIS(sic) PECCA(TA) (Fig. 92). The frame with its triplex

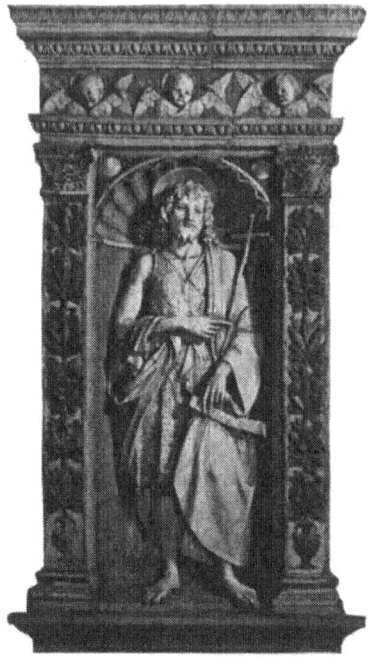

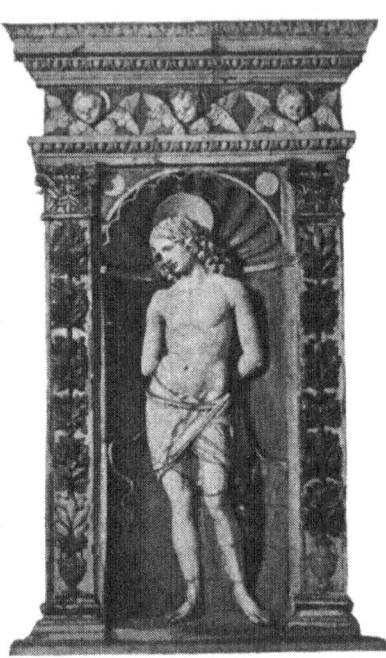

FIG. 92.—S. GIOVANNI BATTISTA.   FIG. 93.—S. SEBASTIANO.

bunches of fruit rising from blue and violet vases and its cherub frieze seems complete in itself. Arranged as at present where the Baptist is pointing toward the entombed Christ it is surely quite as appropriate as if placed alongside of a Madonna suckling the Child.

8. S. Sebastiano (Alinari, 10391). H., 1.80m.; W., 0.84m.

A sympathetic and restrained study of S. Sebastiano (Fig. 93), more charming than the figures of the Saint at Arezzo, and Montalcino. The frame is a counterpart to that of S. Giovanni Battista.

9. Angels adoring the Sacred Relic (Alinari, 10394). H., 0.60m.; W., 2.

This motive of angels adoring a relic (Fig. 94) Andrea learned from his uncle Luca. He employed it in the predella of the Cintola altarpiece at La Verna and most appropriately here.

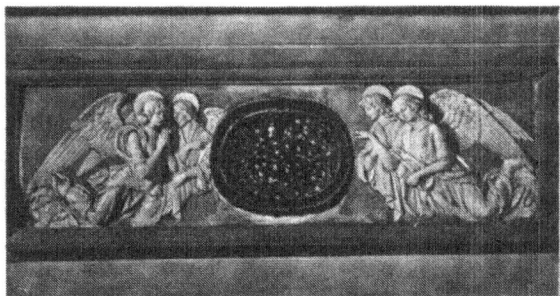

FIG. 94.—ANGELS ADORING RELIC.

Bibl. :

C-M., 240 No. 219; Cr., 221-222, 330, 349; Foratti, *Rass d'Arte,*
XIX(1919), 30-31; M., *Br.,* 1902, 55; *L. D. R.,* 92, Fig. **53**; *R. H.,*
107, Fig. **106**; von Rumohr, II, 296 note; S., 143, Abb. **158**.

85 PUTTI SUPPORTING GARLANDS. Città di Castello, Pinacoteca, Nos. 28, 30. Statuettes, H., 0.92m. Photos., Alinari, 4868-4869.

These putti (Figs. 95-96), according to a Ms. by Certini in the archives
of the Canonica, once adorned a lavabo in the sacristy of S. Giovanni.
Possibly the garland served as a frame for the lavabo, set beneath the
medallion of the Madonna which is now placed between the putti in the
Pinacoteca. This scheme is followed in the lavabo at S. Ansano, near
Fiesole. At S. Ansano the putti do not carry the garland naturally and
stand on nothing. Their designer had probably in mind Giovanni's gar-
land-bearing putti on the cornice of the lavabo at S. Maria Novella. Here,
however, they stand on yellow scrolls. This would seem to imply a niche,
somewhat like that in which stands a figure of S. Domenico, No. 68 in
the Museo Nazionale. A similar niche may be assumed for the garland
bearing putto in the Liechtenstein collection in Vienna. The analogues to
these figures are to be found in the putti bearing stemmi at Montevarchi.

Bibl. :

B., *Denk.,* 86, Taf. **265**; Certini, Ms. quoted by Graziani; Cr., 336;
Graziani, 152-153, pl. 20; Guardabassi, 51; Melani, *A. I. D. I.,* VII
(1898), Tav. **2**; V., VI., 594, Figs. **402-403**.

86 PUTTO BEARING A GARLAND. Vienna. Prince Liechtenstein
Collection. Photo., Bardini.

This putto stands on a yellow spiral and carries a polychromatic fruit

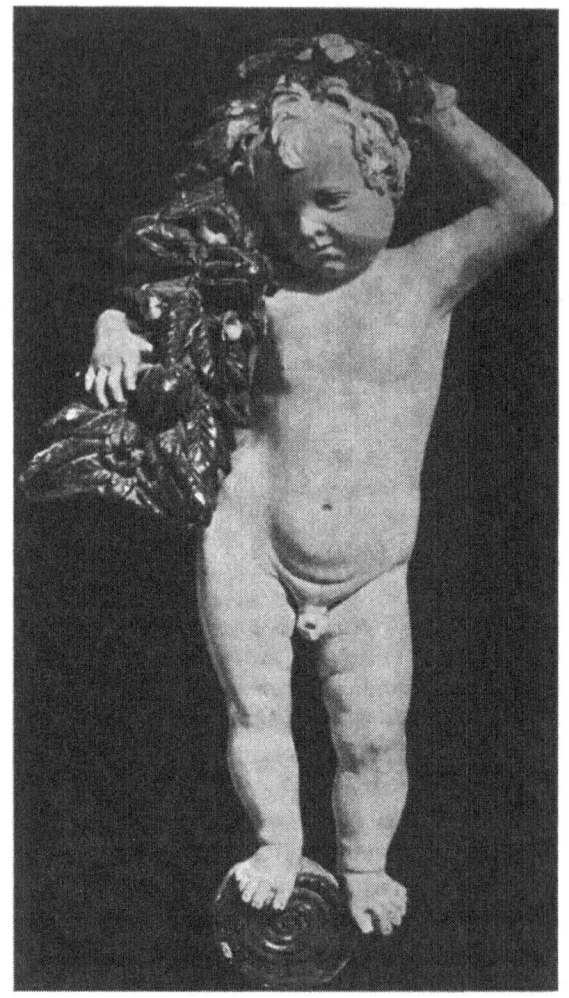

FIG. 95.—PUTTO AND GARLAND.

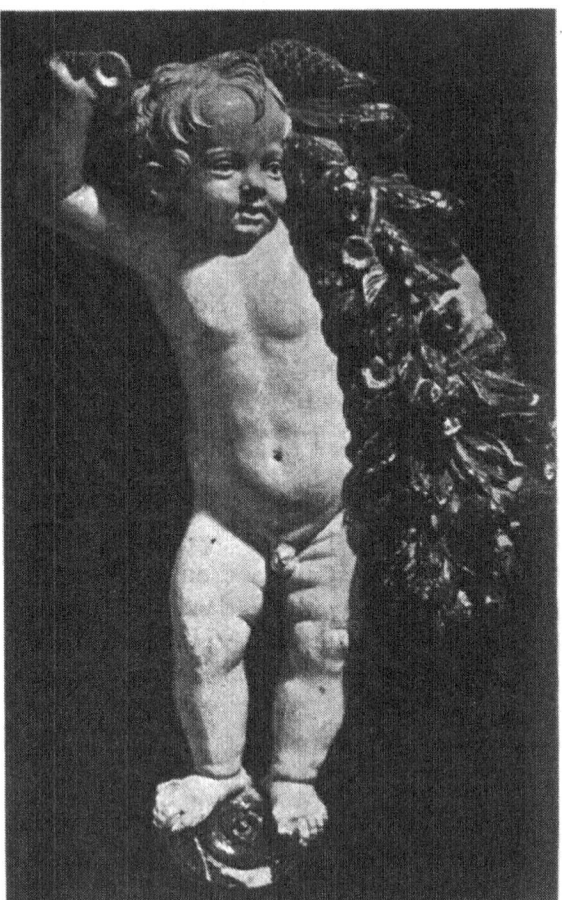

FIG. 96.—PUTTO AND GARLAND.

garland. It formerly stood to the left of a lunette of a niche or tabernacle, possibly a lavabo.

87 MADONNA WITH NUDE, STANDING CHILD. Florence, Piazza dell'Unità. Medallion. Photo., Alinari, 17315.

This Madonna (Fig. 97), now placed in a niche, was formerly a medallion as may be seen from the circular blue background. The composition may be associated with the early Madonnas in which the Child stands in his mother's lap, and even more closely with the type which Dr. Bode has called the Madonna of the Balustrade. As in the Opera del Duomo lunette of 1489 the Child stands in front of his mother on a support over which her mantle is thrown. The introduction of drapery to the left seems to

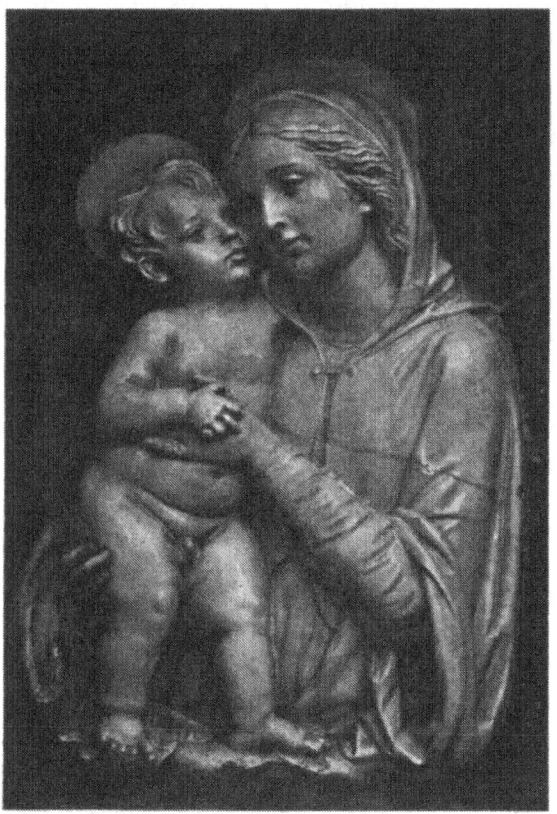

FIG. 97.—PIAZZA DELL' UNITÀ MADONNA.

have been determined by the medallion form. This Madonna, although not well known from publication, appears to have been very popular and was reproduced several times. Her tunic has a decorated neck band and her mantle is held together by a cord and two buttons.

Bibl. :

M., *D. R. A.*, 46, Fig. 20.

88 PORTRAITS AND SAINTS. 1498. Florence. Ospedale di S. Paolo. Loggia. Medallions. Diam., 1m. Photos., Alinari, 2462, 2465-2473; Brogi, 4688; Casts, Lelli, 437.

The hospital of S. Paolo built for convalescents in 1413, in the Piazza di

S. Maria Novella under the patronage of the Pinzocheri or Frati del terz'Ordine Serafico and of the Arte dei Giudici e Notai, became through maladministration so short of funds that in 1425 the Pope interested himself in its reformation, and again in 1451 commissioned S. Antonino, then archbishop of Florence, to restore order to its chaos. At this date some enlargement of the hospital appears to have been made, but the documents discovered by Cavallucci show that the Loggia of the hospital dates from 1489-1498.

This Loggia is not, as Rosselli and others affirm, to be attributed to Brunelleschi and executed after his death, but, as Fabriczy indicates, to a late fifteenth century architect like Antonio da Sangallo, the elder. Like the Loggia of the Innocenti hospital it is decorated with medallions in the spandrels of the arches and half medallions at the extremities. Vasari tells us that all the decorations are by Andrea della Robbia. This statement is somewhat too sweeping, since two medallions, those of the Healing of the Young and of the Old Man, are certainly to be assigned to another hand.

In design these medallions appear to have been thought of as separate entities, not as forming a composition. The two terminal half medallions present busts probably designed to look toward the middle of the Loggia, but as placed, they not only turn their backs on the rest of the medallions, but the inscriptions, if read from left to right, reverse the natural order. Beneath these inscriptions are others effaced by them. These earlier inscriptions are also reversed in order.

1. Half medallion with bust of Benino de'Benini (Fig. 98). Alinari, 2473.

This bust represents the spedalingo or governor of the hospital. Unglazed against blue background. In quality to be classed with Andrea's bust of Almadianus at Viterbo, 1510. The inscription ALL ANNO 1495 replaces an earlier inscription DE BENINI.

2. Medallion of Christ healing a young man. Alinari, 2463.

By some minor sculptor of the Robbia school.

3. Medallion of S. Francesco (Fig. 99). Alinari, 2471.

Andrea's S. Francesco of La Verna is here more sorrowful and sad. Stigmata are shown on hands and side. His nimbus is yellow, his robe gray green. The face and hands are glazed in flesh colour.

4. Medallion of S. Lodovico da Tolosa (Fig. 100). Alinari, 2466.

This resembles Andrea's S. Lodovico of the altarpiece at Gradara Rocca and Prato, grown older and more experienced. His nimbus and crozier are yellow; his tunic light blue, the mantle dark blue lined green. His stole, cord and gloves are white. The white of the eyeball is in strong contrast to the flesh colour of the face.

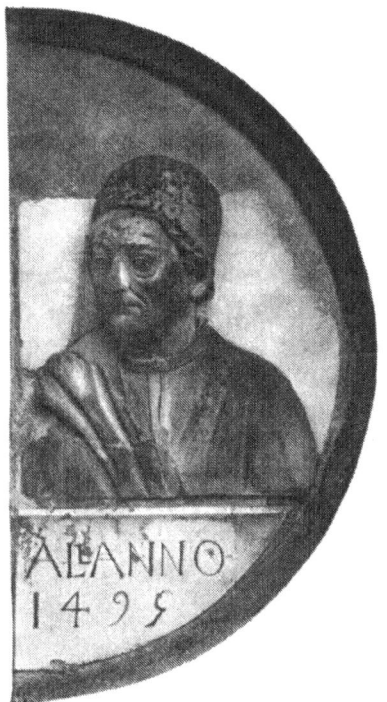

FIG. 98.—PORTRAIT OF PRETE BENINO.

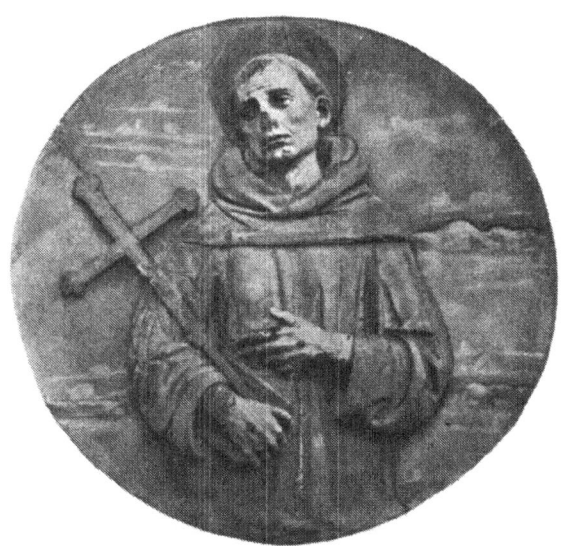

FIG. 99.—S. FRANCESCO.

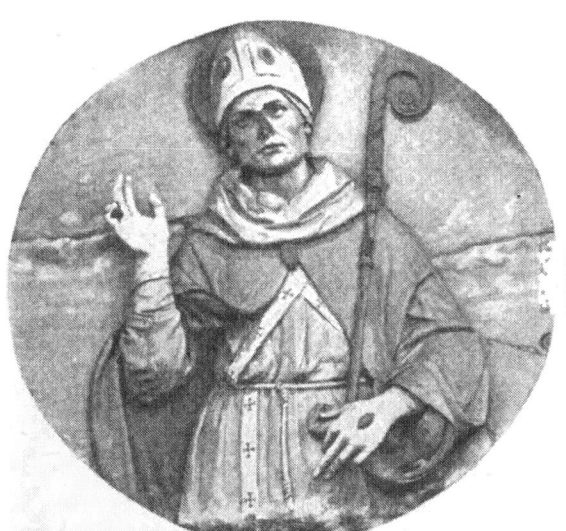

FIG. 100.—S. LODOVICO.

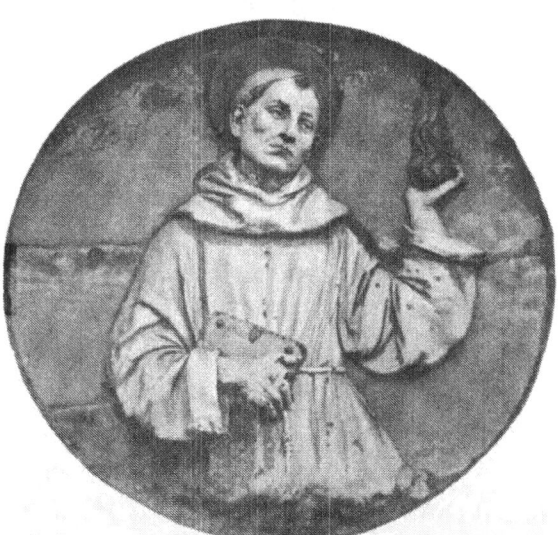

FIG. 101.—S. ANTONIO OF PADUA.

5. Medallion of S. Antonio of Padua (Fig. 101). Alinari, 2470.

This mild S. Antonio of Padua, with book and sacred flame, is here represented by Andrea as more serene than in the altarpiece at the Osservanza. His gown is gray blue, the book blue with yellow fittings, the flame violet. His face and hands are flesh colour.

6. Medallion of S. Bernardino of Siena (Fig. 102). Alinari, 2469.

This is one of the most expressive representations of this saint. His gown is gray blue, the book violet with yellow fittings, the disk blue with yellow monogram of Jesus.

7. Medallion of S. Bonaventura (Fig. 103). Alinari, 2465.

Older and more sorrowful than in the Cintola altarpiece at La Verna or in the vault of the Osservanza, S. Bonaventura, the Seraphic Doctor, wears a gray robe over which is a blue mantle adorned with violet seraph or cherub heads nimbed in yellow. He wears a white mitre, jeweled blue and yellow, and white gloves, and carries a yellow crozier and a violet book with yellow fittings. At his side hanging on a green band is his violet cardinal's hat. His face is flesh coloured.

8. Medallion of S. Elisabetta of Hungary or S. Rosa of Viterbo (Fig. 104). Alinari, 2468.

S. Elisabetta (or S. Rosa) who may be seen as a younger woman in the altarpiece at the Medici chapel in S. Croce, holds roses in her lap. The roses are single and double, as in the Salviati stemma at S. Giovanni in Valdarno. Her nimbus is yellow, her mantle blue gray, her robe greenish gray, her veil white, her face and hands flesh coloured.

9. Medallion of S. Chiara (Fig. 105). Alinari, 2467.

S. Chiara, clad in Franciscan nun's costume, is older and more careworn than in the Osservanza altarpiece. She carries her emblematic lily branch, and a book, green with yellow trimmings. Her face is flesh colour.

10. Medallion of Christ healing an Old Man. Alinari, 2464.

By some minor sculptor of the Robbia School.

11. Half Medallion with bust of Benino de'Benini (Fig. 106). Alinari, 2472.

Unglazed against a blue background. The inscription: DAL LANNO 1451 covers an effaced inscription PRETE + BENINO. That Prete Benino (or Bonino) was the spedalingo of the hospital is confirmed by Document No. 14, from the XVII century Ms No. 176, sent me by Mr. Rufus G. Mather. On the 27th of January, 1451, Pope Nicholas V appointed Prete Bonino di Antonio di Maso Bonini, at that time chaplain to the Archbishop Antonino, to serve as Governor, Chief, and Administrator of the Hospital. On the 13th of April, 1452 this was made an appointment for life. Prete Bonino died in 1497.

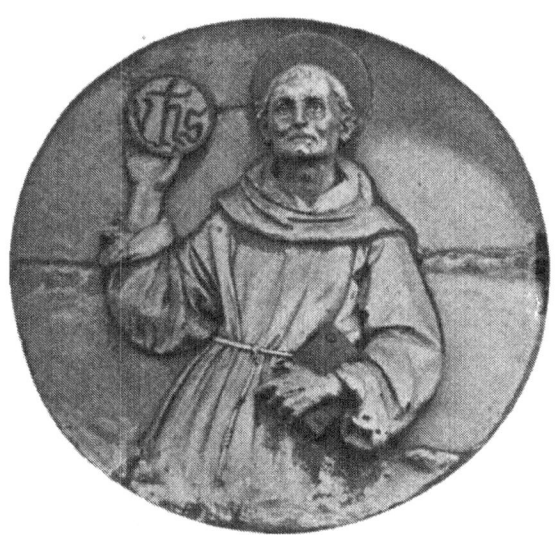

FIG. 102.—S. BERNARDINO.

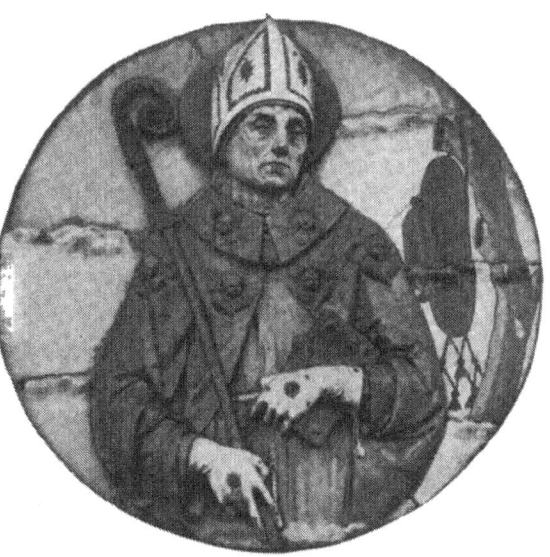

FIG. 103.—S. BONAVENTURA.

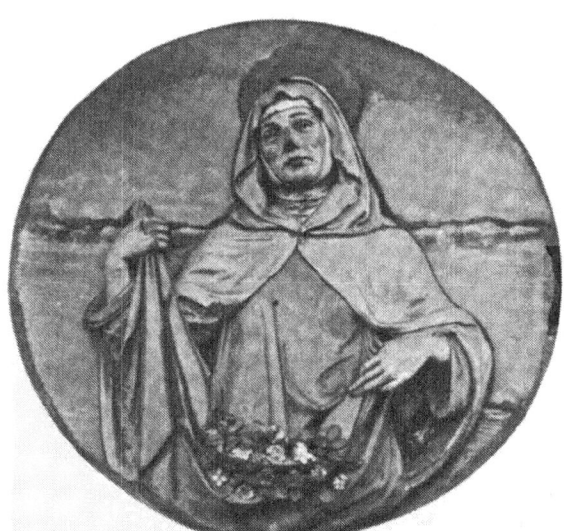

FIG. 104.—S. ELISABETTA.

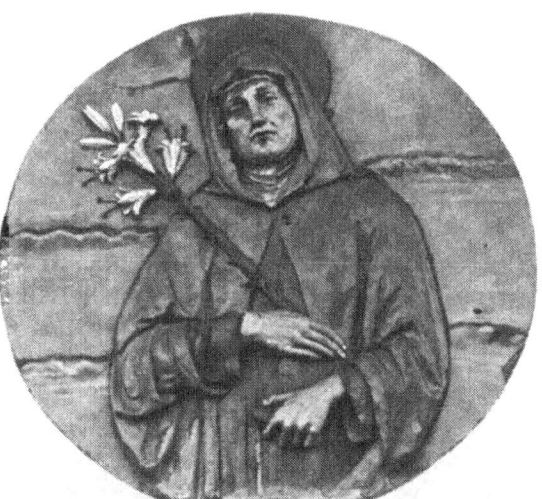

FIG. 105.—S. CHIARA.

Documents: [Revised by Mr. Rufus G. Mather.]

1.

"1490
Alla nostra muraglia e prima per opere e vetture
della pietra forte del pilastro del canto del porticho
e fornitura de capitelli e peducci a ricontro del
pilastro come chiaramente si vede al quaderno di
cassa segnata t a c 36 cosa per cosa l 376 s 19 dj 4
dadi 6 di giugno adj primo daghosto 1489. Resta
indrieto el costo della pietra forte avuta da lorenzo
di leonardo ridolfi posto la muraglia debi dare
alibro debitorj e creditorj segnato C a c 72 f 94 s 19
dj 4 da lire quattro luno — l 376 s 19 dj 4-   l 376 s 19 dj 4"

[Archiv. di S. Maria Nuova, Ospedale di San Paolo, Libro di Entrata e
Uscita, 1485-1496, segnato T, c 82t.]

2.

"1493
A giusto di piero muratore adj 24 di detto (dicenbre)
l 27 s 19 porto contanti sono per opere XV di maestro
e opere 38 di manovalj a s 16 el maestro e s 3
amanovalj misono nel murare la porta della chiesa
nella testa del porticho posto alibro debitorj e creditorj
segnato C. a c. 72 a conto della muraglia   l 27 s 19-"

[Idem, c. 91.]

3.

Alla nostra muraglia lire 14 s 17 chome apare al
quaderno di gabella di vino a c 22 per segatura dasse
correntj dalberj e abetj vechj e dasse di nocj per
le porte del porticho dadj 11 daghosto adi 22
di dicenbre 1494 posto allibro debitorj e creditorj
segnato C a c. 72 a côto della muraglia-   l 14 s 17-"

[Idem, c. 93.]

4.

"1495
A marcho di vicho da santa m' inpruneta f dodicj
larghi a soldi 133 luno pellaltro da di 10 di magio
adj (error in text) 1494 adj 16 di magio 1495 sono per
conto dembricj e gronde avute dalluj pel tetto
del portico e pellamattonato delle volte sopra
il portico sono l 79 s 16 levatj dal quaderno
biancho di gabelle di vino a c 26 posto lamuraglia

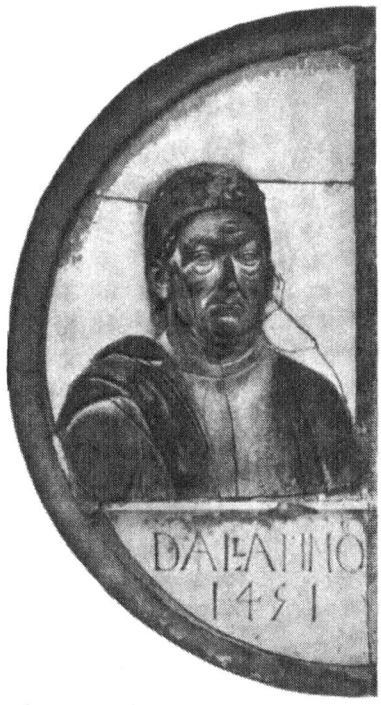

FIG. 106.—PORTRAIT OF PRETE BENINO.

debi debitore alibro debitorj e creditorj segnato
C a c 72-   l 79 s 16"
    [Idem, c. 95ᵗ.]

5.
      "1495
A lucha di tano legnaiuolo da samichele berteldj adj 30 di
detto (genaio) L due e s dieci sono per resto di cio che noj
abiamo avuto a fare insieme per insino a questo dj posto
a conto della muraglio alibro debitorj e creditorj segnato
C   a c 72 -   l 2 s 10"
    [Idem, c 95ᵗ.]

6.
      "1495
A tommaso dambruogio inbianchatore adj 10 di
febraio f 2 larghi per conto della inbianchatura del
porticho dallato di sopra e di sotto monto lire
cinquanta dacordo posto a suo conto alibro
pigionalj segnato C a c 88 al conto della pigione -   l 13 s 8"
    [Idem, c 96.]

7.

"1496
A giovanni di romolo scharpellino lavora gli
schaglionj del portico L 33 s 9 di contanti e
Gabelle dadj 21 di marzo 1494 adj p° di
luglio 1495 al quaderno di gabelle di vino
a c 30 posto a conto della muraglia alibro
debitorj e credi(tori) C a c 76-   l 33 s 9"
8.

"Andrea della robbia de dare L cientoquarantuna
s. 10 sono p(er) un chonto allibro debitorj e creditori
s⁽ᵗᵒ⁾ c c. 74   l 141 s 10 d-
  posto al detto (biancho s⁽ᵗᵒ⁾ E) c. 119
  [Arch. di S. Maria Nuova, S. Paolo, Libro Deb. e Cred., Rosso D. 1497-
1502, c. 22; published in *L'Arte*, XXI(1918), 208.]
9.

"1498 Andrea della Robbia de dare l 141 sol 10"
  [Milanesi Miscell. 40 III P c. 365, from Archiv. di Sa. Ma. Nuova,
Spedale S. Paolo, Deb. e Credit. 1498 al 1503, seg⁽ᵗᵒ⁾ D c 22.]
10.

"+1530
Andrea della robia da dare lib. cēto
quarātuna sol. diecj sono p(er) u°(uno) suo
chōto al detto lib(r)o rosso (D) c. 22 .... fj lib. 141   10"
  [Arch. di S. Maria Nuova, S. Paolo, Lib. Deb. et Cred., Bianco E, 1505-
1543, c. 119.]
11.

"Matt° dipacholo daterrarossa e conpnj (conpagnj) fornaciaj d(e)ono
dare adi 3 di giugn° 1497 f dua larghi doro in oro porto
Matt° angienj a uscita s⁽ᵗᵒ⁾ d c 51 -   f 2 l-   s-   d-
E adi p° di luglio f dua larghi doro porto
Matt° angienj - a uscita s⁽ᵗᵒ⁾ d c 52—   f 2 l-   s-   d-
E adi 14 di d(e)tt° f dua larghi doro porto
Simone dllarobja- a uscita s⁽ᵗᵒ⁾ d c 53—   f 2 l-   s-   d-
E adi 15 dachosto L dodici s 12 porto chontantj
- a uscita s⁽ᵗᵒ⁾ d c 54—   f- l 12 s 12 d-
E adi 18 dachosto f uno doro porto Simone
dllarobja - a uscita s⁽ᵗᵒ⁾ d c 55—   f 1 l-   s-   d-
E adi 9 di settebre f uno doro porto Simone
dllarobja- a uscita s⁽ᵗᵒ⁾ d c 56—   f 1 l-   s-   d-
E adi 17 di novebre f q(u)atr° doro porto
Matt° angienj- a uscita s⁽ᵗᵒ⁾ d c 59—   f 4 l-   s-   d-

E adi 20 di dicēbre f dua doro porto e
dtt° chontantj- a uscita s⁺° d c 62—   f 2 l-   s—   d—
E adi 17 di febraio f dua doro porto Matt°
angienj- a uscita s⁺° d c 65—   f 2 l-   s—   d—
E adi 31 di marzo f uno doro porto Matt°
angienj- a uscita s⁺° d c 66—   f 1 l-   s—   d—

13. 12. 12"

[Archivio di Sa. Ma. Nuova, San Paolo, Libro Rosso D 1497-1502, c
54.]

12.

"A Mattcho (should be Marcho) daterrarossa adi
14 di luglio (1497) f dua doro porto simone
di marcho dllarobja aspese di muraglia-
allibro rosso c 54-   f 2 l-   s—   d-"

[Archiv. idem, San Paolo, Entrata e Uscita D 1497-1502, c. 53.]

13.

"A Marcho dipacholo daterarossa fornaciaio
f uno doro porto simone dllarobja aspese
dimuraglia- allibro rosso c 54—   f 1 l-   s—   d-"

[Idem, c. 55.]

14.

"A Marcho daterrarossa fornacjaio f uno
doro porto simone dllarobja stacholloro
aspese dimuraglia— allibro rosso c 54—   f 1 l-   s—   d-"

[Idem, c. 56'.]

15.

"San Paolo dei Convalescenti.
Et perche in detto spedale e luogo nacevano molte dificulta e
disensione p(er) Breve di Niccola o/5 (quinto) di 27 di genn° delanno 1451
d° spedale e luogo fu visitato dal Reverendisimo Arcivescovo
antonino di Sᵗᵃ Mᵃ insieme con il visitatore di d° spedale
delordine de Minori Conventuali e del Proconsolo e furono
fatte molte ordinazioni e vi fu messo Governatore Capo
et aministratore Prete Bonino di Ant° Masi da Pitigniano
Cappellano in quel tempo di d° Mons Arcivescovo e
perche la sua administratione era ammovibile il d° Prete
ricorse lanno seguente a S sᵗᵃ e sotto di 13 di Aprile
1452 p(er) Breve del medᵐᵒ Niccola o/5 fu confermato in
spedalingo a vita con conditione che fusse obligato ogni
anno a rendere contto della sua administratione all Arcivescovo
di firenze come p(er) d° Breve e con altre conditionj come

p(er) le scritture di n° 25 et 26.

- - - - - -

- - - - - -

L'anno 1497 sendo vacato detto spedale p(er) lamorte di Prete
Bonino etc. etc. - - - -"

[Archivio di Stato, Schedario Manoscritti No. 176, busta 19, Carte del
Sec. XVII.]

Bibl.:

B. J., 20-21 note 3, 39, 62-63; B., *Kf.*, 16, 24; *A. S. A.*, II(1889),
3; *It. Pl.*, 93; *Denkm.*, 86; Burl., 53; C-M., 93-98(Doc.), 212 No. 41;
Cr., **188-192**, 306-307(Doc.), 326; C., s.v. del Benino; Demmin, 218;
D. D., 30; Fabriczy, *Brun.*, 259-262; Fantozzi, Guida, 533; Fov., 112;
M., *R. H.*, 80, 169-170; R. G. M., *L'Arte*, XXI(1918), 208(Doc.);
Michel IV, **125-126**; Perkins, *T.Sc.*, I, 198; *H. H.*, 143; Passerini
174 ff.; R., *D. R.*, **214-215**; *Sc. Fl.*, III, 179, **182**; Richa, III, 130;
Rosselli, 64; von Rumohr, II, 295 note; S., 117-118; Vas., II, 180
note 1; V., VI, 584.

89 MEETING OF S. FRANCESCO AND S. DOMENICO. Florence.
Ospedale di S. Paolo, Loggia. Lunette. H., 1.40m.; W., 2.70m.
Photos., Alinari, 2474; Brogi, 4689-4689a; Casts; Cantagalli, 405;
Lelli, 411-412.

The documents published from the Archives of the Hospital of S. Paolo
mention payments made in 1493 to Giusto di Piero muratore, for building
the doorway of the church at the head of the Loggia (Doc. No. 2 of the
preceding).

Over the doorway a lunette (Fig. 107) represents the meeting of S.
Francesco and S. Domenico. Cavallucci suggests that this had a specific
meaning for the hospital, since the Archbishop S. Antonino, a Dominican,
had struggled from 1451 to 1458 with the proprietors, the Pinzocheri,
Franciscans. But this struggle was long since past when the relief was
put in place. The union of Franciscans and Dominicans was the object
of the prayers and sermons of Savonarola and had a general significance
at the end of the XV century.

There can be little doubt that this fine composition came from the hands
of Andrea himself. It shows his sympathetic treatment of the faces and
hands of elderly people, such as we see in the medallions in the exterior of
the Loggia, in the bust of Almadianus (1510), and elsewhere. The demand for naturalistic colouring led to the imitation of flesh colour in glazing faces and hands, but in the medallions of the saints this was not alto-

gether successful, and here was abandoned altogether. Henceforth, the followers of Andrea frequently left the representation of flesh unglazed. Superficial painting was substituted for glazing. We may also note in the case of S. Domenico a somewhat sentimental pose, such as is found in Andrea's later lunettes at Pistoia and Viterbo. These characteristics are

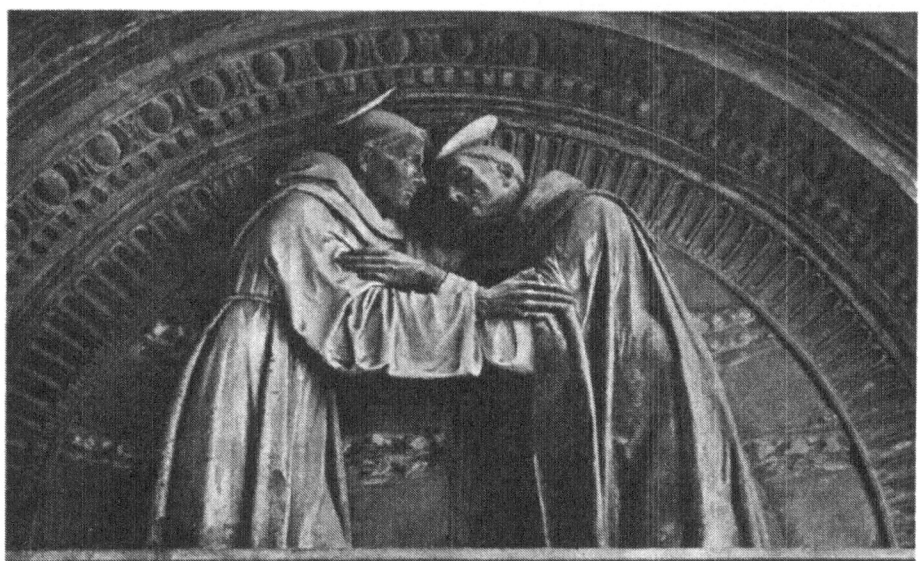

FIG. 107.—MEETING OF S. FRANCESCO AND S. DOMENICO.

not found in Luca's more majestic Visitation of Mary and Elizabeth in S. Giovanni fuorcivitas, Pistoia, to which this relief has been compared by André Michel.

S. Francesco is here clad in greenish gray and S. Domenico in violet black monastic gowns. The clouds in the background are in relief and exhibit more than the white and black of Andrea's earlier reliefs. They are here touched with a greenish yellow—forerunners of the golden clouds in the reliefs of some of Andrea's followers.

Bibl.:

See preceding; also: B., *Denk.* Taf. 270; *W. D. R.*, 8, Taf. 39; C-M., 79-80, 96 (Doc.); Cr., 189-190, 307 (Doc.); D. D., 31, Abb. 46; Fov., 112-113; R., *D. R.*, 212-214; *Sc. Fl.*, III, 179; S., 118-119, Abb. 127.

90 STEMMA OF LARIONE MARTELLI. 1498. Pistoia, Companile. Photo., Private.

Unframed and lacking the inscribed tablet is a shield of unusual form (Fig. 108) with decorated apices and a raised border. It bears the Martelli arms: gules, a griffin segreant or.

According to the official records Narione di Bartolommeo Martelli was

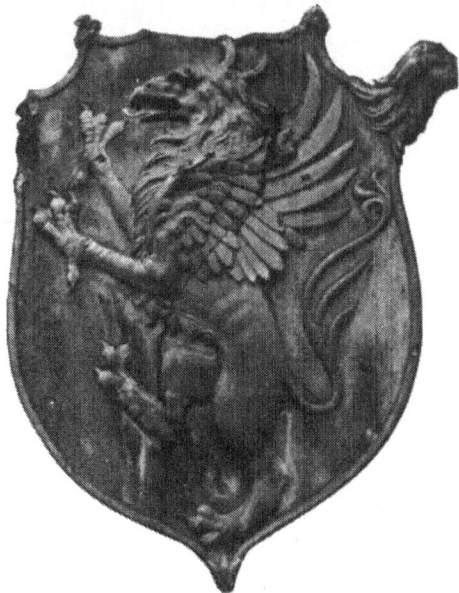

FIG. 108.—MARTELLI STEMMA.

appointed Podestà of Pistoia for 6 months, beginning Jan. 3, 1498. The Princeton Museum Priorista records a Larione di Bartolo Martelli as Prior of Florence in 1498 and 1511.

Document:

1. "1498 Nariono dj Bartolom° Martellj P⁴ 9 Gen°'"
[Archivio. di Stato, Sched. Mss. no. 496, c. 415.]

2. "Potãs Pistorij Reduct pro 6 mensibus cũ

Uno judice doctorato	cum sal(ario) libra
Uno Milite socio not°	rum duarum
Duobus alijs not(ar)ijs	milium quod
Quattuor domicellis	ringentarum
xv famulis inter	pro quolibet
quos sit unius constabilis	semestrj sibi
Quatuor equis	dand(o) a dicta
	comunitate pistorij

Ilarion bart' nic' de martellis - 6 mesi et di 15 init die 3 januarij 1498"
    [Archiv. di Stato, Reg. Extrins., 1508-1529, Segnãlo Tratte 71, c. 27.]

Bibl.:
    C., s.v. Martelli; Litta, s.v. Martelli; M., *L. D. R.*, 247-248; *R. H.*,
    115-116, Fig. 113; P., **451-453**; W., 152.

91 STEMMA OF GIOVACHINO GUASCONI.   1499.   Certaldo,
    Palazzo Pretorio.   Photo., Alinari, 8534*.

Within a wreath of eight bunches of fruit and flowers, of triplex with
tendency to quinqueplex composition, separated by transverse fluted rib-

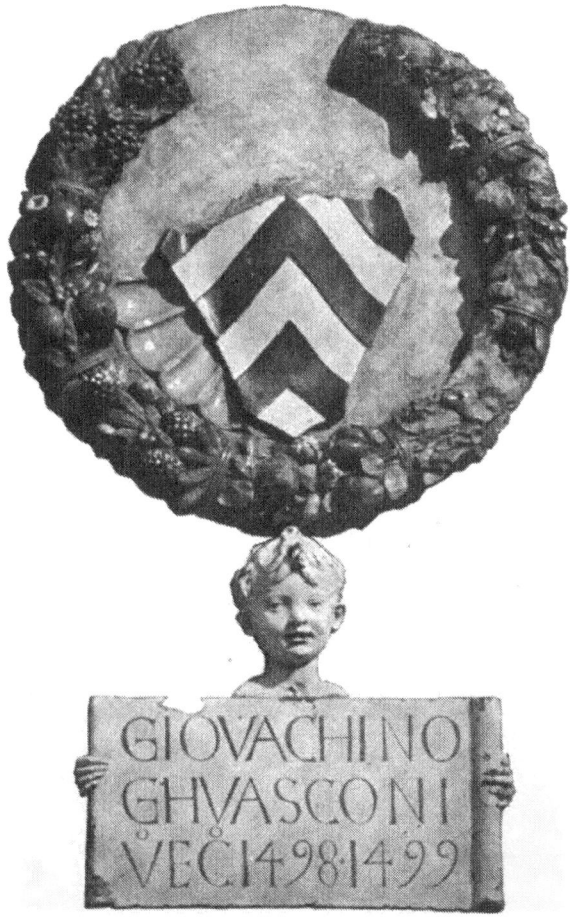

Fig. 109.—Guasconi Stemma.

bons, is a blue fluted disk against which is set a kite shaped shield (Fig. 109) bearing the Guasconi arms: Argent, three chevronels sable (the second surmounted by a crosslet of the same).

Below, a putto of unusual beauty unfolds a horizontal scroll inscribed:

GIOVACHINO
GHVASCONI
V(ICARI)O E C(OMMISSARI)O 1498 ✦ 1499 ·

Bibl.:

C., s.v. Guasconi; M., *R. H.,* 117, Fig. 114; W., 147.

ANDREA DELLA ROBBIA

1500-1510

92 THE ASCENSION. La Verna. Chiesa Maggiore. Altarpiece. H., 4.57m.; W., 3.08m. Photo., Alinari, No. 9834.

This altarpiece (Fig. 110), at one time the Altare Maggiore, has been in the Ridolfi chapel at La Verna since 1601. It may have been ordered by Ridolfo di Pagnozzo Ridolfi who in 1477 set up in Robbia ware his stemma at S. Giovanni in Valdarno, and who in Florence was a Prior in 1480, Gonfaloniere in 1486 and 1490. The Christ raises both hands to exhibit the stigmata. The four couples of adoring angels, though not so elaborately conceived as those of the Crucifixion altarpiece at La Verna, are nevertheless full of Andrea's grace and charm. The landscape, with its bluish green mountains and its brown and green trees, is somewhat more realistic than that in Luca's Ascension relief in the Cathedral of Florence. The kneeling group, consisting of the Madonna and the Eleven Apostles, is perhaps less noble than the group in Luca's Ascension, but is more skilfully composed than the other similar groups from Andrea's atelier. Their eyes have yellow irises, and violet brows, lashes and pupils.

The double frame, with its fruit and cherub friezes, its billet and cord mouldings, is closely related to the frame of the Crucifixion altarpiece in the Cappella delle Stigmate, and the predella is decorated with the network of cubes found upon the wall tiles of that chapel. We may note that the bunches of fruit are more complex and rise from slenderer blue vases; at the top of the frame is a disk enclosing a cherub head from which radiate golden streams of light. The cherub heads of the inner frieze are all set perpendicular to the direction of the frieze, and clouds beneath or beside them are omitted.

Bibl.:

Beni, 360; B., *Kf.*, 16; Burckhardt, II, 434; Burl., 119; Compendio della Divozione e Meraviglie del sagro Monte della Verna (Cesena, 1826), 83; C-M., 92, 256 No. 331; Cr., 170, 220, 331; Fov., 108; Graziani, 147-148; M., *Scribner's*, 1893, 697; Mencherini 251-254; P., Pr. Mus. Copy, 282; Reumont, *Kunstbl.* No. 206(1831); R., *D. R.*, 178; *Sc. Fl.*, III, 163; Vas., II, 198.

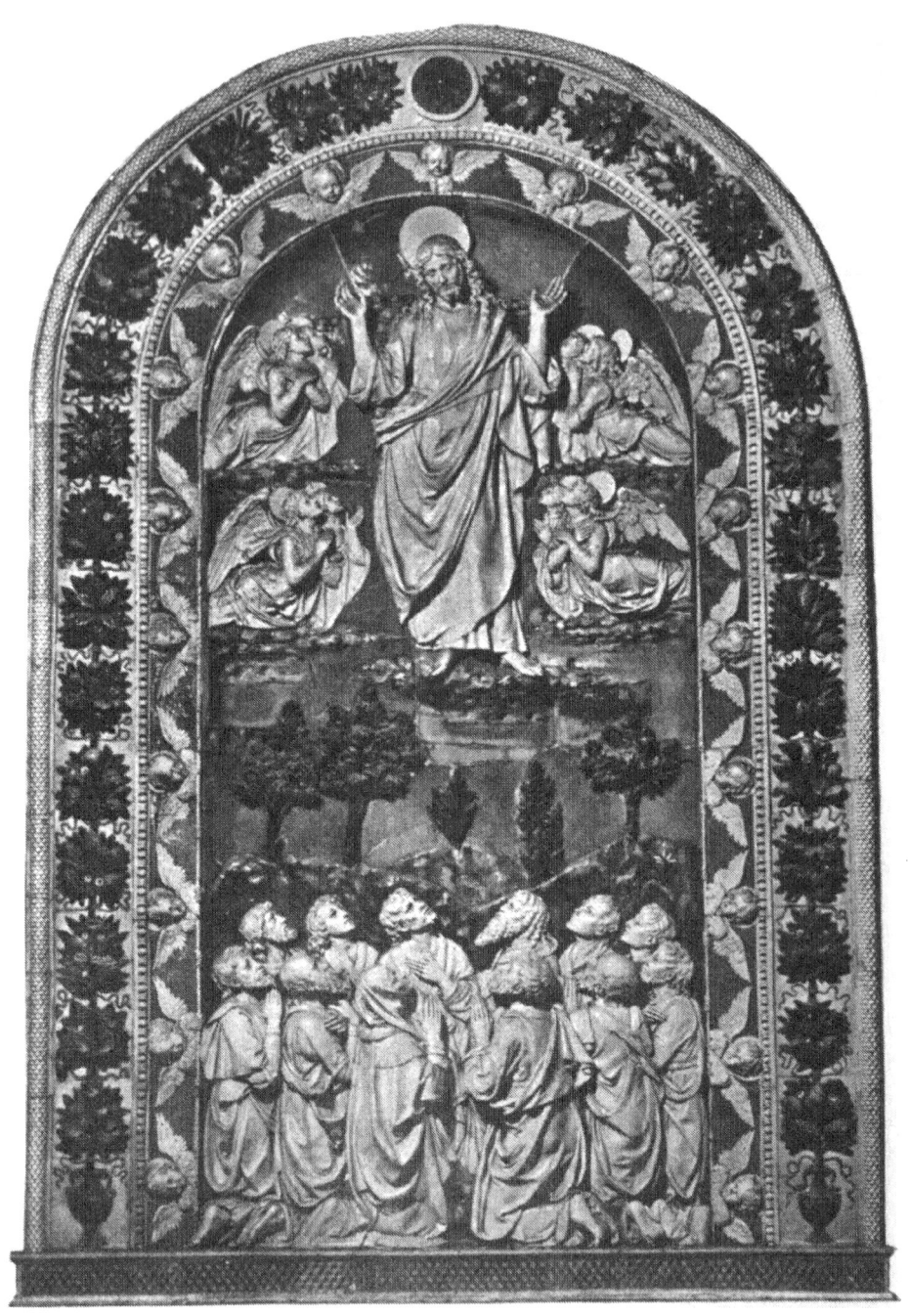

FIG. 110.—THE ASCENSION. LA VERNA.

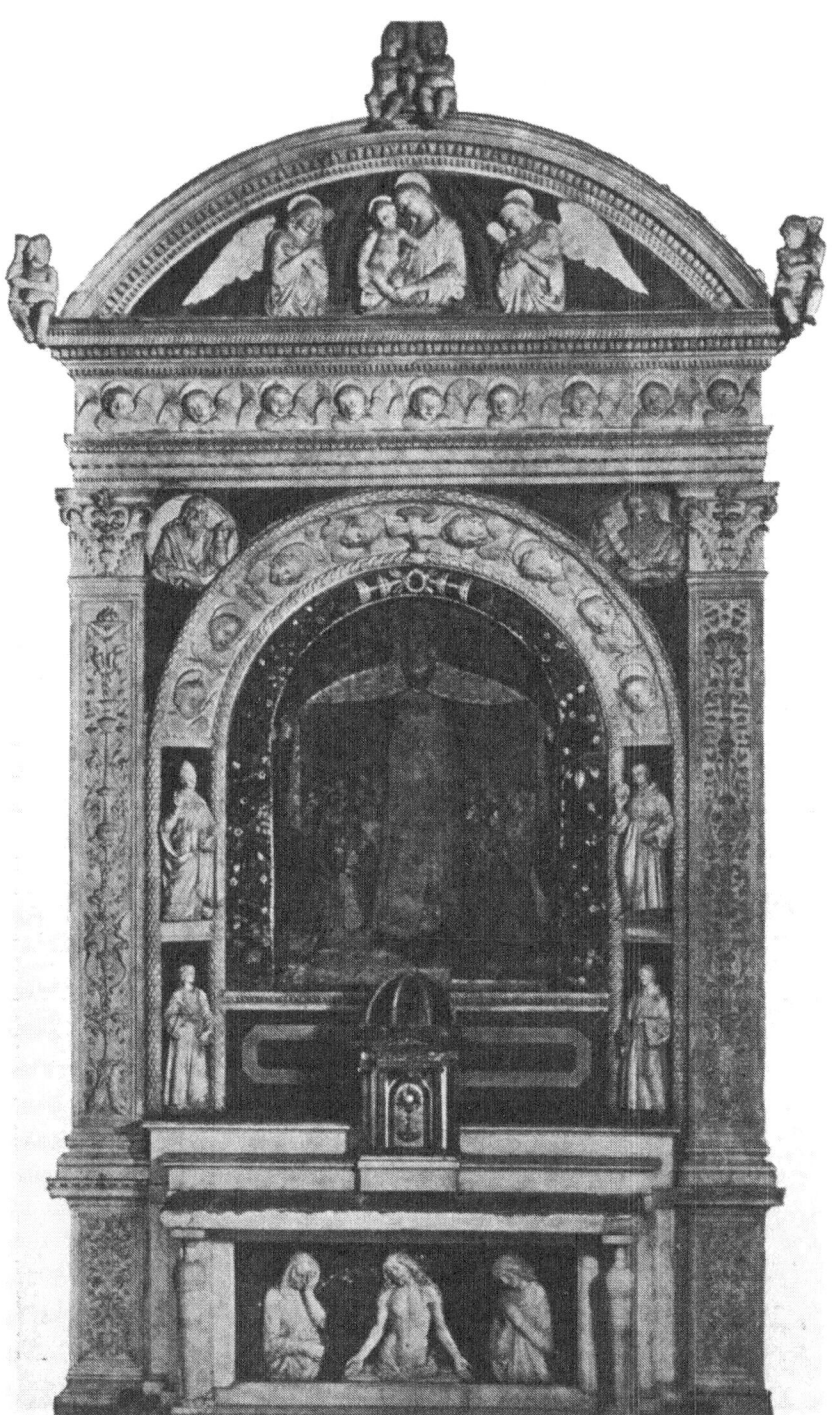

FIG. 111.—MARBLE ALTARPIECE. S. MARIA DELLE GRAZIE, AREZZO.

93 ALTARPIECE, CHIEFLY MARBLE; WITH MADONNA. PROPHETS, SAINTS, PIETÀ. Arezzo. S. Maria delle Grazie. Altarpiece. H., 7.20m.; W., 3.70m. Photos., Alinari, 9759-9766.

Vasari opens his account of Andrea della Robbia with praise for his work in marble and cites this altarpiece as evidence of his skill. It is strange that no other work of Andrea's in marble is known to exist. The general composition of the altarpiece (Fig. 111) may have been due to Benedetto da Maiano, who designed the porch of this church in 1495. The slender

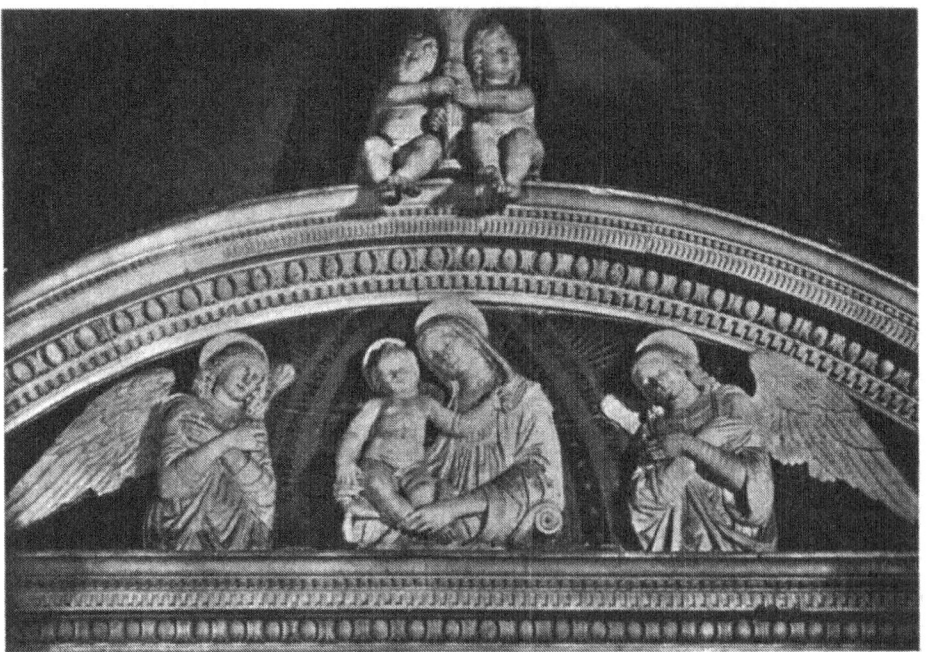

FIG. 112.—LUNETTE, MADONNA AND ANGELS.

pilasters with their candelabra decoration do not suggest Andrea della Robbia and could never have been designed or executed by Giovanni della Robbia. Giovanni, however, may well have executed the hanging garlands and some of the architectural details. The Madonna and angels of the lunette (Fig. 112) are related to Andrea's Madonnas of 1489 and 1505; and the four Saints in niches—S. Donato, with the grotesque symbol (for the dragon's head) (Fig. 113), S. Bernardino of Siena, with the monogram of Jesus (Fig. 114), and the two deacon martyrs SS. Stefano and Lorenzo—are reflections of the same saints as portrayed during this period by Andrea della Robbia.

The altar front (Fig. 115), representing the Pietà or Christ in the sepulchre, flanked by his Mother and S. Giovanni, may without hesitation be attributed to Andrea himself. It recalls to mind Luca's treatment of the same theme as a background to the Federighi tomb, but chastened by Andrea's greater refinement. The Mater Dolorosa is superior to Luca's as an

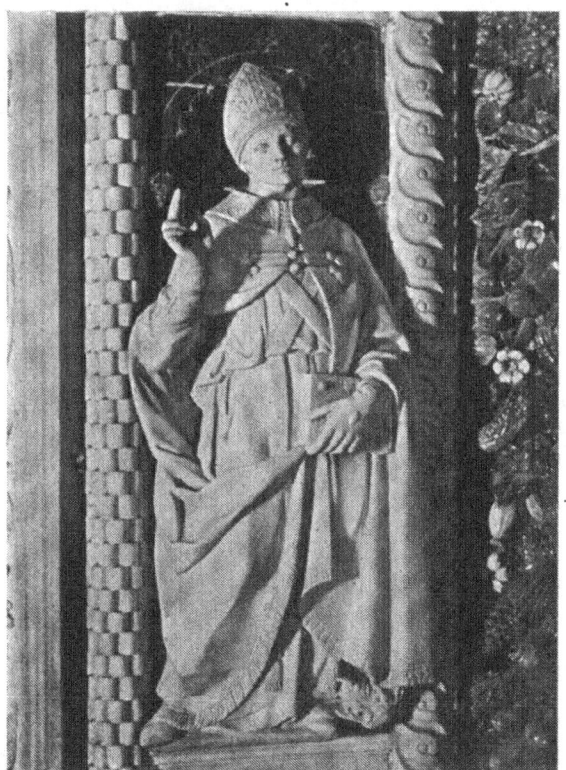

FIG. 113.—S. DONATO.

expression of natural sorrow; the Christ standing in his tomb displaying the stigmata was admired enough to be repeated several times in terracotta; and the S. Giovanni, with folded hands, though somewhat sentimental is at least the equal of Luca's.

Bibl.:

B. J., 39-42, 72-73; B., *Kf.*, 15; *Denk.*, 84, Taf. 263; *A. S. A.*, II (1889), 3;·Burl., 112; C-M., 82-88, 224 No. 114; Cr., 191-195, 325; 327; Fov., 111; Geymüller, II, 3-4, Bl. 1; M., *Sc. Mag.*, 1893, 697; Michel, IV, 121-122; Perkins, H. H., 144; R., *D. R.*, 195-197; *Sc. Fl.*, III, 171-172; S., 120-121, Abb. 132; *Tour du Monde*, 1880, 238-240; Vas. II, 179; Vita, 55.

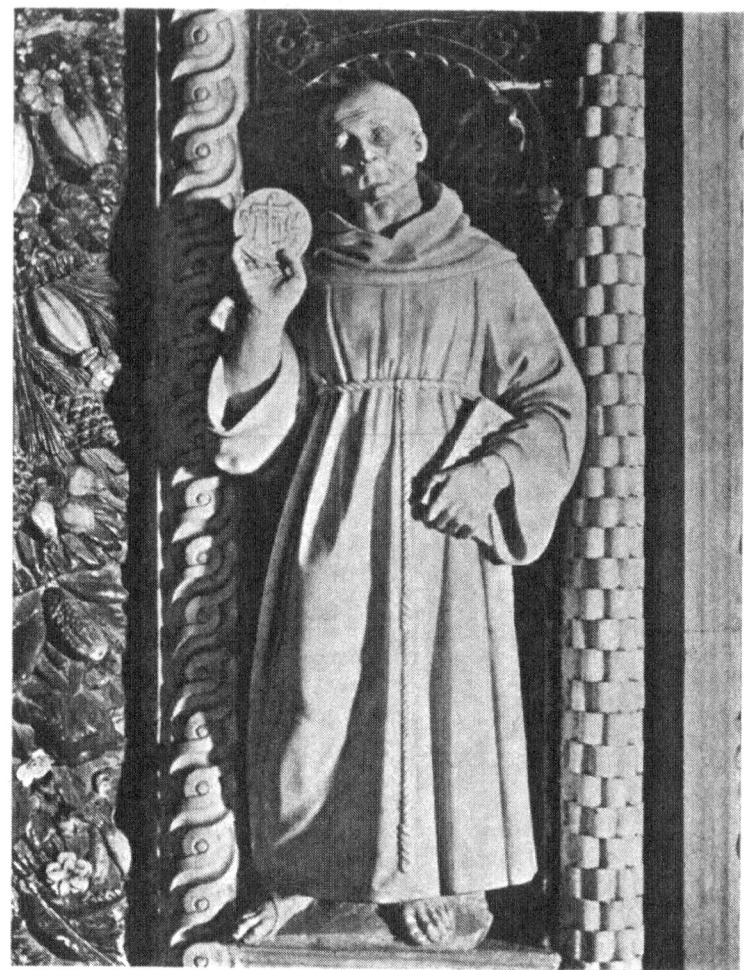

FIG. 114.—S. BERNARDINO.

94 PIETÀ OR CHRIST IN SEPULCHRE.   Florence.   Piazza di S. Spirito.   Monte di Pietà.   Lunette.   Photo., Alinari, 2514; Casts, Cantagalli, 403; Lelli, 383.

A fine replica (Fig. 116), with slight variations, of the Pietà in the marble altar at S. Maria delle Grazie, Arezzo.   White figure on blue, sepulchre violet.

Bibl.:

B., *Denk.*, 86, Taf. 262; Cr., 195, 325; D. D., 30, Abb. 45; R., *D. R.*, 200; *Sc. Fl.*, III, 173; S., 121, Abb. 133.

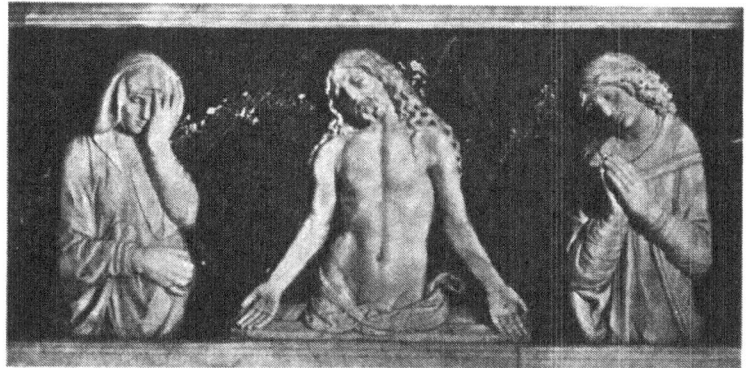

FIG. 115.—PIETÀ.

95 FRAGMENTS OF AN ALTARPIECE. S. Angelo in Vado (near Pesaro). S. Chiara and S. Maria. Photos., Private.

The two churches S. Chiara and S. Maria share between them fragments of this fine altarpiece (Figs. 117-121). It was apparently a round-headed relief with a frame consisting of a garland of fruit rising probably from blue and violet vases and set between an outer egg and dart and an inner cord moulding. Two fragments of the curved portions of the frame are in S. Chiara and two vertical sections are in S. Maria. The predella must have been unusually attractive. The church of S. Chiara preserves

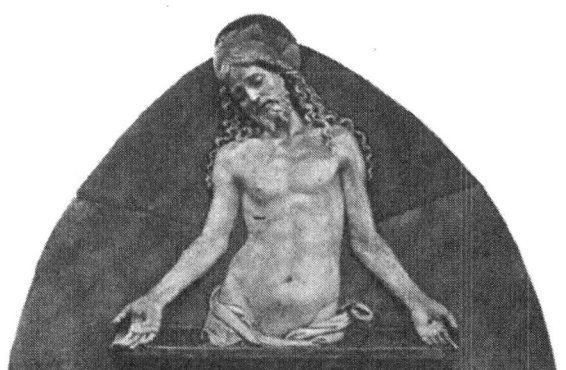

FIG. 116.—PIETA. PIAZZA DI S. SPIRITO.

three reliefs: (1) a Deposition or Lamentation over the dead Christ; (2) the kiss of Judas; and (3) two soldiers, a portion of the preceding composition or of a relief representing the Capture of Christ. The latter reliefs are unique in Robbia monuments.

The subject of the main relief is not clearly revealed by the fragments. At the top we may place the bust of God Father and angels (Fig. 117), awkwardly recomposed in rectangular form in S. Chiara. He probably had both hands raised, as at Montepulciano, Foiano, and Memmenano, but was surrounded by angels rather than cherub heads. From him radiate plastic

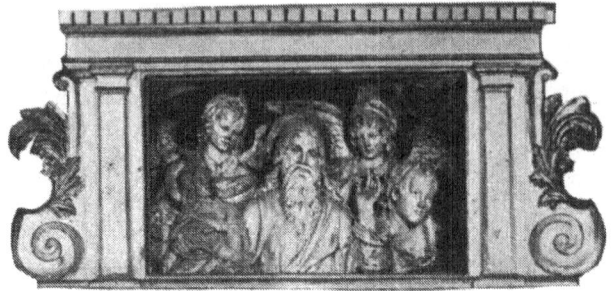

FIG. 117.—GOD FATHER.

streaks of golden light, to be seen also in the blue background of the adoring angels (in S. Maria). Between these angels we may place the Dove (in S. Chiara). There still remain two busts and two heads—the bust of a youthful saint or angel is exceptionally fine—for which it is not easy to find an appropriate position. Possibly as was the case at Montepulciano the altarpiece served as a ciborium, with a central recess for a painting. In this case the busts and heads might be in someway arranged as adorers of the Sacred Host.

It is a great misfortune that of this central relief there are such scanty remains.

Bibl. :

Anselmi, *A. S. A.*, VIII(1895), 447; Antaldi, *A. e S.*, 1887, 226, 234, 243; Cr., 354; V., *A. S. A.*, I(1888), 90.

96 CORONATION OF THE VIRGIN AND RESURRECTION OF CHRIST. Aquila. S. Bernardino, Cappella Oliva-Vetusti. Round-headed relief. H., 3.10m.; W., 2.50m. Photo., Fallerini.

The church of S. Bernardino at Aquila was begun in 1454 and finished in 1472. In the chapel of the Oliva-Vetusti family are busts of Canon Ascanio Oliva and other distinguished members of the family. The altarpiece (Fig. 122) was ordered from Florence by some member of this family. Originally it was probably surrounded with a Robbia frame, of cherub heads and possibly a fruit garland; later the frame was abandoned and

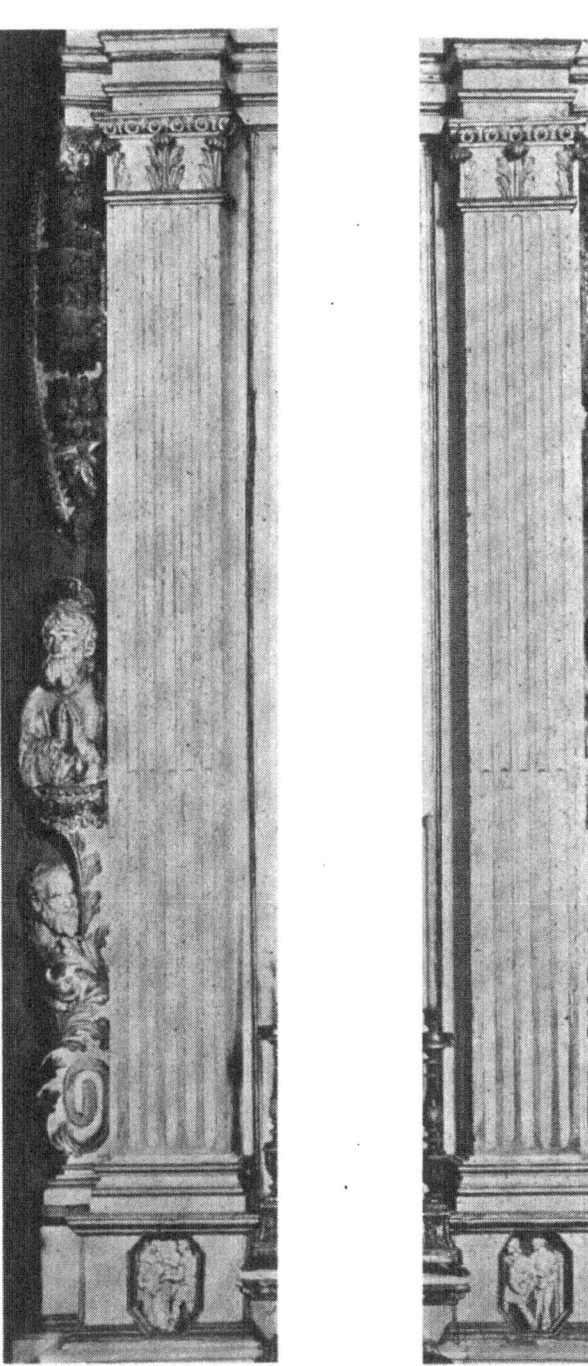

FIGS. 118-119.—FRAGMENTS OF ALTARPIECE. S. ANGELO IN VADO.

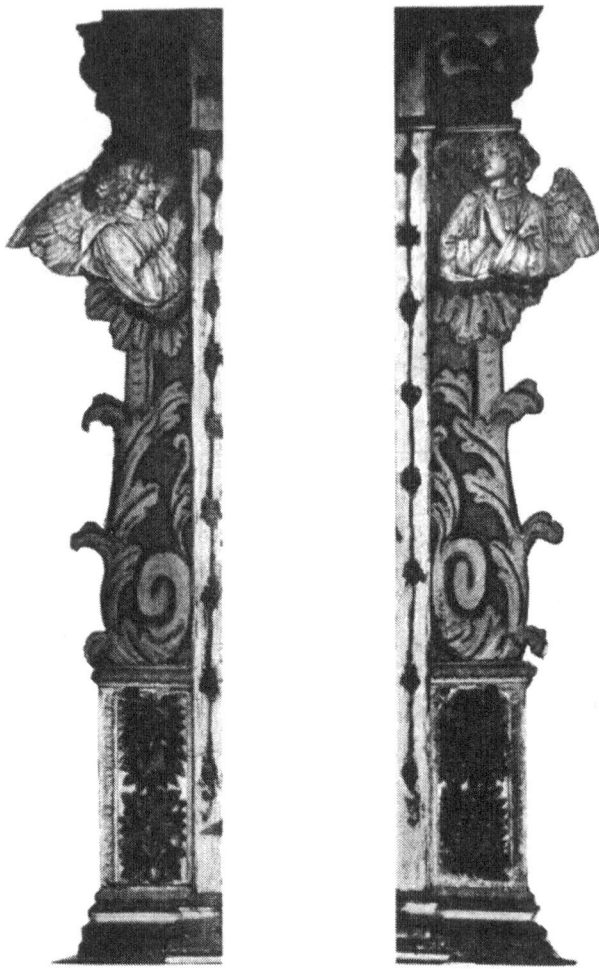

FIGS. 120-121.—FRAGMENTS OF ALTARPIECE. S. ANGELO IN VADO.

greater height given to the central relief by the addition in plaster of Rococo angels and clouds.

The composition is a combination of the Coronation and the Resurrection. The unity of the scene as to subject consists in the thought of a resurrected Christ about to ascend to a heaven where his Mother is being crowned as Queen. About the sarcophagus are four sleeping soldiers and a civilian (donor? or Joseph of Arimathea). The four standing saints are S. Benedetto with his aspergill, accompanied by his sister S. Scholastica to the left, and S. Chiara and S. Francesco to the right.

The Coronation scene is more closely related to the Assisi than to the

Siena composition. The mandorla or glory is composed of cherub heads with a single pair of wings, emphasized above and below by larger cherubs with two pairs of wings. Four couples of trumpeting angels surround this group. These are arranged so as to form a group with the four couples of adoring angels in the Resurrection scene. Some of these angels seem to have been modelled by an apprentice hand, but the principal figures may be attributed to Andrea himself. The Coronation scene is finer than that at S. Fiora and very nearly equal to that at Assisi; the Resurrection is Andrea's best interpretation of that subject, possibly similar to the Resurrection he made for S. Frediano in 1501, certainly finer than the Resurrections at the Accademia, at S. Fiora, and in the Berlin Museum.

The predella scenes of the Annunciation, the Nativity and the Adoration of the Magi (head of kneeling king and of Child repaired) are modifications of those at Assisi. The Circumcision scene, based possibly on the Circumcision made for the Bacci family at Arezzo, is somewhat similar to that in the Ascension relief at Foiano. Mouldings and pilasters as in the altarpiece in S. Francesco, Foiano.

Bibl. :
Bindi, 324, Tav. 162; B., *Kf.*, 25; Bonafede, 137; Burl., 65, 112; C-M., 223 No. 109; Cr., 331; Leosini, 202; Manieri, *Faenza*, VI(1918), 30-32; Perkins, *H. H.*, 143; Serra, 53-55, Tav. 34-35.

97 THE CIRCUMCISION. Arezzo. S. Francesco, Cappella Bacci. Altarpiece (formerly).

Vasari mentions an altarpiece by Andrea della Robbia representing the Circumcision, made for the Bacci family and presumably for a chapel of theirs in S. Francesco. The whereabouts of this altarpiece, if it still exists, is unknown. The composition however, is probably preserved in a predella piece of the large altarpiece in S. Bernardino at Aquila.

Bibl. :
Vas., II, 179.

98 MADONNA AND CHILD BETWEEN ANGELS. 1505. Pistoia. Duomo. Over entrance portal. Lunette. H., 1.60m.; W., 2.20m. Photo., Alinari, 10159.

This relief (Fig. 123) is important as an example of Andrea della Robbia's work when he was seventy years of age. Documents show that it was completed in August 1505.

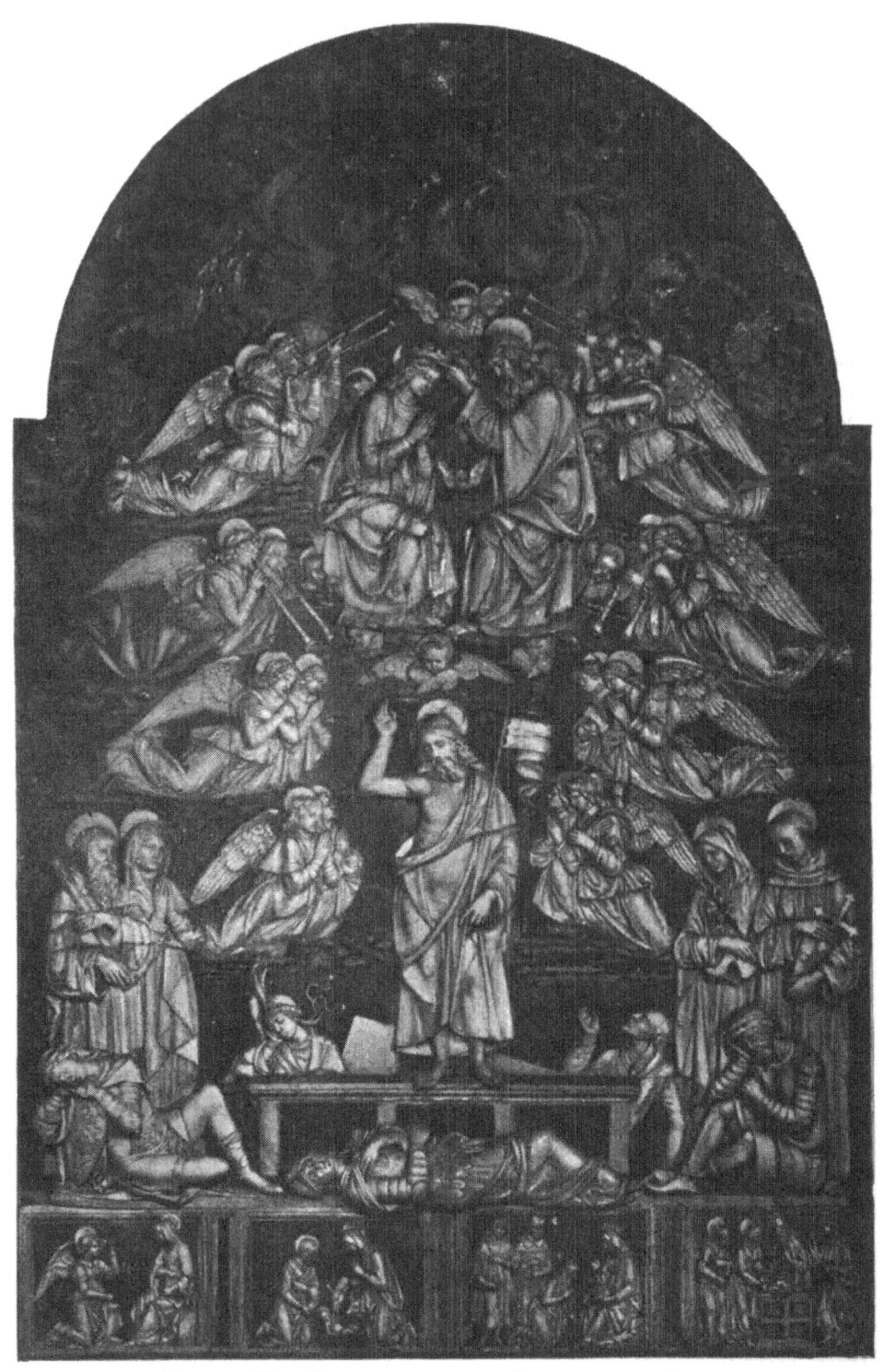

FIG. 122.—THE CORONATION AND THE RESURRECTION. AQUILA.

The fact that the relief was widened, thus decentralizing the composition and necessitating some patchwork to the right was probably not Andrea's fault. Let us note some of the details. The Madonna is the same individual who presides over the entrance of the Cathedral at Prato, but here somewhat older, modelled more summarily and with less effort. Her eyes have violet brows, lashes, pupils, and yellow irises. The nude standing Child has one arm about her neck, the other rests against her breast—a

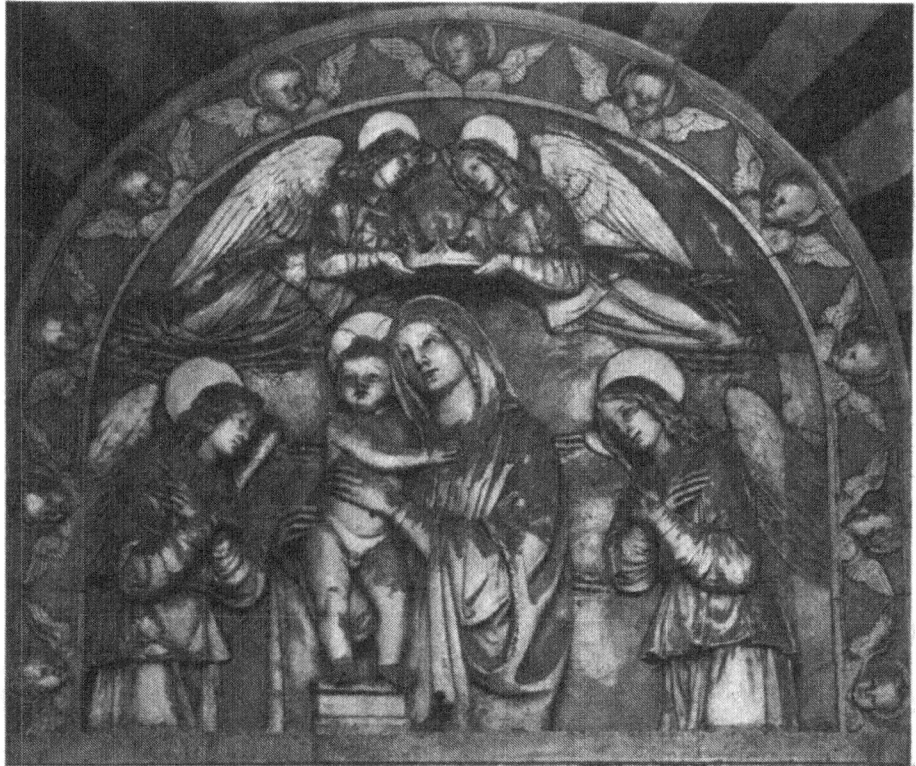

FIG. 123.—LUNETTE OF MADONNA AND ANGELS. PISTOIA CATHEDRAL.

motive inherited from Luca and used a number of times in Andrea's atelier. For the first time the Child is posed upon a pedestal. At either side is an adoring angel. Above are two angels wearing pectorals, holding a lilied crown over the Madonna's head. The cloud shadows are marked with dark violet. A frieze of eleven cherub heads, white on blue, set between plain mouldings frames the relief.

Documents: [Quoted from Bacci, II, 167-185.]

1.

"Lunedi a di xxx detto [di decembre 1504].

Da entrata di denari per debiti vecchi a dì soprascritto da l'opera di san jacopo contanti lib. lxx e per detta da pietro del benino e giovanni binducci proveditore e per noi pagorno a andrea di marcho dalla robbia pago lui per arra di uno mezo tondo e una nostra donna s'è obrigato a fare sopra alla porta del duomo, di terra chotta smaltata, per prezo di fior. cinquanta d'oro larghi chome piú larghamente apare per uno foglio, schritto per me bartolomeo zeloni e soscritto di mano di detto andrea, el quale è in mano di pietro del benino proveditore soprascritto   lib. 70, sol. -.

Posto a libro [A] cc. 170, 171."

[Arch. comunale di pistoja — Opera di s. Giov. e Zenone, Giornale del libro A, cod. 236, c. 148.]

2.

"Andrea di marcho dalla robbia de' dare a dì 30 di dicembre [1504] contanti lib. lxx ebbe per noi da l'opera di san jacopo e per detta da pietro del benino e giovanni binducci proveditore pago lui per arra di uno mezo tondo e una nostra donna s'è obrigato a fare di terra chotta smaltata sopra alla porta del duomo choperto il mezo tondo di schagle di quella medesima materia per prezo di fiorini cinquanta d'oro in oro larghi chome apare per uno foglio di mano di bartolomeo zeloni e soscritto di mano di detto andrea cioè in questo a uscita a c. 171   lib. 70, sol. —.

E a dì 3 di maggio 1505 contanti fior. ij d'oro larghi e per noi da pietro del benino pago el figliuolo c. 171   lib. 14, sol. —.

E a dì detto per staia xij di grano a lib. vj, sol. vij li mandai a firenze e sol. xxviij pagai di vettura in tutto c. 171   lib. 41, sol. 12.

E a dì 22 detto lib. lx ebbe per noi da pietro sino a dì 17 di detto in tanto vino c. 171   lib. 60, sol. —.

E a dì 15 di luglio contanti fior. iiij° d'oro larghi ebbe per noi da pietro del benino c. 171   lib. 28, sol. —.

E a dì 9 d'ogosto contanti lib. xxxv sol. vij ebbe lui per noi da pietro a c. 172   lib. 35, sol. 7.

E a dì 19 detto contanti lib. xxv sol. v ebbe lui per noi da Pietro a c. 172   lib. 25, sol. 5.

E a dì 22 detto contanti lib. lxij sol. iiij.° ebbe per noi da pietro a c. 172   lib. 62, sol. 4.

E sino a dì 7 detto contanti sol. vj pago lui per chomprare spugna e cholla c. 172   lib. —, sol. 6.

E sino a dì 16 detto per once 5 di linseme cioè olio di linseme ebbe da gherardo dondoli c. 172   lib. —, sol. 5.

E a dí 25 detto contanti lib. 13 pago lui per noi da pietro per resto di fior. 50 d'oro larghi monta la vòlta c. 172   lib. 13, sol. –."

[Arch. comunale di pistoja — Opera di s. Giov. e Zenone, Libro A, cod. 235, c. 172'.]

3.

"Sabbato a dí iij di maggio [1505].

A uscita di denari per le porti del duomo a dí soprascritto, a andrea di marcho dalla robbia a dí soprascritto contanti fiorini dua d'oro larghi e per noi da pietro del benino pago el figluolo   lib. 14, sol. –.

E a dí detto per staia xij di grano a sol. lxvij lo stajo montano lib. xl sol. iiij.ᵉ e sol. xxviij pagai di vettura a mandarlo a lui a firenze in tutto

Posto a libro [A] cc. 170, 171.   lib. 41, sol. 12.

...A uscita di denari per le porti a dí soprascritto [giovidí a dí xxij detto] a andrea di marcho dalla robbia lib. lx ebbe per noi da pietro del benino sino a dí 17 detto in tanto vino cioè   lib. 60, sol. –.

Posto a libro [A] c. 171."

[Arch. comunale di pistoja — Opera di s. Giov. e Zenone, Giornale del libro A, cod. 236, cc. 150'.]

Bibl.:

Bacci, II, 167-185 (Doc.); B. J., 71-72; Beani, 33; B., *Kf.*, 16, 24; *A. S. A.*, 1889, 3; *Denk.*, 87, Taf. 271; Burckh., 360; C-M., 106 (Doc.), 243 No. 232; Cr., 195-196, 310 (Doc.), 330; Fov., 115; Gualandi, VI, 33-35 (Doc.), Giglioli, 85-87 (Doc.); Repetti, IV, 433 (Doc.); R., *D. R.*, 201-202; *Sc. Fl.*, III, 173-175; Tigri, *Discorso* (Doc.); Vas., II, 197.

99 ARCHIVOLT AND VAULT DECORATION.   1505.   Pistoia. Duomo, Porch decoration.   Photo., Alinari, 10160.

In front of the Cathedral at Pistoia is a porch of which the central opening is arched, giving access beneath a barrel vault to the main entrance. (1) The exterior arch is decorated with a terra-cotta fruit frieze, capped with a white shell set against a blue background.   (2) The vault has a charming coffered ceiling (Fig. 124), large yellow rosettes against a blue ground, framed by a series of leaf and dart and egg and dart mouldings. On each side of these square coffers are broad bands, each containing two bunches of fruit and flowers of triplex composition, set dos-a-dos, white on blue.   At the angles are smaller cofferings, each with a white ball against blue backgrounds.

Documents: [Quoted from Bacci, II, 167-185.]
I.

"A uscita di detto [martedí a dí xv di luglio (1505] per la vòlta a di soprascritto sino a dí soprascritto sino a di xij detto a tonio di giovanni vetturale da san donnino contanti sol. xxx pago lui per noi da pietro del

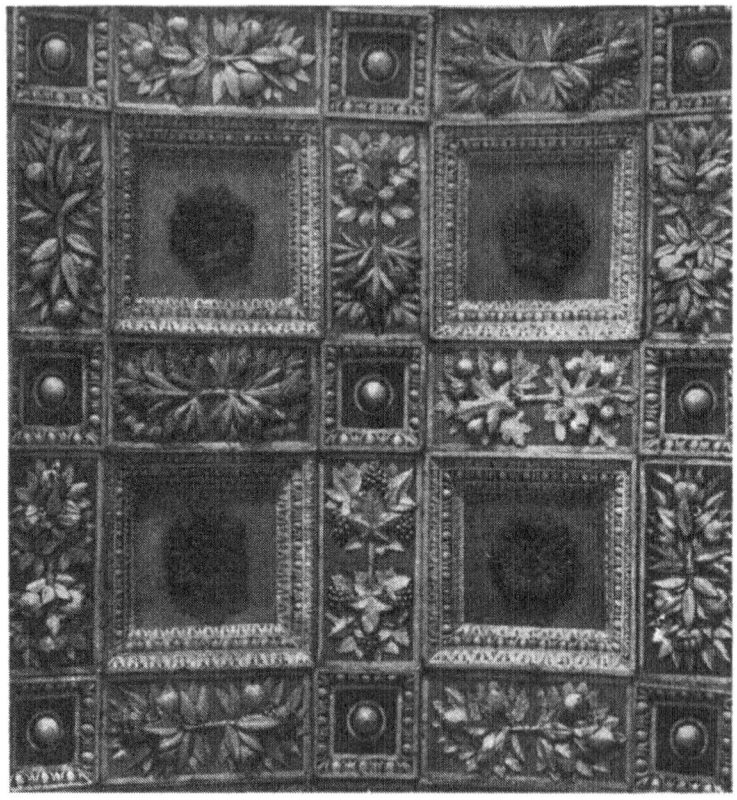

FIG. 124.—COFFERING OF VAULT.

benino per parte di vettura della vòlta rechò da firenze   lib. -, 30 sol.

...E a dí 15 detto a andrea dalla robbia contanti fior. iiij.° d'oro larghi ebbe per noi da pietro   lib. 28, sol. -.

...E a dí 19 detto per libbre 1, once 8 d'auti, per uno choppo e per spugna per lavare e marmi   lib. -, sol. 7, 4.

E a dí detto a Filippo di m.° marcho contanti sol. xx pago lui per parte di 2 opere di muro e 3 di manuale aiutò alla vòlta   lib. 1, sol. -.

E a dí detto per 12 some di rena a mariotto del frascha contanti pago lui posto a libro c. 171   lib. -, sol. 10."

[Arch. Comunale di Pistoja — Opera di s. Giov. e Zenone, Giornale del libro A, cod. 236, c. 152.]

2.

"Die xxvj augusti 1505.

Prefati etc. servatis servandis etc. stentiorno ad andrea de la rubia per havere fatto quello megio tondo, sopra la magiore porta della Chiesa Catedrale, di terra cotta, ducati cinquanta larghi d'oro nuovo etc. mandarunt.

Die dicta.

Item, simili modo et forma etc. stentiorno lire setanta sol. sette piccoli i quali si sono spesi in pezi 1900 d'oro fino comprato a firenze a lire tre soldi x piccoli il cento et peza cinquanta d'oro comprato qui in pistoja a lire quattro soldi 4 piccoli il cento per mettere a oro il soprascritto lavoro, in tutto lire setanta soldi x piccoli etc. mandarunt.

Die dicta.

Item, simili modo et forma etc. stentiorno ad antonio da san donino vetturale per la vectura di some xjx del soprascritto lavoro di firenze qui et per la gabella del dicto lavoro et la gabella de' 1900 pezi d'oro fino di firenze in tutto lire xjx soldi octo piccoli etc. mandarunt etc.

Die dicta.

Item, simili modo et forma etc. stentiorno lire quarantadue piccoli per le spese facte ad andrea de la rubia, uno suo figlio et uno gargione et il cavallo dí xxviij, cioè·da dí xxvj di luglio insino a dí 24 d'agosto presente, stati in pistoja per fare murare et mettere a oro il soprascritto lavoro etc. mandarunt etc."

[Arch. Comunale di Pistoja — Opera di s. Giov. e Zenone, cod. 227, c. 62'.]

3.

"A uscita de' denari per le porti a dí soprascritto [mercholedí a dí xxx di luglio 1505] contanti fior. cinque d'oro larghi per 1000 pezi d'oro fine pago andrea dalla robbia per adornare la vòlta   lib. 35, sol. -.

E a dí detto a antonio di giovanni da san donnino per gexo e chalcina e vettura di detto gexo recò per la vòlta contanti lib. v, sol. ij, den. 6 pago lui
      lib. 5, sol. 2, 6.

E a dí detto sol. xxij contanti sono per tanti si spese in el charretto di santa Maria dell'Umiltà el quale s'achattò per portare via pietra essen'è auto marmi   lib. 1, sol. 2.

Posto a libro c. 171.

...A uscita de'denari per la vòlta a dí soprascritto [sabbato a dí ij d'ogosto 1505] a giovanni binducci contanti sol. xlv ebbe per ghabella di due some della vòlta di terra chotta   lib. 2, sol. 5.

E adi detto a giuno chontanti f iiij doro larghi pago lui per sue fatiche delle fighure depinse sopra alle porta   lib. 28 sol. -.

posto alibro c 171

...A uscita de' denari per la vòlta a dí soprascritto [lunedí a dí iiij·

d'ogosto 1505] a Filippo di m.° marcho contanti sol. xxx pago el suo gharzone. Posto a libro c. 171   lib. 1, sol. 10.

...A uscita di denari per la vòlta a dí soprascritto [giuovidí a dí vij, d'ogosto 1505] a filippo di m.° marcho contanti sol. xlij pago lui e staio uno di grano del mio ebbe el fratello per sol. xlj in tutto   lib. 4, sol. 3.

E a dí detto a andrea dalla robbia per uno penello e libbre 1/2 di cholla. Posto a libro c. 171   lib. -, sol. 6.

...A uscita di denari per la vòlta a dí soprascritto [sabbato a dí viiij.° d'ogosto 1505] a andrea dalla robbia contanti lib. xxxv, sol. vij ebbe lui per noi da pietro   lib. 35, sol. 7.

E a dí detto a filippo di m.° marcho contanti lib. iiij.° sol. vj pago lui el gharzone   lib. 4, sol. 6.

E a dí detto a Maso di tovano per viij some di rena a bigongia contanti sol. 7   lib. -, sol. 7.

E a dí detto a niccolo zeloni per 1205 mattoni chotti lib. x, sol. xvij per sol. 18 il cento   lib. 10, sol. 17,

E a dí 12 detto a filippo di m.° marcho contanti sol. xx pago el fratello e sol. xxv pago el gharzone suo in tutto   lib. 2, sol. 5.

E a dí detto a giusto d'antonio scarpellino contanti fior. tre d'oro larghi per noi da allexandro fabroni   lib. 21, sol. -.

E a dí detto per uno manovale per portatura di 300 mattoni s'ebbeno di chaxa bernardo sozifanti contanti sol. ij den. 8. pago lui   lib. -, sol. 2, 8.

Posto a libro c. 172.

...A uscita di denari per la vòlta a dí soprascritto [sabbato a dí xvj d'ogosto 1505] contanti fior. tre d'oro larghi per 600 pezi d'oro fine chonprò pietro del benino per la vòlta   lib. 21, sol. -.

E a dí detto a gherardo dondoli per once v d'olio di linseme ebbe da lui andrea dalla robbia   lib. -, sol. 5.

E a dí detto a filippo di m.° marcho contanti lib. tre ebbe lui   lib. 3, sol. -.

E a dí 19 detto contanti lib. x, sol. x pago antonio di giovanni da san donnino vetturale per la vòlta cioè per 300 pezi d'oro fine recò da firenze   lib. 10, sol. 10.

E a dí detto a andrea dalla robbia contanti lib. xxv, sol. v pago lui per noi da pietro   lib. 25, sol. 5.

E a dí detto per piú cholori e fare portare le scagle in sul tetto contanti sol. xiiij.° pago andrea dalla robbia   lib. -, sol. 14.

E a dí 21 detto a francesco centi contanti sol. xlij per 50 pezi d'oro manchò   lib. 2, sol. 2.

Posto a libro c. 172.

...A uscita di denari per la vòlta a dí soprascritto [giuovidí a dí xxj d'oghosto 1505] a andrea di cino per xvij subielli s'ebbeno da lui per fare centine contanti sol. xxxxiiij.° pago lui   lib. 1, sol. 4.

E a dí detto a niccolò zeloni per subielli di braccia 5 l'uno contanti sol.

lib. -, sol. -.

Posto a libro c. 172.

...A uscita di denari per la vòlta a dí soprascritto [venardí a dí xxij detto 1505] a andrea dalla robbia contanti lib. lxij, sol. iiij.° ebbe per noi da pietro del benino   lib. 62, sol. 4.

E a dí detto a dua fachini per riportare el legname del ponte lib. -, sol. 6.

E a dí detto a filippo di m.° marcho contanti lib. ij pago el figliolo

lib. 2, sol. -.

E a dí detto a niccolò zeloni per ischafili di chalcina contanti lib. viij, sol. ij pago lui   lib. 8, sol. 2.

E a dí detto a uno manovale per spegnere chalcina e rendere di quella s'acchattò contanti sol. otto

lib. -, sol. 8.

E a dí detto a Mariotto del frascha per some xxvj di rena

lib. -, sol. 17, 4.

E a dí 23 detto a filippo di m.° marcho contanti sol. l pago al figlio

lib. 2, sol. 10.

E a dí detto a antonio di giovanni da san donnino per ghabella e vettura di 19 some di terra chotta recò da firenze contanti lib. xliiij.° sol. iij ebbe per noi da pietro del benino   lib. 44, sol. 3.

E a dí detto a giusto d'antonio scharpellino contanti lib. xiiij° ebbe per noi da pietro   lib. 14, sol. -.

Posto a libro c. 172.

...A uscita di denari per la vòlta a di soprascritto [lunedí a dí xxv detto 1505] a andrea dalla robbia contanti lib. xiij ebbe per noi da pietro del benino per resto di fiorini 50 d'oro montò la vòlta   lib. 13, sol. -.

E a dí detto a pietro del benino contanti lib. xlij ebbe per la spesa fece a andrea soprascritto e dua gharzoni e la mula da dí 26 di luglio sino a dí 24 d'ogosto [1505]   lib. 42, sol. -.

Posto a libro c. 172.

...A uscita di denari per la vòlta a dí soprascritto [giuovidí a dí xxviij detto 1505] a filippo di m.° marcho contanti sol. xxx pago michele suo gharzone   lib. 1, sol. 10.

E a dí detto a Mariotto del frascha per 42 some di rena recò a san zelone contanti sol. xxviij pago lui   lib. 1, sol. 8.

E a dí detto a filippo di m.° marcho contanti sol. xliiij.° pago el figlio

lib. 2, sol. 4.

E a dí 30 detto a filippo soprascritto contanti sol. xlij pago el figlio e sol. x pago michele in tutto   lib. 2, sol. 12.

E a dí detto a giusto d'antonio scarpellino contanti pago lui lib. 14, sol. -."

[Arch. Communale di Pistoja — Opera di s. Giov. e Zenone, Giornale del libro A, cod. 236, c. 153.]

4.

"Filippo di m.° marcho dí detto de'avere a dí 13 d'ogosto [1505] per opere 14 di m.°[aestro] cioè di lui e opere 18 di manovale aiutorno a andrea dalla robbia achonciare la vòlta a sol. 22 el m.°, e sol. 10 el m.°[manovale] montano   lib. 24, sol. 8.

E a dí 22 detto per opere 2 di m.° e 2 di m.° aiutò a choprire la vòlta
                                                                          lib. 3, sol. 4.

E a dí 30 detto per una opera di m.° e una di m.° aiutò rimettere per mano el porticho del duomo   lib. 1, sol. 12.

E de' avere per le 5 partite prime rinpetto che sono opere 5 di m.° e 6 di m.° aiutò alla vòlta   lib. 8, sol. 10.

[*Aggiunta*] E de' avere a dí 17 di dicembre 1506 per iiij opere di m° e iiij m°(manovale) certi legni mese a tetto dettino di suo d'achordo chon lui
                                                                          lib. 6, sol. 7.

[Arch. Comunale di Pistoja — Opera di s. Giov. e Zenone, Libro A, cod. 235, c. 174.]

Bibl.:

B. J., 71-72; Bacci, II, 167-185 (Doc.); Car., A. I. D. I., V (1896), Tav. 21; Cr., 196, 326; M., Sc. Mag., 1893, 694; R., *D. R.*, 205-206; *Sc. Fl.*, III, 176-177; Repetti, IV, 438 (Doc.).

100 MADONNA, SAINTS AND ANGELS. 1507-1508. Viterbo. S. Maria della Quercia. Three lunettes. One, H., 1.20m.; W., 2.80m.; the others, H., 0.82m.; W., 1.62m. Photos., Alinari, 11847, 11849, 11851; Moscioni, 4256-4258.

In 1417 a pious peasant of Viterbo, for the protection of his vineyards, ordered of Maestro Martello, known as Monetto, an image of the Madonna. This rude painting, executed on a roof tile, was suspended on an oak tree by the roadside. It performed miracles, became the object of worship, and to it pilgrimages were made. Its history is preserved in a series of frescoes in the Palazzo Comunale of Viterbo. On this site the Jesuits were permitted in 1464 to erect a church and monastery, but their tenure was short lived and on September 29, 1469 it came into the possession of the Dominicans. It is to the efforts of Fra Filippo Strozzi of Florence, who with his brothers ruled the monastery in 1507 and 1508, that we owe the façade of the church and its decoration. The architectural design is attributed to Giuliano da San Gallo, but the central portal was executed by Bernardino di Giovanni, a sculptor of Viterbo, and the lateral portals by Domenico da Firenzuola, in 1504 to 1506. The three terra-cotta lunettes over the

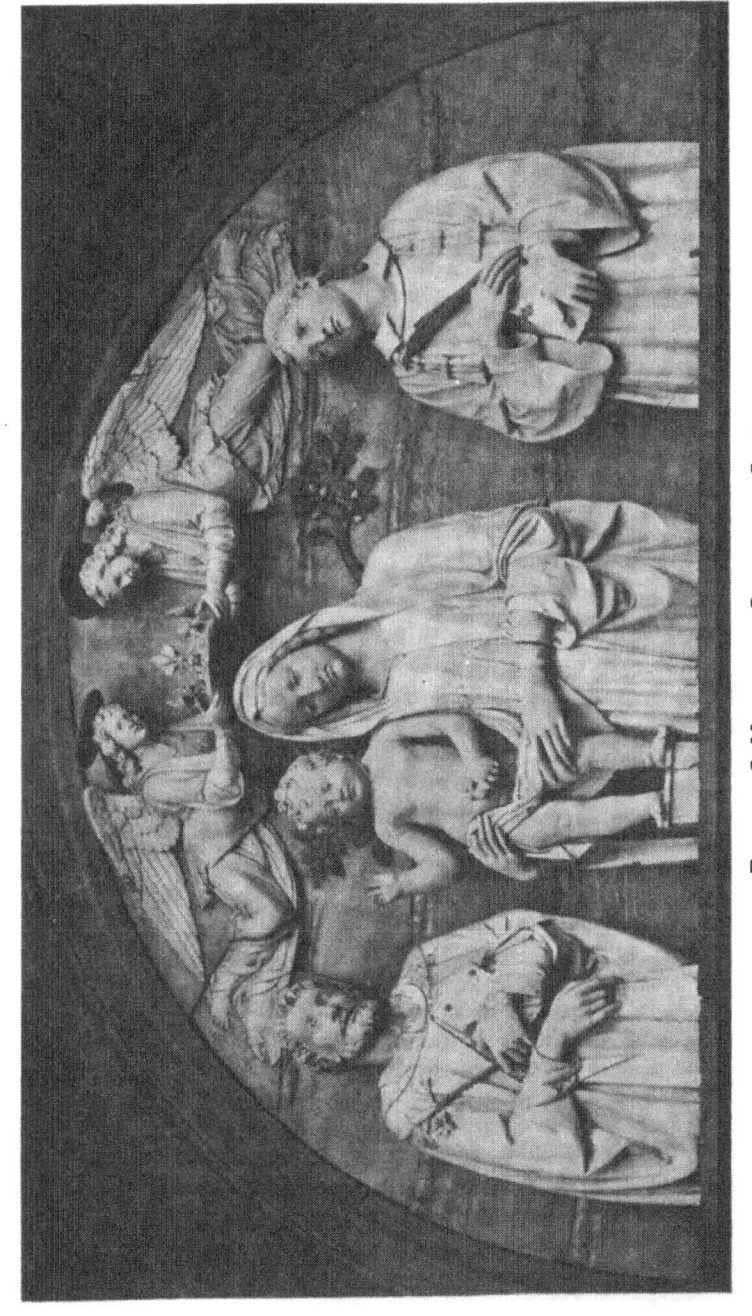

FIG. 125.—S. MARIA DELLA QUERCIA AND SAINTS.

doors are documented works of Andrea della Robbia, made in Florence in 1507 and 1508.

1. The central lunette (Fig. 125) represents the Madonna della Quercia crowned by angels between S. Domenico and S. Lorenzo. The figures are glazed white and set against a blue sky with clouds in relief. Green is used for the oak tree, lily stem and palm; yellow for the clasps and studs of the books, also for the irises of the eyes; green and blue and yellow for the jewels of the crown.

S. Domenico, patron saint of the monastery, carries a book and lily. His hands are carefully modelled. His present head is modern and forms a discordant note in the composition. The Madonna is less graceful than Andrea's Madonnas at Prato (1489) and Pistoia (1505) and recalls somewhat Giovanni's Madonna of 1497 at S. Maria Novella. The Child stands upon a pedestal, as at Pistoia; holds a bird as in Monetto's painting, and is blessing. His sparse curly hair recalls Giovanni's Christ Child in the lavabo at S. Maria Novella. S. Lorenzo, patron saint of Viterbo, is less charming than Andrea's representation of that saint in the lunette of the Prato Cathedral (1489), but superior to Giovanni's S. Lorenzo in the Tabernacolo delle Fonticine (1522). The angels holding the jewelled crown lack the grace of the angels in the S. Croce altarpiece. They alone wear haloes, set almost perpendicular to the plane of the relief.

2. The lunette over the door to the left represents S. Pietro Martire between two adoring angels (Fig. 126). His hood and mantle should be conceived of as black over the white tunic. He carries a book with yellow fittings and a green palm. A dagger is plunged into his shoulder and a large knife into his head. The huge knife resulted in splitting the head from the crown to the neck.

3. The lunette over the door to the right represents S. Tommaso d'Aquino between two adoring angels (Fig. 127). S. Tommaso is represented as the founder of the order, holding in his right hand a model of a church or monastery and in his left a book with yellow fittings. On his breast is the fixed star or sun, golden in colour, one ray pointing to the model of a church.

Documents: [Revised by Mr. Rufus G. Mather.]

1. "MDVIJ adj 30 giugnio

. . . . . .

. . . . . .

. . . . . .

e addj xviii detto (settembre) ducati

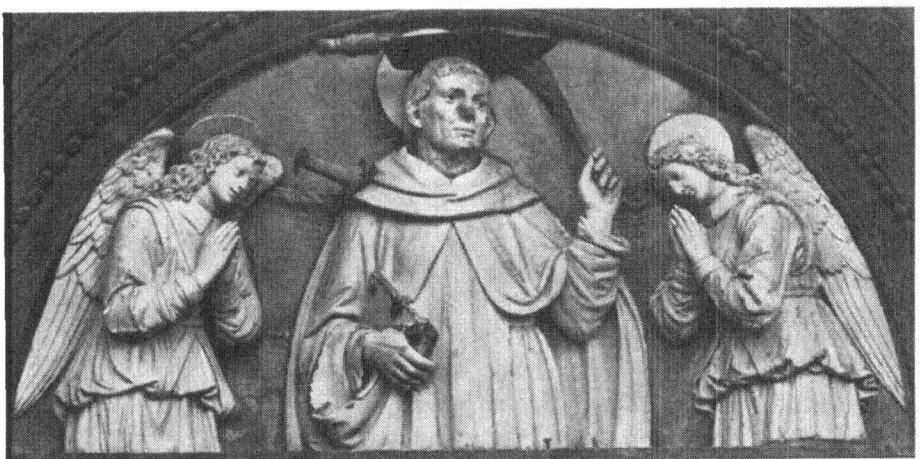

FIG. 126.—S. PIETRO MARTIRE AND ANGELS.

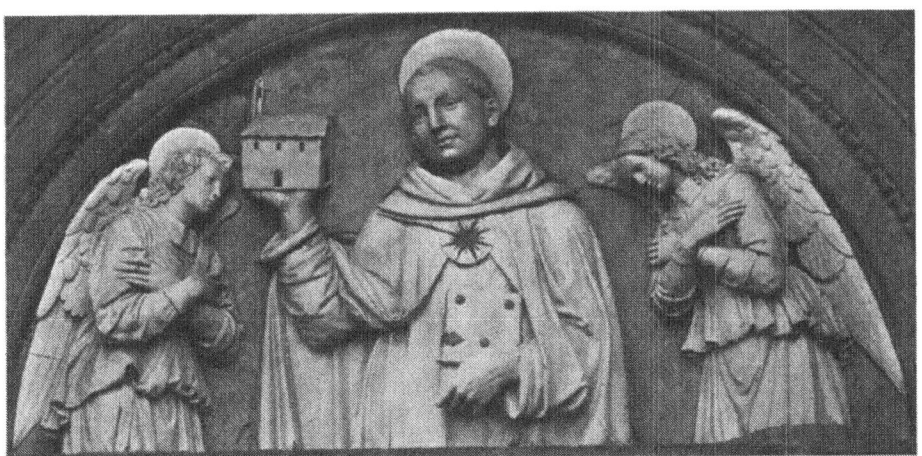

FIG. 127.—S. TOMMASO D'AQUINO AND ANGELS.

quatro et mezzo a gianpiero scharpellino
sopradetto portò gli valerio charci
et sono pel resto dell'arme di papa
lulio si misse nella facciata della chiesa - d. 4.37.10"

[Archivio di S. M. della Quercia, Viterbo, Libro di Entrata e Uscita della Fabbrica, segnato Cod. 116 c. 65.]

2. "+yhs 1507 —

. . . .

. . . .

e adj decto (23 novembre) ducati dieci

a Andrea della robia porto contantj
per arra dj tre archettj sopra le
porte della chiesa di terra cocta invetriata chome appare per una scripta
dj sua mano equalj tre archettj montorno
ducatj 10 dj charlinj in firenze —   d. 10 —"
   [Idem, idem, c. 66ᵗ.]

3. "Jesus 1508 —

. . . .

. . . .

e adj decto (7 giugnio) ducatj diecj ad
andrea della robia per parte di suo
cottimo dj tre mezi tondj sopra le portj
della chiesa et per noi dal bancho de chigj
per una lettera di chambio facta a girolami
in firenze presentj fratj ambrosio suo figluolo — d 10 —"

. . . .

. . . .

e addj iij di luglio carlinj cinquantaquatro
a domenicho vecturale per meta dela vectura
dj some tre di tre ½ (mezzo) tondi di terra cocta
per di sopra le tre portj della chiesa venute
da firenze da Andrea della robia porto
fratj ambrosio — — —— — — ——   d 5 — 30 -
   [Idem, idem, c. 69.]

4. —"+yhs 1508 —
addj xiiij dottobre 1508 fu alloghato a
bernardino di giovanni et a charlo dj
mariotto et a domenicho di jachopo da
firenzuola tutti scharpellinj la facciata
della chiesa chol suo frontone per prezo
di ducati quatrocentoquaranta di charlini
in tutto"
   [Idem, idem, c. 168ᵗ.]

5.
"1508 novembre 1 Bernardino di Giovanni
da Viterbo Carlo dj mariotto et domenicho
di jachopo da firenzuola tutti scharpellini
deono dare adi primo di novembre 1508 ducati settanta et bol xviij dj 15 ebbe Charlo
et domenicho sopradetti per parte del chottimo

della facciata et frontone chome si vede in questo
168 et ecene(?) scripta di mano di detto bernardino — — —— — —— — —— — — d 70 b 18 dj 15."
   [Idem, idem, c. 96'.]

6. "+ Jesus 1508
Mariano chigi a cõp'(compagnia) dicõtro(di viterbo)
deono havere adj   di magio ......
. . . . . .
. . . . . .
e adj decto(7 giugnio) d(ucati) dieci di c'(charlini)
paghatj p(er) noi ad andrea della robia p(er) una
lett'(lettera) a girolami ī firēze p(er) cõto delle tre
mezitõdi diterachotta sop(r)a le tre po(r)tj della chiesa — d 10—"
   [Archiv. idem, Libro Deb. & Cred. 1495-1517, segnato Cod. 139 c. —]

7.
"Memorie delli miglioramentj fatti ī nella chiesa et
cõvento di Scā Maria della Quercia ch(e) fu dato alla
cõgregat" (congregatione) chiamata di Scõ Marco
cioe nel 1496 p(er) sino al p(re)sente āno 1519
. . . .
. . . .
Item le figure liquali suno di sop' le tre
portj della chiesa ch(e) sono di piet" cocta
e vennono da firenze"
   [Archiv. idem, Cronaca 1506-1845 c. 11 — no/segnatura.]

Bibl.:
   B., *Denk.*, 87, Taf. 273; Burl., 119; Cahier, *Car. des Saints*, I, 98, 390,
   note 4; C-M., 257-258, Nos. 340-342; Cr., 196-197, 331; Erculei,
   162 (Doc.); Ferretti, *Ill. Fior.*, 1905, 126-130 (Doc.); Guérin, *Vies
   des Saints*, III, 247; Fov., 115; M., *Sc. Mag.*, 1893, 683, 697; R. H.,
   163-165; Mortier, 84-88, 154-155; Pinzi, *A. S. A.*, III (1890), 300-
   332 (Doc.); *Guida*, 160-161; R., *D. R.*, 210; *Sc. Fl.*, III, 177-179;
   V., VI, 584.

ANDREA DELLA ROBBIA

1510-1525

101 GIOVANNI BATTISTA ALMADIANO. 1510. Viterbo. Museo Comunale. Bust. Photos., Alinari, 11840; Moscioni, 3473.

This fine bust of Almadiano (Fig. 128), proto-notary and private chaplain to Leo X, was formerly in the church of S. Giovanni dei Fiorentini,

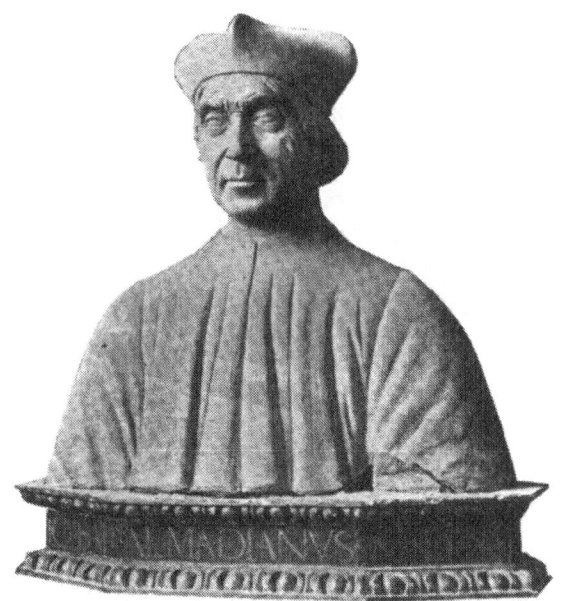

Fig. 128.—Bust of Almadiano.

Viterbo. It was set above a doorway, to the left of the altar accompanied by the inscription:

QVEM STRVIS IN TERRIS
BAPTISTA JOANNES EXTRVET
IN COELIS ALMADIANE TIBI

According to the registers of the church it was paid for on February 7, 1510. It exhibits the same sense of portraiture seen in the busts of the S. Paolo Hospital, and like them was left unglazed. It was many times painted and in recent times thoroughly cleaned. It now rests on a wooden base inscribed :

▲ IO(hannes) ▲ BAP(tistes) ▲ ALMADIANVS▲ M ▲ D X▲

Document : [Quoted from Gentile, in *A. S. A.*, II (1889), 411, note 1. Venturi considers the document fictitious.]

"11 Ottobre 1509 ad Andrea de'Robbia per le figure sopra la porta ducati sedici. 7 Febraio 1510. per il busto pagati per conto Almadiano del banco Chigi ducati sette."

Bibl. :

Cr., 197-198, 310 (Doc.), 327; D. D., 30; Gentili, *A. S. A.*, II, (1889), 410-411 (Doc.); Guasti, *Cafaggiolo*, 156; R., *D. R.*, 209-210; *Sc. Fl.*, III, 177-179; S., 122, Abb. 135; V., VI, 584.

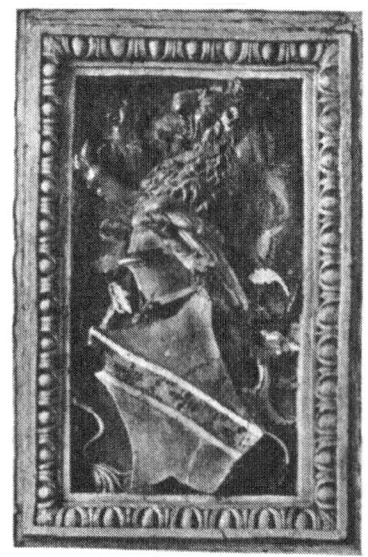

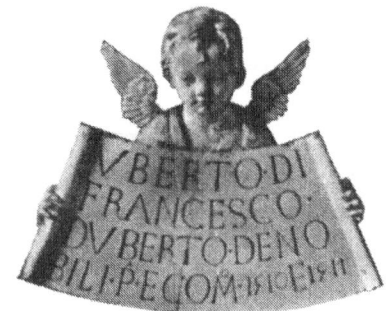

FIG. 129.—DE NOBILE STEMMA.

102 STEMMA OF UBERTO DI FRANCESCO DE NOBILI. 1511.
Arezzo, Palazzo Comunale, Inside.   Photo., Private.

Within a rectangular frame consisting of an egg and dart between fillet mouldings is a tournament shield (Fig. 129) bearing the *arma moderna* of the de Nobili family: Azure, a bend of France (semé of lilies or) fimbriated argent. The shield is surmounted by a helmet with torse and mantlings and crested with a demi-lion rampant.

Below, a charming cherub bears a curved scroll inscribed:

VBERTO ✦ DI
FRANCESCO ✦
DVBERTO ✦ DENO

BILI ✦ P(ODEST)A ✦ E COM(MISSARI)O ✦ 1510 E 1511

Uberto di Francesco de'Nobili had been a Prior in Florence in 1497 and 1501.

Bibl.:
C., s.v. Nobili; M., *R. H.,* 190, Fig. **178**; P., 481-483; W., 159.

103 CRUCIFIXION AND SAINTS.   Fiesole.   S. Maria Primerana. Round-headed altarpiece.   H., 2.62m.; W., 1.68m.   Photos., Alinari, No. 3271; Brogi, No. 9864.

This altarpiece (Fig. 130) appears to belong to the period of the Bibbiena altarpieces (1513-1520).   This is indicated by the concave background, the heavy proportions of all the figures, the advanced knowledge of anatomy displayed in the torso of the crucified Christ, the relief of the clouds, the expressive character of the skull beneath the cross.   The facial types of the Christ, the Madonna, the S. Maria Maddalena and S. Giovanni Evangelista are Andrea's, and the inscription: ✦ INRI ✦ above the cross shows letters of the same form as those at La Verna.   We can hardly hold him personally responsible for the spelling of the inscription on the predella (not shown in the photograph):   O VOS OMNES QVI TRANSITIS P(ER) VIAN ATENDITE E VIDETTE SI ES DOLOR SICVT DOLOR MEVM ✦

Bibl.:
B. J., 70-71; B., *Kf.,* 24; Carocci, *Dint.,* I, 137; C-M., 232 No. 174; Cr., 343; R., *D. R.,* 217-218; *Sc. Fl.,* III, 181, 183; Vas., II, 194.

104 LAMENTATION OVER THE DEAD BODY OF CHRIST.
London. Victoria and Albert Museum, No. 409-'89. Statues. H.,
c. 0.90m. Photo., Private.

Lamentations, like Adorations, occur logically in the works of Andrea,
though more common in that of his successors. The influence of Savon-

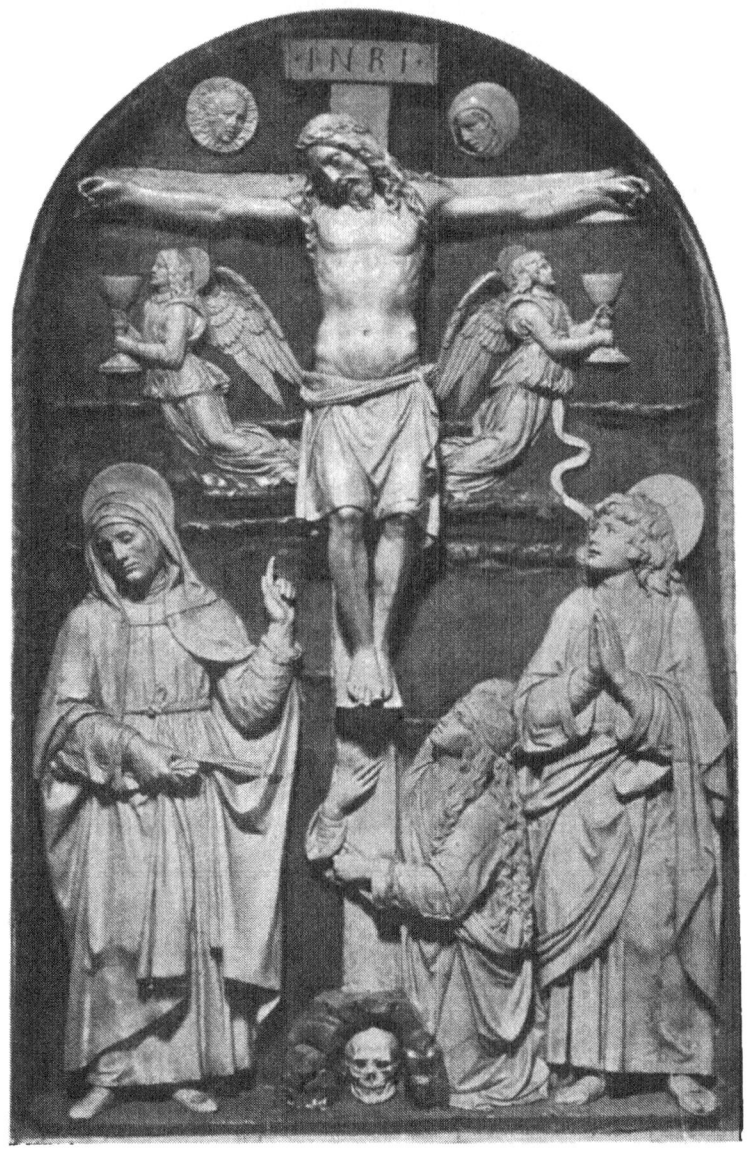

FIG. 130.—CRUCIFIXION AND SAINTS.

arola and the Piagnoni was doubtless shown in the multiplication of tragic religious subjects. Rarely was an actual Entombment represented, as in the predella of the Cintola altarpiece at S. Fiora. Lamentation over the Crucified One were more frequent, as in the altarpiece at S. Maria Primavera, Fiesole. Lamentations over the Body of Christ extended in the Virgin's lap are most common, especially in Giovanni's atelier. Here is another composition, a Lamentation over the Body of Christ extended on the ground (Fig. 131). Giovanni signed a lunette of this subject in 1521,

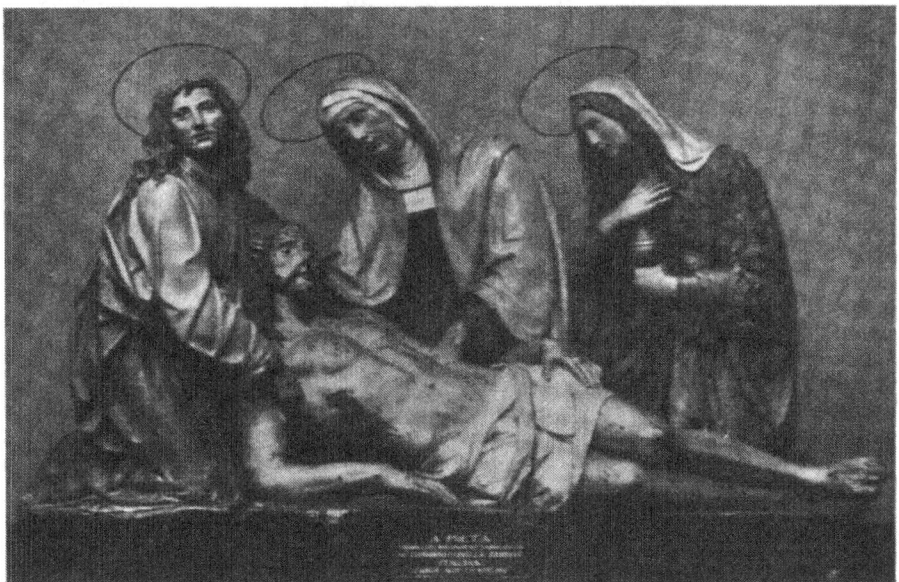

FIG. 131.—LAMENTATION OVER DEAD CHRIST.

but this London group is closer in its types to the Bibbiena altarpiece, to which it seems to be closely related.

These statues are only partially glazed. S. Giovanni's robe is glazed blue, and the lining of his mantle yellow; the loin cloth of Christ is white; the Madonna's mantle is blue lined green, her neckerchief is white; all the rest is unglazed, including the entire figure of La Maddalena.

It was acquired in Siena in 1869.

Bibl.:
Cr., 345; S., 142 Abb. 156.

105 THE RESURRECTION, ALSO FRAME FOR PAINTING. 1517-1518. Florence. S. Frediano, Cappella della Compagnia di S. Frediano. Lunette (missing).

The Cappella della Compagnia di S. Frediano is described in the documents as the last chapel on the right in the church of S. Frediano, and as opposite the Cappella di S. Lorenzo. According to Richa (IX, 177) the latter was founded in 1490. The Cappella di S. Frediano was probably founded at the same time, and as we have already noted, was decorated with a Robbia frieze of cherub heads in 1494-1502. Its altarpiece as we gather from Richa and Rosselli, represented a Pietà. Richa adds that it included as lateral saints, S. Girolamo and S. Frediano; and was painted by Ghirlandaio. From the documents and from Rosselli we gather that it was set in a Robbia frame with architrave, frieze and cornice; the frieze being decorated with cherub heads. Arcangelo di Jacopo a painter and Niccolò del Tatta a goldsmith were employed to do the necessary gilding. Rosselli says of it "Passata il Pulpito segne un altare con Tavola antica della Pietà e con ornamenti di terra-cotta della maniera di Luca della Robbia—vi e il segno della compagnia di S. Friano—Croce e Lettere rosse in azz." This emblem he depicts in the margin. The documents imply also that there was an inscription and seem to distinguish between the cherubs of this frame and those of the frieze of the chapel "che furono fatti e pagati per altro tempo."

It is probable that the emblem of the compagnia was placed at either end of the predella and that the centre contained the inscription: O VOS OMNES QVI TRANSITIS VIAM ATTENDITE ET VIDETE SI EST DOLOR SICUT DOLOR MEVS.

The form of the relief noted by Richa was probably a lunette, as is indicated by its position "sotto l'arco della cappella (Doc. No. 111)." It is further defined by Bocchi-Cinelli as above an altar and framed by many beautiful seraphim. Its subject is indicated in the Documents and by Richa as a Resurrection and its author Andrea della Robbia. His treatment of this theme is familiar to us from the altarpiece at Aquila, and from the relief in the hallway of the Accademia, Florence.

In 1827 von Rumohr records cherub heads and other fragments as in the Casa Mozzi, Florence. In 1855 Barbet de Jouy specifies as in the cortile of the Casa Mozzi (later Bardini), four angels, fifteen heads of seraphs, and four sleeping guards which seem to have formed part of a Resurrection relief. These, Milanesi in 1878 identified, probably correctly, as from the Cappella di S. Frediano. Their whereabouts now is unknown.

Documents: [Copied by Mr. Rufus G. Mather.]

1.

"+ yhs m(aria) MDXVIJ
Gino chaponj n° k° di chontro de avere
addi 6 di mago lxxij...........................l 22 s–
- - - - - - - -
E addi 6 di settenbre............................l 60
- - - - - - - -
E addi 6 detto 18 e l 5. 14 andrea
dela Robia in 2 partite in questo
a c 201   l 13 s 14
- - - - - - - -
- - - - - - - -
E addi 26 di novenbre 1518 lvj   16 s–
E addi .... detto lvij s x andrea
della Robbia sino adi 18 in questo
a c 201   16 s 10"

[Archiv. di Stato. Compagnia di San Frediano. Libro Debitori e
Creditori, anni 1467 al 1522, segnato No. 112, c. clxxxxvj.]

2.

"E de dare l cinquantanove s x dj iiij
picciolj pachati andrea dellarobbia
In piu volte sono per una Resurressione
di terra cotta fatta sotto larcho di
detta chapella per adornamento fatto
fare e sindachj accio deputati posto
andr° della robia avere per dette
fichure In questo a c 201"   l 59 s 10 dj 4
[Idem, c. 112.]

3.

a. c. 201   a. c. ccj

"+ yhs m(aria) MDXVIIJ   "+ yhs m(aria) MDXVIJ
Andrea di .... della Robbia de dare   Andrea della Robbia de avere
sino addi 28 settenbre 1518 l otto porto l cinquanta nove s x dj iiij picciolj
nicholo martellinj contanti disse per   se gli fano buonj per piu lavoro di
arra della Resurezione fatta sotto   terra cotta per una Resuressione
larco della Chapella di s° friano   fatta per adornamento della nostra
nostra in chiesa s° friano et In questo capella a s° frediano lultima a
non sono e cherubinj che furono   manritta in detta chiesa posto
fattj e pachatj per altro tempo dison   dare In questo a c 112
per arra a uscita di Gino Caponi   l 59 s 10 dj 4"

n° k° a c 183 avere In questo a c 196 18 s-
E addi 6 detto l cinque s xiiij porto
nicholo martellinj de avere detta
c 184 avere In questo a c 196   15 s 14
E addi 18 di novenbre 1518 1 sette
s x porto nicholo martellinj contanti a
uscita di Gino Caponj n° k° a c 184
In questo a c 196   17 s 10.
E addi 30 daprile 1519 l xxviij porto
contanti chome disse nicholo martellinj e fatti buonj a detto nicholo
dise l- adi 31 di dicēbre 1518 e l- adi
22 di genaio 1518 chome a uscita
dant° di neri biccj k° a c 186
avere In questo a c 203   1 28 s-
E addi detto lx s vj dj iiij porto
e disse avere pachatj nicholo martellinj
sindacho a detto andrea e a altri per luj
per piu cag(i)one schritte di neri biccj
k° a uscita a c 186 posto avere In questo
                    a c 203   1 10 s 6.4
                         1 59 . 10 . 4"
    [Idem, c. 201, ccj.]

4.
          "+ yhs m(aria) MDXVIIJ
Ant° di neri biccj n° cam° fatto per
nic° scharlattj de avere addi 6 di
dicenbre 1518 1 sei per noi a Rede di
Lo (Lorenzo) fornaio dare in questo a c 202   16
- - - - - -

- - - - - -
E addi 30 daprile 1519 1 iiij a spese di conp(agnia)
in questo a c 197   14
E addi detto 1 xxviij a andrea dellarobia
in questo a c 201   1 28
E addi detto 1 x s vj dj iiij a andrea
della Robbia in questo a c 201   1 10 s 6 . 4"
    [Idem, c. cciij.]

5.
    [Idem, c. ccxxj.]
Nicholo di maestro lorenzo Martelinj uno

de sindachj della Conp' de avere perinsino addi 18 di maggio 1519
l quindici s xiiij piciolj
pachatj per la chapella nostra murata In
sanfriano e per luj antonio di nicholo deltatta
battiloro per pezzi 450 doro messj per mettere
doro agliarchitravj e cherubinj posto chapella dare
In questo a c 112   l 15 s 14
E addi detto l otto s iij dj iiij piccholj pachatj
appiu persone dipintore per mettere doro scharpelinj fabro
legnaiuolo..............posto dare In questo a c 112   18 s 3 dj 4"
    [Idem, a c. ccxxj.]

6.   c. 112

    "+ Mdj
E de dare adi primo di settembre 1520
l settanta s x picciolj fattj buonj a archangelo
di jacopo dipintore posto avere In questo a
c 214 sono per ornamento fatto nella
tavola dellaltare di detta chapella etc.........   l 70 s 10
- - - - -

- - - - -

E de dare l trenta cinque s vij piccholj
fatti buonj a 3 operaj avere In questo
a c 213 sono per pezzi 1010 doro a l 3
s 10 il cento per dorare e cherubinj e
adornamento della tavola dellaltare   l 35 s 7
· · · · · ·

E de dare l xv s xiiij picciolj per tanti
disse avere pachati nicholo martelini
a antonio di nicholo deltatta battiloro
per pezzi 450 doro autj dalluj a l 3 s 10
il cento per mettere nellarchitrave e
cherubinj di terra della robbia a detto
altare sino a di 18 di maggio 1519
posto nicholo avere In questo a c 221   l 15 s 14
E addi detto l otto s 3 dj 4 picciolj
sono per piu spese pachate per detta
capella al dipintore che messe doro
al chornicione e cherubinj sopradetti
di per mettere 2 puleggi e alfabo
etc.... posto nicholo avere In questo a c 221   18 s 3 dj 4"
    [Idem, c. 112.]

Bibl.:

B. J., 97; B., *Kf.*, 24; Bocchi-Cinelli, 162; C-M., 106, 215 No. 56; Cr., 199-200; Fov., 115; R., *D. R.*, 150; *Sc. Fl.*, III, 147; Richa, IX, 177; von Rumohr, II, 295 note; Vas., II 180-181 note 4, 192.

Lightning Source UK Ltd.
Milton Keynes UK
UKOW07f1220170415

249828UK00007B/119/P